SIMONE WEIL: AN ANTHOLOGY

SIMONE WEIL (1909–1943) is one of the most important thinkers of the modern period. The distinctive feature of her work is the indissoluble link she makes between the theory and practice of both politics and religion and her translation of thought into action. A brilliant philosopher and mathematician, her life represents a quest for justice and balance in both the academic and the practical spheres. A scholar of deep and wide erudition, she became during the thirties an inspired teacher and activist. So as to experience physical labour at first hand, she spent almost two years as a car factory worker soon after the Front Populaire and later became a fighter in the Spanish Civil War. When her home city of Paris was occupied, she joined the Resistance in the South of France and became for a time an agricultural labourer before acceding to her parents' wish to escape Nazi persecution of the Jews by fleeing to New York. Leaving America, she joined the Free French in London where, frustrated by the exclusively intellectual nature of the work delegated to her, and weakened by a number of physical and emotional factors, she contracted tuberculosis and died in a Kentish sanatorium at the age of thirty-four. The bulk of her voluminous *oeuvre* was published posthumously.

SIÂN MILES was born and brought up in the bi-cultural atmosphere of Wales and educated there and in France where she has lived for many years. She has taught at a number of universities worldwide, including Tufts University, Massachusetts, Dakar University, Sénégal and York University, Toronto. She now teaches at Warwick University in England. Her other publications include: *George Sand: Marianne*; a translation of Violet Trefusis' *Echo*; in collaboration, Paul Valéry's *Cahiers/Notebooks*; and Guy de Maupassant: *A Parisian Affair and Other Stories* (Penguin Classics).

SIMONE WEIL

An Anthology

Edited and Introduced by SIÂN MILES

PENGUIN BOOKS

PENGUIN BOOKS

Published by the Penguin Group
Penguin Books Ltd, 80 Strand, London WC2R 0RL, England
Penguin Group (USA) Inc., 375 Hudson Street, New York, New York 10014, USA
Penguin Group (Canada), 90 Eglinton Avenue East, Suite 700, Toronto,
Ontario, Canada M4P 2Y3 (a division of Pearson Penguin Canada Inc.)
Penguin Ireland, 25 St Stephen's Green, Dublin 2, Ireland
(a division of Penguin Books Ltd)
Penguin Group (Australia), 250 Camberwell Road,
Camberwell, Victoria 3124, Australia (a division of Pearson Australia Group Pty Ltd)
Penguin Books India Pvt Ltd, 11 Community Centre,
Panchsheel Park, New Delhi – 110 017, India
Penguin Group (NZ), cnr Airborne and Rosedale Roads, Albany,
Auckland 1310, New Zealand (a division of Pearson New Zealand Ltd)
Penguin Books (South Africa) (Pty) Ltd, 24 Sturdee Avenue,
Rosebank 2196, South Africa

Penguin Books Ltd, Registered Offices: 80 Strand, London WC2R 0RL, England

www.penguin.com

First published by Virago Press 1986
Published in Penguin Classics 2005

2

Copyright © Introductions and arrangements Siân Miles, 1986, 2005
All rights reserved

The moral right of the author has been asserted

Simone Weil's writings are copyrighted as follows: *Attente de Dieu* © La Colombe Edition du
Vieux Colombier 1950; *Waiting on God* © G. P. Putnam's Sons and Routledge & Kegan Paul
1951, renewed 1979. *Cahiers de Simone Weil* Vol I. © Librairie Plon 1951, Vol. II © Plon 1953,
Vol III © Plon 1956; *The Notebooks of Simone Weil* © G. P. Putnam's Sons 1956. *La Pesanteur et
la Grâce* © Librairie Plon 1947; *Gravity and Grace* © G. P. Putnam's Sons and Routledge &
Kegan Paul 1952, renewed 1980. *L'Enracinement* © Editions Gallimard 1949; *The Need for Roots*
© Simone Weil 1952, preface by T. S. Eliot © G. P. Putnam's Sons and Routledge & Kegan Paul
1952, renewed 1980. *Oppression et Liberté* © Gallimard 1955; *Oppression and Liberty* © Routledge
and Kegan Paul 1958. *Leçons de Philosophie* © Librairie Plon 1959; *Lectures on Philosophy*
© Cambridge University Press 1978. *Condition première d'un travail non-servile* from *La
Condition Ouvrière* © Editions Gallimard 1951; *Prerequisite to Dignity of Labour* © Siân Miles
1986. *L'Iliade ou le poème de la force* from *La Source Grecque* © Editions Gallimard 1953; *The
Iliad or the Poem of Force* © Mary McCarthy 1945. *Seventy Letters* © Oxford University Press
1965. *La Vie de Simone Weil* © Librairie Arthème Fayard 1973; *Simone Weil: A Life* © Pantheon
Books 1976. *Ecrits de Londres et Dernières Lettres* © Gallimard 1957 and *Ecrits historiques et
politiques* © Gallimard 1960. *Selected Essays 1934–43* © Oxford University Press 1962.

Printed in England by Clays Ltd, St Ives plc

CONTENTS

FOREWORD
to the Penguin Edition

In the decade and a half since the first publication of this anthology, the influence of Simone Weil's life and work has spread and deepened in many different spheres. Some of these include the familiar fields of philosophy and religion with which her name has traditionally been most closely associated. Some, however, represent other areas where the seeds of her understanding have taken strong root and produced the kind of interdisciplinary cross-fertilization characteristic in aspiration of both her formal and informal writings. These include the political, the educational, the psychological as well as the cultural, in which strands of her thinking have developed in ways marking it as having been unusually prescient, innovative for its time and spectacularly applicable to our own.

In the fields of politics and economics her many persuasive arguments on the inherent tendency of power to over-extend itself have an all too resonant ring. 'If we want to consider power as a conceivable phenomenon, we must think it can extend the foundations on which it rests up to a certain point only, after which it comes up, as it were, against an impassable wall. But even so it is not in a position to stop; the spur of competition forces it to go ever farther, that is to say, to go beyond the limits within which it can be effectively exercised.' (Weil, 1958) Some might argue that the imperative which drives the US and her allies to attempt to control ever greater proportions of the world's dwindling oil resources does indeed lead them into ever wider confrontations, creating opposition which they can neither understand nor overcome.

Claiming that wherever small is possible, big is bad, she anticipates by several decades the notion, though not the sadly revelatory name of subsidiarity now enshrined in the European Community Treaty, and Schumacher's 'small is beautiful' ethos which emerged in parts of the West after her death and is ever more widely accepted as a means of controlling irresponsible expansion. Small-scale production, localized economies and greater emphasis on regionaliza-tion are expressed as objectives and consummations devoutly to be wished in the many essays on the nature of work and on industrial relations written after her own experiences as a factory hand and agricultural labourer in the late thirties and soon after the occupation of France by the Nazis.

Some readers have been tempted to muse on the contem-porary relevance of her proposition that the complexity of relations between developed states and a perceived need for co-ordination lead to increased hegemony and consequent domination. Advanced nations (including especially the UK since the demise of virtually all its manufacturing sector), exercise control and exploitation over the world economy through the manipulation of information in ways she anticipates with chilling accuracy. The intense discussion which took place a few years ago about the poten-tially revolutionary influence of the internet because of its decentralized structure and the at least theoretical possi-bility that information would be available to all equally has proved something of a chimera due to the fact that information remains heavily controlled.

Others have noted her influence in the area of resistance

to war and argue that the industry of war in consumer societies is supported by two factors: the objectives of statecraft and the desires of consumers. Thus pacifist platforms, even if supported by millions of people, are likely to fail primarily because the roots of consumption and the inability to give up socialized ways of thinking about needs are obstacles to anti-war movements. Statecraft implicates, at the occupational level, workers who might be opposed to imperialism or war, but as soldiers or technicians or specialized skill workers, like miners or drillers, they have a job to perform and keep. This locates both the routes of recruitment to war and the movements to protest along specific class channels. Simone Weil's ideas on bureaucracy and work are particularly useful in helping to understand the limits of freedom as well as the necessity of *enracinement* or rootedness for survival.

Even more importantly, perhaps, something of the unreality of fictive nature of the language of war is strongly foreshadowed by her argument that winning itself is an illusion which discounts the sufferings and impermanence of victory. Underlying much feminist thought and expression is the implicit understanding that the language of war is deliberately obfuscatory, not to say absurd. Since Simone Weil's time, one of the most important movements to have arisen is of course feminism itself, and it is interesting to compare and contrast the influence of her work in its development. Unsurprisingly, it is among feminist theologians as well as philosophers that it appears to figure most prominently. Some of the latter are deeply disturbed, not to say repelled, particularly by the later mysticism in her work, seeing in it an unhealthy or even morbid fascination with pain and suffering as well as passive acceptance of a traditionally masculinist and necrophilic language of discourse.

Others, however, see in her thought elements with which more recent developments in both philosophy and theology may be strongly linked. Her dazzling insights, often expressed with both terseness and conviction, include the claims that all error, suffering and unhappiness stem from forgetting one is God. Though Simone Weil makes no special claims for women (quite the contrary, in fact) debate has arisen among contemporary feminist thinkers, particularly in France, beginning with the work of Irigaray, to centre on the idea of 'becoming divine' as opposed merely to probing and testing the validity of essentially patristic doctrines and terminology.

Here again, at the interface of religion and philosophy, language is of crucial and exciting importance. Simone Weil's conception of 'creative attention' is grasped as an individual's just and loving gaze directed upon an individual reality and the potential of the former to transform both the one who attends and the other who is attended to. This understanding has modified, amongst other orthodoxies, the view of prayer as petition or intercession. Rowan Williams, writing exactly fifty years after her death, in an article examining the strength and ambiguity of her work claims: 'Weil's analysis of how God is to be spoken of remains one of the most difficult and challenging of this century and for that reason it is important not to canonize it or domesticate it.' (Williams, 1995). He goes on to suggest that it collapses under the weight of what he terms 'contradictory pressures'. Simone Weil, as a mathematician and particularly as a geometer, positively invites discussion of such phrases and embraces with a boldness both untypical of her times and an enthusiasm connected with her love of Eastern religion the whole notion of seizing contradiction as a means to understanding.

If her thought continues to influence philosophers and theologians, who struggle with the task of tracing a linguistic dividing line between their two fields, it provides illumination for those whose interests combine the philosophic with the cultural and in the first instance, the literary. Iris Murdoch, writing of her first encounter with the work of Weil, recalls with great and affecting simplicity just being moved by such deep, radiant thinking. As George Steiner has remarked on Murdoch in his Introduction to her *Existentialists and Mystics*:

Properly grasped, the 'mystical' pursuit of the Good, of perfect unison with moral truths arises out of a rootedness in common humanity, in 'ordinary' being, far more concrete than either the 'language-games' of analytic-academic philosophers or the ideologies of the existentialists. For Iris Murdoch, there is in 'mysticism', when it its attached to life, a deep-lying utilitarianism. In all this, the absolutely key *persona* is that of Simone Weil.

Iris Murdoch herself has much to say about the process towards a state of mind and body closely akin to Weil's *attention*. Quoting the poet Valéry and his assertion that 'the proper, unique and perpetual object of thought is that which does not exist', she describes the state aspired to as 'an orientation of the soul towards something which one does not know but whose reality one does.' (Murdoch, 1992.) Her admiration for Weil's work is both deep and enduringly evident throughout both her philosophical and novelistic *oeuvre* and to read her, Murdoch asserts, is to be reminded of a standard.

George Steiner's phrase 'deep-lying utilitarianism' suggests the theme of another twentieth-century writer similarly influenced by the work of Simone Weil. Seamus Heaney, in the first of his lectures as Professor of Poetry at Oxford, acknowledges the temptation to show how poetry's existence as a form of art relates to our existence as citizens of society – how it is 'of present use'. His lecture, entitled 'The Redress of Poetry' quotes a familiar argument of Weil's, most lucidly expressed in *Gravity and Grace* where she writes:

If we know in what way society is unbalanced, we must do what we can to add weight to the lighter scale ... we must have formed a conception of equilibrium and be ever read to change sides like justice, 'that fugitive from the camp of the conquerors ... Obedience to the force of gravity. The greatest sin.' (Weil, 1952a).

Heaney notes that this work is informed by:

... the idea of counterweighting, of balancing out the forces, of redress – tilting the scales of reality towards some transcendent equilibrium. And in the activity of poetry too, there is a tendency to place a counter-reality in the scales – a reality which may be only imagined but which nevertheless has weight because it is imagined within the gravitational pull of the actual and can therefore hold its own and balance out against the historical situation. This redressing effect of poetry comes from its being a glimpsed alternative, a revelation of potential that is denied or constantly threatened by circumstances. (Heaney, 1995.)

Interestingly and appropriately enough, he illustrates his remarks with 'The Pulley' and 'Love', the latter of George Herbert's poems being particularly influential in turn on Simone Weil herself.

Heaney is not the only poet of our times to have gained major insights from the work of Simone Weil. Adrienne Rich, his American near-contemporary is another, who, in her *Lies, Secrets and Silence* evokes a familiar image from Weil's work; that of some hapless inarticulate in the dock, listening mutely while the judge and learned counsel keep up a flow of witticisms:

Those who suffer from injustice most are the least able to articulate their suffering ... the silent majority, if released into language, would not be content with the perpetuation of the conditions which have betrayed them. But this notion hangs on a special conception of what it means to be released into language; not simply learning the jargon of an elite, fitting unexceptionably into the status quo, but learning that language can be used as a means of changing reality. (Rich, 1980).

Nor is her cultural influence limited to literature. In the *Notebooks* she writes of 'the beauty of a landscape just at the moment when nobody is looking at it, absolutely nobody ... To see a landscape as it is when I am not there.' Painters too may have much to learn from her work. This was the opinion expressed with some conviction for the first time by Herbert Read in his *Letter to a Young Painter* soon after the first publication of Simone Weil's *Cahiers*. Traces of the connections he makes may be seen in the writings of the contemporary minimalist Agnes Martin, whose own advice and strictures to young artists resemble Weil's with regard to training the intuitive attention which alone in her view is the source of perfectly beautiful art. Reflecting the tension often experienced in Weil's work, she urges them to 'feel the pull' of life. 'We must', she says, surrender the idea that this perfection that we see in the mind or before our eyes is obtainable or attainable, a rather more austere view of Heaney's 'glimpsed alternative.' (Martin, 1991)

The value in Simone Weil's work attributed to being able to perceive without reverie, and to make an effort of attention empty of all content, places her thinking within the family of humane ideas which anticipates much in *Gestalt* and its later development in present-day psychologies. These in turn are intimately connected with Eastern mysticism and their application, in the form of contemporary therapies, has permeated common experiences of healing. The process of *décréation* which she uses to describe the kind of spiritual stripping-down which enables a person to perceive and bear an undistorted truth, is an exercise now familiar to many who decide to make a radical reassessment and re-creation of their lives.

REFERENCES

———— ◎ ————

Heaney, Seamus, *The Redress of Poetry*, Faber and Faber, London and Boston, 1995.

Martin, Agnes, *Agnes Martin*, Kunstmuseum Winterthur, Cantz Verlag, Ostfildern, 1991.

Murdoch, Iris, *Metaphysics as a Guide to Morals*, Chatto and Windus, London, 1992.

Ibid. Existentialists and Mystics, Chatto and Windus, London, 1997.

Rich, Adrienne, *On Lies, Secrets and Silence*, Virago, London, 1980.

Weil, Simone, *Oppression and Liberty*, trans. Arthur Wills and John Petrie, Routledge and Kegan Paul, London 1958. Originally published as *Oppression et Liberté*, Gallimard, Paris, 1955.

Williams, Rowan, 'The Necessary non-existence of God' from Richard H. Bell, ed. *Simone Weil's Philosophy of Culture*, C.U.P., Cambridge, 1993.

PREFACE TO THE VIRAGO EDITION

———————— ◎ ————————

The Introduction is based on the biographies and exegeses of Jacques Cabaud, *L'Expérience vécue de Simone Weil avec de nombreux inédits*, Paris, Plon, 1957, translated into English as *Simone Weil: A Fellowship in Love*, London, Harvill, 1964: New York, Channel Press, 1965; and Simone Pétrement, *La Vie de Simone Weil*, Paris, Fayard, 1973, translated into English as *Simone Weil: A Life*, translated by Raymond Rosenthal, London, Mowbrays, 1977: New York, Random House, 1976; on interviews with the late Sir Richard Rees and with Simone Weil's mother, the late Mme. Selma Weil. The latter, already very old and frail, was still actively editing when I first met her in 1964. She was kind enough to befriend me while as a recent graduate, under a British State Studentship, I was conducting my own research in Paris on the work of her daughter. I am extremely grateful to all the many other Simone Weil scholars upon whose work I have drawn and which is cited in the References.

ACKNOWLEDGEMENTS

———————— ◎ ————————

Grateful acknowledgement is made to the following for permission to reprint previously published material:

CAMBRIDGE UNIVERSITY PRESS for excerpts from *Simone Weil: Lectures on Philosophy*, translated by Hugh Price, 1978, with an Introduction by Peter Winch. Originally published as *Leçons de philosophie* by Librairie Plon, 1959.

EDITIONS GALLIMARD for permission to translate excerpts from *La Condition Ouvrière* by Simone Weil, 1951.

MARY McCARTHY for her translation of Simone Weil's 'L' *Iliade* ou le Poème de la Force'. 'The *Iliad* or the Poem of Force' first published in *Politics*, November 1945.

OXFORD UNIVERSITY PRESS for excerpts from *Simone Weil: Seventy Letters*, translated and arranged by Richard Rees, 1965; *Selected Essays, 1934–43* by Simone Weil, chosen and translated by Richard Rees, 1962.

RANDOM HOUSE INC. for excerpts from *Simone Weil: A Life* by Simone Pétrement, translated by Raymond Rosenthal, 1976. Originally published as *La Vie de Simone Weil* by Librairie Arthème Fayard, 1973.

ROUTLEDGE and KEGAN PAUL and THE PUTNAM PUBLISHING GROUP for excerpts from *Waiting on God* by Simone Weil, translated by Emma Craufurd, 1951. Originally published as *L'Attente de Dieu* by La Colombe, Editions du Vieux Colombier, 1950; *The Notebooks of Simone Weil Vols I and II*, translated by Arthur Wills, 1956. Originally published as *Les Cahiers de Simone Weil* (3 vols), by Librairie Plon, 1952–5; *Gravity and Grace* by Simone Weil, translated by Emma Craufurd, 1952. Originally published as *La Pesanteur et la Grâce*, by Librairie Plon, 1947; *The Need for Roots: Prelude to a Declaration of Duties towards Mankind* by Simone Weil, with a Preface by T. S. Eliot, translated by A. F. Wills, 1952. Originally published as *L'Enracinement: Prélude à une déclaration des devoirs envers l'être humain*, by Gallimard, 1949.

Excerpts from *Oppression and Liberty* by Simone Weil are reprinted by permission of THE UNIVERSITY OF MASSACHUSETTS PRESS © 1958 by Routledge and Kegan Paul.

For their contributions both direct and indirect to the Penguin edition, I should like to thank most warmly the following: Pamela Anderson, Christine Battersby, Barrie Hinksman, Catherine Hoskyns, Peter Larkin, Simon Lewty, Elsbeth Lindner, Pauline Matarasso, Patti Owens, James Ryan, Maggie Ross, Susan Visvanathan and Sylvie Weil.

INTRODUCTION

———————— ◎ ————————

Simone Weil completed her last work in 1943 when at the age of thirty-four she died in an English sanatorium. Two weeks earlier she had written to her parents:

When I saw *Lear* here, I asked myself how it was possible that the unbearably tragic character of these fools had not been obvious long ago to everyone, including myself. The tragedy is not the sentimental one it is sometimes thought to be; it is this:

There is a class of people in this world who have fallen into the lowest degree of humiliation, far below beggary, and who are deprived not only of all social consideration but also, in everybody's opinion, of the specific human dignity, reason itself – and these are the only people who, in fact, are able to tell the truth. All the others lie.

In *Lear* it is striking. Even Kent and Cordelia attenuate, mitigate, soften, and veil the truth; and unless they are forced to choose between telling it and telling a downright lie, they manoeuvre to evade it.

I do not know if it is the same in the other plays, which I have neither seen nor re-read here (except *Twelfth Night*). Darling M., if you were to re-read a bit of Sh[akespeare] with this in mind, perhaps it would reveal some new aspects.

What makes the tragedy extreme is the fact that because the fools possess no academic titles or episcopal dignities and because no one is aware that their sayings deserve the slightest attention

– everybody being convinced a priori of the contrary, since they are fools – their expression of the truth is not even listened to. Everybody, including Sh.'s readers and audiences for four centuries, is unaware that what they say is true. And not satirically or humorously true, but simply the truth. Pure unadulterated truth – luminous, profound, and essential.

Is this also the secret of Velasquez's fools? Are their eyes so sad because of the bitterness of possessing the truth and having won at the price of nameless degradation, the power to utter it and then being listened to by nobody (except Velasquez)? It would be worth while to look at them again with this idea in mind.

Darling M., do you feel the affinity, the essential analogy between these fools and me – in spite of the Ecole and the examination successes and the eulogies of my 'intelligence'?

This is another reply on 'what I have to give'.

In my case, the Ecole, etc., are just another irony.

Everyone knows that a high intelligence is often paradoxical and sometimes a bit wild. . . .

The eulogies of my intelligence are positively *intended* to evade the question: 'Is what she says true?' And my reputation for 'intelligence' is practically equivalent to the label of 'fool' for those fools. How much I would prefer their label.

Nothing new about your prospects since my last letter (of 28 July; let me know by cable if you don't receive it). Nor about mine.

★

A thousand kisses, darlings. Hope, but with moderation. Be happy. I hug you both again and again.

Simone (Weil, 1965)

Since then she has become known as one of the foremost thinkers of modern times, a writer of extraordinary lucidity and a woman of outstanding moral courage.

Most of her work has been published posthumously under the editorship of a number of people including Albert Camus, Simone Pétrement, and her mother, Selma Weil. Several of the earliest English translations of her work appeared in American political journals of the late thirties and early forties. It was not until the fifties, however, with the publication of *Gravity and Grace, The Need for Roots, Oppression and Liberty, Intimations of Christianity, Waiting on God,* and the two volumes of *Notebooks,* that she became known to British readers. In the following decade two important anthologies of her essays and letters, translated, edited and prefaced by her English biographer, Richard Rees, made more of her work available (Rees, 1962, 1966; Weil 1965). With it came a fuller account of her extraordinary life and the publication of Jacques Cabaud's *L'Experience vécue de Simone Weil.* A translation of some of her essays on mathematics, on scientific methods and on the teaching of mathematics as well as essays connecting these with the religious and Hellenist aspects of her work, followed in 1970 with the publication of *Science, Necessity and the Love of God.* In 1973, the authoritative biography *La Vie de Simone Weil,* by Simone Pétrement appeared and J.P. Little's comprehensive bibliography. Now in its second volume the latter shows the growing interest in the work of Simone Weil in most countries of the world. The *Association pour l'étude de la pensée de Simone Weil* was formed in the seventies and in 1978 the *Lectures on Philosophy* appeared in this country. Prodigious as this output is, it represents only part of her writing. Numerous articles, papers and notes remain uncollected and more importantly still, her entire written *œuvre* in turn represents only part of her life's work.

Although her academic influence has come to bear principally in the fields of philosophical and religious thought, Simone Weil's chief significance has been otherwise twofold. She is recognized first for her unique combination of thought and action and secondly for being one of the most remarkable polymaths of this century. She has come to symbolize a paradoxical, active non-membership of the contemporary Church as a social structure and to stand for those who resist the natural tendency which she saw within it, as within every collectivity, to abuse power.

What frightens me is the Church as a social structure. Not only on account of its blemishes, but from the very fact that it is something social. It is not that I am of a very individualistic temperament. I am afraid for the opposite reason. I am aware of very strong gregarious tendencies in myself. My natural disposition is to be very easily influenced, too much influenced – and above all by anything collective. I know that if at this moment I had before me a group of twenty young Germans singing Nazi songs in chorus, a part of my soul would instantly become Nazi. That is a very great weakness, but that is how I am. I think that it is useless to fight directly against natural weaknesses. One has to force oneself to act as though one did not have them in circumstances where a duty makes it imperative; and in the ordinary course of life one has to know these weaknesses, prudently take them into account, and strive to turn them to good purpose; for they are all capable of being put to some good purpose.

I am afraid of the Church patriotism which exists in Catholic circles. By patriotism I mean the feeling one has for a terrestrial country. I am afraid of it because I fear to catch it. It is not that the Church appears to me to be unworthy of inspiring such a feeling. It is because I do not want any feeling of such a kind in myself. The word want is not accurate I *know*, I feel quite certain, that any feeling of this kind, whatever its object, would be fatal for me. (Weil, 1951b)

André Gide called her the saint of all outsiders and she wrote:

... I should betray the truth, that is to say the aspect of truth that I see, if I left the point, where I have been since my birth, at the intersection of Christianity and everything that is not Christianity, I have always remained at this exact point, on the threshold of the Church, without moving, quite still *en hypomene* (it is so much more beautiful a word than *patientia*) ... (Weil, 1951b)

By a strange irony, she who remained at great personal, some might say fatal cost, deliberately and conspicuously outside the Church, is known principally today as one of its modern martyrs. During her lifetime she wrote that she would only feel free to enter it if there were a notice on the door of every church forbidding access to those in receipt of an income above a certain figure and that a fairly low one. Yet after her death there can hardly be a large church or cathedral in the world where her work is not now permanently on display for sale.

This anthology, a selection of some of her major works, is an attempt to connect the social, political and public writings of Simone Weil which she intended for publication, with the private and religiously based. Essays from the former alternate with excerpts from the latter. It is intended as an introduction to the work of an extraordinary woman, the ecumenical character of whose writing carries the pre-Christian meaning of being addressed to the inhabited earth.

Belief. Very different meanings $2 + 2 = 4$, or: I am holding this pen. Here, belief is the feeling of evidence. I cannot, by definition, believe in mysteries in this way. But I believe that the mysteries of the Catholic religion are an inexhaustible source of truths concerning the human condition. (And further, they are for me an object of love.) Only nothing prevents me from believing that some of those truths have been directly revealed elsewhere. Adherence of the mind analogous to what is obtained by a work of art (the very greatest art) ... (Weil, 1956)

A bibliography is included for those who want to read more of her work. Much of the latter is in the form of fragments or notes, short 'pensées' sometimes not exceeding seven or eight lines, many of which are brief injunctions, reminders or questions to herself, e.g. 'To look at a landscape as it would be if I were not in it', 'God-*fearing* man. What does this mean?'; 'Laughter. Contradiction. Bergson. Value of comedy. Analogy between comedy (including Rabelais, etc.) and *ko-an*'; 'Must not read into.' Some depend on a key word or phrase; 'lever', 'blind man's stick', 'Louis XIV's smile', (Weil 1956), which has particular significance in her vocabulary. Alternating with the essays are extracts from the notes entrusted to her great friend Gustav Thibon, and classified by him under certain categories. These were to become known in English as *Gravity and Grace*. Extracts from the *Notebooks* themselves, though they would give a more complete idea of the astounding breadth of her knowledge and interests, might have proved too cryptic for the purposes of the present volume.

Philosopher, sociologist, mystic, teacher and political activist, Simone Weil was many things to many people. Gabriel Marcel, the existentialist philosopher, represents the view of the majority when he warns against attempting to place her thought within any formula or to enclose it within any category. Whatever is said about Simone Weil, he added, is liable to distort her; she must be allowed to speak for herself. T.S. Eliot, in his introduction to *The Need for Roots*, describing his first encounter with her 'great soul and brilliant mind' is similarly reluctant to use conventional methods of evaluating her work. He advocates exposure 'to the personality of a woman of genius, of a kind of genius akin to that of the saints' in lieu of the orthodox search for points of agreement or disagreement. (Eliot, 1952) Comparing her work with that of Wittgenstein, Peter Winch and Hugh Price are struck by the 'almost visionary ability' she possesses 'to draw together strands of knowledge from many different fields'. (Price, 1978) They propose her *Lectures on Philosophy* as a companion to Russell's *Problems of Philosophy*, in intro ucing students to the subject. Her pupils themselves speak of her as a uniquely gifted and sympathetic teacher. Anne Reynaud-Guérithault was careful to preserve all the notes she took in Simone Weil's classes and writes lovingly about the integrity and humility of the young graduate. The miners' groups in Saint-Etienne remember her with great and lasting affection and refer to the deep joy of having known and loved her while she was with them. To her family she was the tenderest of daughters and sisters.

Simone Weil was born in Paris on 3 February 1909 into an agnostic French-Jewish middle-class family. She and her brother André were brought up in a comfortable, cultivated background. Their unorthodox and energetic mother, Selma, oversaw their schooling and the French educational system of the time allowed her a fair measure of autonomy in choosing appropriate courses for each child and in combining state with private education. The two children were very close and both were intellectually precocious. After André was sent to the boys' lycée it was decided that Simone should attend that of the girls. André, three years his sister's senior, already showed a remarkable gift for mathematics and relished school. Simone, suffering from a physical disability, had a less happy introduction to the classroom. Her hands were too small in proportion to her body and she experienced great difficulty in using them. They were frequently swollen and painful so that throughout her life the act of writing was for her slow and laborious. This in turn caused her mother some anxiety and she ruefully compared Simone's lack of confidence with André's joy in his lessons. As a young girl, Selma Weil had wanted to study medicine but her father refused to allow her to do so.

At the age of fourteen, André had passed his *premier bac* and at sixteen was accepted at the Ecole Normale Supérieure, France's most prestigious *grande école*. It was at about this time that Simone was to fall into what she subsequently described as a bottomless despair at being excluded from the 'transcendent realm only truly great men enter and where truth resides' [my translation: S.M.]. A careful writer, mindful of the significance of every word she wrote (Alain said that she hammered her points home as if writing with a navvy's pick) it is interesting to note that she uses the word 'men' specifically (*les hommes authentiquement grands*). However, it was then too that 'suddenly and forever' she gained the conviction that by longing for truth and making a constant effort of attention so as to reach it, anyone can attain it, whatever one's natural faculties. 'Under the name of truth' she adds 'I also included beauty, virtue and every kind of goodness'. (Weil, 1951b)

The word 'attention' in Simone Weil's vocabulary has

particular significance, crucial to an understanding of her thought. It is not the kind of concentrated mental effort normally suggested by the expression 'paying attention', nor is it any particularly careful kind of scrutiny. It is rather a form of stepping back from all roles, including that of observer. It is a distancing of one's self not only from the thing observed, but from one's own faculties of observation.

Attention consists of suspending our thought, leaving it detached, empty and ready to be penetrated by the object. It means holding in our minds, within reach of this thought, but on a lower level and not in contact with it, the diverse knowledge we have acquired which we are forced to make use of. Our thought should be in relation to all particular and already formulated thoughts, as a man on a mountain who, as he looks forward, sees also below him, without actually looking at them, a great many forests and plains. Above all, our thought should be empty, waiting, not seeking anything, but ready to receive in its naked truth the object which is to penetrate it. All wrong translations, all absurdities in geometry problems, all clumsiness of style and all faulty connection of ideas . . . all such things are due to the fact that thought has seized upon some idea too hastily and being thus prematurely blocked, is not open to the truth. The cause is always that we have wanted to be too active; we have wanted to carry out a search. (Weil, 1951b)

So despite what she believed to be the mediocrity of her talents this conviction carried with it hope for inclusion in the realm of truth not only for herself, but for all, including the least endowed and most unfortunate, with whom she quickly aligned herself.

A few years earlier, when she could be found nowhere in the apartment, she was discovered in the Boulevard Saint-Michel below, attending a meeting of the unemployed. In her early teens, when the Weil family took a holiday in the spa town of Challes-les-Eaux, Simone got to know the staff of the hotel where they were staying and to discuss with them their working conditions. Scandalized by what she learned, she scandalized the residents even more by suggesting to the personnel that they should form a union.

Thus the first stirrings of her interest in labour relations and in the nature of labour itself occurred long before Simone Weil became an undergraduate.

In 1924, the Ecole Normale Supérieure was opened to women for the first time. The year after, Simone Weil entered the *khagne* (a class preparing to compete for entrance to training college for professionals) at the Lycée Henri Quatre in order to prepare for entrance to the Ecole Normale. Unlike most British state schools, the French provide their sixth-formers with a very strong grounding in philosophy. The legendary Alain or Emile Chartier was at this time teaching at the Henri Quatre and his influence over Simone Weil, as over Sartre and Merleau-Ponty, also students of his, was considerable. A friend of his, Lucien Cancouet, worked as a railwayman and was active in the C.G.T.U., Communist-affiliated union. He was anxious to make further education available to his fellow trade-unionists and enlisted the aid of some of Alain's pupils in order to help his fellow-workers gain qualifications after leaving school and also to provide them with the broad general culture which they lacked. Classes were held at a school in the rue Falguière, in French, maths and physics with some sociology and political economy. Simone Weil contributed to some of these classes while she was preparing for her own entrance examinations to the Ecole Normale.

Her first attempt was unsuccessful, largely because of a low mark in history. Simone de Beauvoir, who met her as a student for the first time during this period, was impressed by her capacity to feel the suffering of others. In reply to Simone de Beauvoir's suggestion that the main problem in life was not to make people happy but to discover the reason for their existence, Simone Weil said it was easy to see she had never been hungry. Her second attempt at entry to the Ecole Normale was successful. She came top of the list, Simone de Beauvoir second, and in 1928 they entered the Ecole Normale joining the three women already there, nick-named 'The Gleaners'. While there, Simone Weil continued to attend, illegally, Alain's classes at the Henri

Quatre. It was in one of the 1929 issues of his journal *Libres Propos*, that her earliest essay concerning the nature of labour was published. 'Concerning Perception, or The Adventure of Proteus' was an attempt to define work. She regarded it as true action, not that which emanates from the passions, from the unbridled imagination but action that conforms to geometry, that is to say which is brought into being through knowledge of the world that is gained by moving progressively from one simple idea to another. It is through work that reason seizes hold of the world.

Simone Weil lays stress on the importance of advancing from one clear notion to the next. She believed, like Alain, that philosophy is the explanation of the obvious through the obscure. The connection between her experiences at the working men's school in the rue Falguière and her studies at the Ecole Normale Supérieure was crucially important. It provided the link between her most deeply held beliefs and the means of their implementation. At the School, re-nowned for the independence of spirit of its students, Simone Weil acquired a reputation for eccentricity. Hers was not, however, the cultivated originality typical of both youth in general and of that decade in particular. It was a genuine nonconformity with contemporary social standards that required courage to maintain and which must have made her miserable. She worked phenomenally hard and whether as a result of doing so or of other factors, severe and near-incapacitating headaches, from which she was never entirely free, began during this time.

She became associated with various pacifist movements. By brusque and uncompromising demands for support in signing petitions connected with them, in drawing up mani-festoes and in particular with soliciting contributions for trade-union strike funds, she made several enemies. She was not widely popular with her peers but it was by the School's Administration that she was viewed with the great-est hostility. This was to have serious repercussions when it came to her placement after she had received a brilliant degree in 1931. Having expressed a preference for a post in a port or in an industrial town in the North or the Centre, she was posted almost as far away as possible, to Le Puy, allegedly at the request of the Dean.

During her university career, Simone Weil had joined a group associated with the review '*La Révolution Prolétarienne*'. Upon her arrival in Le Puy she contacted syndicalist groups at the large industrial town of Saint-Etienne, some seventy miles away. It was here that she began to frequent industrial workers' milieux for the first time. Although she was working as an intellectual and being well paid for it, she regarded this as a mere quirk of fate and considered that since so many others had the right to nothing, she too had a right to nothing.

Her career at Le Puy was dramatic and short. While teaching at the lycée she made weekly trips to Saint-Etienne to attend and teach at workers' study circles and to attend meetings of the militant trade-union groups under the leadership of Pierre Arnaud, recently expelled from the Communist Party. 'La Ponote' as she became known, donated the supplementary pay she got for being an *agrégée* towards the purchase of books for these study groups. She lived on the five francs a day then being allocated as unemployment benefit and thereby contributed substantially to the miners' strike fund. She very soon ran into trouble with the educational authorities in Le Puy, leading deputations of unemployed workers into council meetings, writing strongly-worded letters of protest to the local press, carrying the red flag in demonstrations and allegedly inciting workers to strike. She scandalized the people of Le Puy and was twice requested to resign her post at the lycée and to ask for a change of placement. Her awkwardness and dislike of compromise often caused distress to those immediately around her. Recognizing her clumsiness, this time it was her pupils who were her protectors. There is no doubt that in practical terms they suffered directly in consequence. At the end of her year at Le Puy, the examination results of her teaching were catastrophic. Only a fraction of her class got through their *bachot* in philosophy, whether through unfair marking or because of her unorthodox teaching methods is not clear. Nevertheless, her teaching was unforgettable. Anne Reynaud-Guérithault, her student at Roanne, writes:

Simone Weil is by now already well known and is portrayed by some as 'the greatest mystic of the century' and by others as 'a revolutionary anarchist'. So I thought it would be of interest to introduce her, quite simply, as a teacher of philosophy.

She taught me at the girls' secondary school at Roanne during the school year 1933–4. Our class was a small one and had a family atmosphere about it: housed apart from the main school buildings, in a little summer house almost lost in the school grounds, we made our first acquaintance with great thoughts in an atmosphere of complete independence. When the weather was good we had our lessons under the shade of a fine cedar tree, and sometimes they became a search for the solution to a problem in geometry, or a friendly conversation.

I could waste time by reminiscing at some length about some strange rows that took place: the headmistress coming to look for marks and positions which Simone Weil usually refused to give: our orders to rub out the platonic inscription we had written above our classroom door: 'No one admitted unless he knows geometry'.

But I share the distaste of Gustave Thibon for such reminiscences: like him, 'I loved her too much for that'.

If 'a brother cannot speak of his sister as a writer can about a fellow writer', neither can a pupil speak in that way of a teacher she admired so much and who has had such a profound influence on her.

One must aim higher than that. Long before she became famous, I had carefully kept all my notes of her lessons. Simone Weil was too straightforward, too honest to 'cram us for exams' in lessons and keep her real thinking for other times. . . .

I think I can declare that there are not 'two Simone Weils' as people are beginning to say. And that is why I have stifled my scruples, although at first I was afraid of shocking people. (People do not like to be suddenly presented with an image of an artist, writer, hero or saint which is quite different from the one they had previously formed in their minds.) My scruples were vain. The Christian (by instinct if not by baptism) who, in 1943, died in a London hospital because she would not eat 'more than her ration', was the same person I had known, sharing her salary in 1933 with the factory-workers of Roanne.

The same person, too, were the mystic putting the 'void' before the 'real' (the well-known call, as she put it, of the 'void' for grace), and the physicist who, when speaking to us of 'verification' humbly allowed the facts to speak for themselves. ... (Reynaud-Guérithault, 1978)

Simone Weil described her own teaching in a letter to a colleague:

Dear Comrade,
As a reply to the Inquiry you have undertaken concerning the historical method of teaching science, I can only tell you about an experiment I made this year with my class (philosophy class at the Lycée for Girls at Le Puy).

My pupils, like most other pupils, regarded the various sciences as compilations of cut-and-dried knowledge, arranged in the manner indicated by the textbooks. They had *no idea* either of the connection between the sciences or of the methods by which they were created.

In short, such knowledge as they possessed about the sciences could not be described as culture but the opposite. This made it very difficult for me to deal with that part of the philosophy syllabus entitled 'Method in the Sciences'.

I explained to them that the sciences were not ready-made knowledge set forth in textbooks for the use of the ignorant, but knowledge acquired in the course of ages by men who employed methods entirely different from those used to expound them in textbooks. I offered to give a few supplementary lectures on the history of science. They agreed, and all of them attended the lectures voluntarily.

I gave them a rapid sketch of the development of mathematics, taking as central theme the duality: continuous-discontinuous, and describing it as the attempt to deal with the continuous by means of the discontinuous, measurement itself being the first step. I told them the history of Greek science: similar triangles (Thales and the pyramids) – Pythagoras' theorem – discovery of the incommensurables and the crisis it provoked – solution of the crisis by Eudoxus' theory of proportions – discovery of conics, as sections of the cone – method of exhaustion – and of the geometry of early modern times (algebra – analytic geometry – principle of the differential and integral calculus). I explained to them – as no one had troubled to do – how the infinitesimal calculus was the condition for the application of mathematics to physics, and consequently for the contemporary efflorescence of physics. All this was followed by all of them, even those most ignorant in science, with passionate interest and was very easily fitted into six or seven extra hours.

Lack of time and my own insufficient knowledge prevented me from doing the same for mechanics and physics; all I could do was to tell them some fragments of the history of those sciences. They would have liked to have more.

At the end of the series I read them the terms of your Inquiry into the historical method of teaching science and they all enthusiastically approved the principle of such a method. They said it was the only method which could make pupils see science as something human, instead of a kind of dogma which you have to believe without ever really knowing why.

So this experiment completely confirms your idea, from every point of view.

Simone Weil,
Lecturer in philosophy at the Lycée for Girls, Le Puy.
(Weil, 1965)

She shocked inspectors and rectors alike when, eventually relieved of her position, she announced that she had always regarded dismissal as the normal culmination of her career.

While at Le Puy she had been allowed to go down a mine and described the inappropriateness of the tool used (the pneumatic drill) to its operator. 'At present he [the worker] forms a single body with the machine and is added to it like a supplementary gear vibrating with its incessant shaking. This machine is not modelled on human nature but rather on the nature of coal and compressed air.' (Pétrement, 1977) To her mind, distortion of the correct relation of tool to user, one might almost say the reversal of that relation in capitalist production was the major problem to be solved in industrial relations.

She visited Germany in 1932. On her return she expressed her respect and admiration for the German working class and in a series of articles pointed out the similarities between national socialism and Russian communism, to the detriment of both. No nationalist movement based on solidarity between classes would, she believed, avert the disaster to which the German proletariat was rapidly being led. Upon her return to France she was heartbroken and events were soon to justify her acute distress. Hitler ordered the arrest of the most influential communists and after the burning of the Reichstag, at the beginning of the new parliamentary session in 1932, he announced that he had no further use for the socialists.

It was at this time that Simone Weil wrote one of her most passionate political articles. Entitled 'Towards the Proletarian Revolution?' it was a scathing attack on orthodox Russian communism which she saw as a dictatorship of a bureaucratic class. She believed that no proper socialist system would emerge until productive labour itself became the dominating factor. She castigated a new form of oppression which she called the oppression of the function. Trotsky, she said, had not gone nearly far enough in his criticism of Stalinist communism which she viewed as a system of production in which labour itself is subordinated, by means of the machine, to the function consisting in coordination of labour. This article provoked Trotsky himself who accused her of holding such views so as to defend her personality. She had written that true democracy is, by definition, nothing other than the subordination of society to the individual and that this was also the true definition of socialism. She had seen society as a force of nature as blind as all other natural forces and no less dangerous to people unless they could achieve mastery over it. (Cabaud, 1964)

After her transferral from Le Puy she was posted to a school in Auxerre near Paris. Her reputation had preceded her and relations between herself and both the administration and colleagues were extremely strained. Her sojourn fell into the now familiar pattern of so-called tendentious teaching, angry complaints from school inspectors and anxious parents, examination failures from the ranks of the best students, followed by ultimate transferral. Much of her time and energy now, however, was devoted to taking care of some of the refugees who began to flee Germany. Her severe headaches continued and if she made enemies from amongst her colleagues at school she was not to find sympathetic supporters within the C.G.T.U., the most powerful of the French trade unions. Her article had aroused the strongest resentment and many workers considered that by it the actions of the Communist Party in the USSR, had been hideously distorted. However, her association with union members continued throughout the time she spent teaching at a different school, this time at Roanne in the Rhône Valley. No amount of pressure or persuasion could influence her to behave with greater restraint. She still continued to take part in protest marches under the noses of alarmed parents whose children she taught every day. Accounts of her teaching show how deep was the affection and respect in which she was held by her students. Anne Reynaud-Guérithault remembers that amongst the most enduring lessons she learned from Simone Weil was that the intelligence shows one must not *seek* to understand, that one cannot do good consciously, that all value and all virtue cannot of their very essence be understood as such.

While at Roanne, a post which she had requested so as to be close to her revolutionary-syndicalist friends in Saint-Etienne, seventy or so miles away, she visited them regularly. She continued to teach in the study groups she had helped to set up there and to promote discussion of the issues she had raised in courageous speeches made at the Trade Union Congress in Rheims some time previously. There, though threatened with physical assault, she had openly asserted that Stalin was collaborating with Hitler. She described the realities facing those now in flight from the Nazis and the betrayal by the Soviet Communists of their German comrades. These unpalatable truths were difficult to utter in such places and Simone Weil was not helped by her physical appearance and manner of speech.

She looked and sounded like an intellectual. She was careless in her dress, often had cigarette burns in her clothes, and spoke in a rather monotonous tone. Largely thanks to her considerable powers of analysis and expression, and the strength and passion of her conviction, she became a rallying-point in the stormy meetings and demonstrations that took place during the famous general strikes in Saint-Etienne in 1932. She was not, however, relieved of her post at Roanne. At the end of her year there, she applied for a leave of absence for personal studies in order to put into action a plan which she had had in mind since leaving the Ecole Normale. In her application she expressed it as follows:

I would very much like to prepare a philosophical treatise dealing with the relationship between modern technology, the basis of large-scale industry, and the essential aspects of our civilization by which I mean, on the one hand, our social organization and on the other our culture. (Pétrement, 1977)

Simone Weil was anxious to become an industrial worker and a bona-fide member of the groups she had represented intellectually at meetings and demonstrations at Saint-Etienne, Le Puy, Auxerre and Roanne. Before entering the factory she wrote as follows:

Monsieur,
I am late in replying, because the rendezvous has been difficult to arrange. I cannot get to Moulins until quite late on Monday afternoon (about 4 o'clock) and I would have to leave at 9. If you are free to give me an hour or two between those times I will come. In that case you have only to fix a definite meeting place, remembering that I don't know Moulins. I hope it will be possible, as I think it will be an advantage to talk rather than write.

So the thoughts which your letters have suggested to me can wait until we meet. I will mention only one doubt which already occurred to me when I heard your lecture.

You say: Every man is both a link in some automatic series and *also* an instigator of trains of events.

First of all, it seems to me one must distinguish the various degrees of activity and passivity in a man's relations with the trains of events which enter into his life. A man may originate trains of events (be an inventor ...) – he may re-create them in thought – he may enact them without thinking them – he may be the occasion of trains of events thought or enacted by others – and so on. But this is something obvious.

What worries me a little is this. When you say that an assembly line worker, for example, as soon as he comes out of the factory is free from the domain of the automatic series, you are clearly right. But what do you conclude from this? If you conclude that every man, however oppressed, still has the opportunity every day to act as a man and therefore never entirely forgoes his human status, very well. But if you conclude that the life of a worker at a conveyor belt in Renault or Citroën is an acceptable one for a man who wants to preserve human dignity, I cannot follow you. I don't think that *is* what you mean – in fact I am sure it isn't – but I would like to get the point perfectly clear.

'Quantity changes into quality', as the Marxists say, following Hegel. Both automatic series *and* motivated trains of events occur in all human lives, of course; but the question of proportion enters in, and it can be said in a general way that automatic series cannot occupy more than a certain proportion of a man's life without degrading it.

But I think we are agreed about this. ... (Weil, 1965)

She wished, by entering the manual workforce, to examine for herself the meaning of the phrase 'workers' control of production'. This is the pivot upon which both her social and philosophical concerns rest. 'She defined liberty as being neither absence of constraint nor a relationship between desire and its satisfaction, but as a relationship between thought and action. The free person is he or she whose every action proceeds from a preliminary judgement concerning the end which he or she has set and the sequence of means suitable for attaining this end.' (Pétrement, 1977) Human beings are constantly aware of an unbending necessity or series of constraints which bind their existence, even if it be only the constraint of mortality. Being capable of thought, they may choose between responding like robots to stimuli that act upon them from outside or adapting to an inner representation of that necessity which is formed idiosyncratically.

That choice determines whether they are free or not and it is the possibility of making precisely that crucial choice which she believed had been removed from the lives of the factory workers.

While near Saint-Etienne, she had made many friends, amongst them Urbain and Albertine Thévenon, militant trade-union teachers. The manner of their first meeting shows a certain ruthlessness in Simone Weil's character which many people found intolerable. She rang the bell and the door was opened by Albertine, one hand inside a sock that she was in the middle of darning. Having ascertained that M. Thévenon was in, she roughly shouldered his wife aside and walked past her into the room where he was sitting. The Thévenons record their surprise. Albertine subsequently became a close friend and wrote the introduction to Simone Weil's posthumously published factory journal. She, as well as others, objected strongly to Simone Weil's proposal of becoming a factory worker and said her miner friends had no sympathy for *roi-charbon* experiments of this kind in which the boss's son works in his father's mine incognito for a year before joining the board of directors. Secondly, they advised against this form of study on physical grounds. She was more ill-suited than most to perform the kind of work she proposed. However, she ignored her friends' advice and on her return to Paris took lodgings in the rue Lecourbe close to the Alsthom electrical factory where she eventually found a job as a power-press operator. To Albertine soon afterwards she wrote:

Dear Albertine,
I am obliged to rest because of a slight illness (a touch of inflammation of the ear – nothing serious) so I seize the opportunity for a little talk with you. In a normal working week it is difficult to make any effort beyond what I am compelled to make. But that's not the only reason I haven't written; it's also the number of things there are to tell and the impossibility of telling the essential. Perhaps later on I shall find the right words, but at present it seems to me that I should need a new language to convey what needs to be said. Although this experience is in many

ways what I expected it to be, there is also an abysmal difference: it is reality and no longer imagination. It is not that it has changed one or the other of my ideas (on the contrary, it has confirmed many of them), but infinitely more – it has changed my whole view of things, even my very feeling about life. I shall know joy again in the future, but there is a certain lightness of heart which, it seems to me, will never again be possible. But that's enough about it: to try to express the inexpressible is to degrade it.

As regards the things that can be expressed, I have learnt quite a lot about the organization of a firm. It is inhuman; work broken down into small processes, and paid by the piece; relations between different units of the firm and different work processes organized in a purely bureaucratic way. One's attention has nothing worthy to engage it, but on the contrary is constrained to fix itself, second by second, upon the same trivial problem, with only such variants as speeding up your output from 6 minutes to 5 for 50 pieces, or something of that sort. Thank heaven, there are manual skills to be acquired, which from time to time lends some interest to this pursuit of speed. But what I ask myself is how can all this be humanized; because if the separate processes were not paid by the piece the boredom they engender would inhibit attention and slow down the work considerably, and produce a lot of spoiled pieces. And if the processes were not subdivided. . . . But I have no time to go into all this by letter. Only when I think that the great Bolshevik leaders proposed to create a *free* working class and that doubtless none of them – certainly not Trotsky, and I don't think Lenin either – had ever set foot inside a factory, so that they hadn't the faintest idea of the real conditions which make servitude or freedom for the workers – well, politics appears to me a sinister farce.

I must point out that all I have said refers to unskilled labour. About skilled labour I have almost everything still to learn. It will come, I hope.

To speak frankly, for me this life is pretty hard. And the more so because my headaches have not been obliging enough to withdraw so as to make things easier – and working among machines with a headache is painful. It is only on Saturday afternoon and Sunday that I can breathe, and find myself again, and recover the ability to turn over a few thoughts in my head. In a general way, the temptation to give up thinking altogether is the most difficult one to resist in a life like this: one feels so clearly that it is the only way to stop suffering! First of all, to stop suffering morally. Because the situation itself automatically banishes rebellious feelings: to work with irritation would be to work badly and so condemn oneself to starvation; and leaving aside the work, there is no person to be a target for one's irritation. One dare not be insolent to the foremen and, moreover, they very often don't even make one want to be. So one is left with no possible feeling about one's own fate except sadness. And thus one is tempted to cease, purely and simply, from being conscious of anything except the sordid daily round of life. And physically too it is a great temptation to lapse into semi-somnolence outside working hours. I have the greatest respect for workmen who manage to educate themselves. It is true they are usually tough; but all the same it must require a lot of stamina. And it is becoming more and more unusual with the advance of rationalization. I wonder if it is the same with skilled workers.

I am sticking it, in spite of everything. And I don't for one moment regret having embarked on the experience. Quite the contrary, I am infinitely thankful whenever I think of it. But curiously enough I don't often think of it. My capacity for adaptation is almost unlimited, so that I am able to forget that I am a 'qualified lecturer' on tour in the working class, and to live my present life as though I had always been destined for it (which is true enough in a sense), and as though it would last for ever and was imposed on me by ineluctable necessity instead of my own free choice.

But I promise you that when I can't stick it any longer I'll go and rest somewhere – perhaps with you. [...]

I perceive I haven't said anything about my fellow workers. It will be for another time. But once again, it is hard to express. ... They are nice, very nice. But as for real fraternity, I have hardly felt any. With one exception: the storekeeper in the tool-shop, a skilled worker and extremely competent, whom I appeal to whenever I am in despair over a job which I cannot manage properly, because he is a hundred times nicer and more intelligent than the machine-setters (who are not skilled workers). There is a lot of jealousy among the women – who are indeed obliged by the organization of the factory to compete with one another. I only know 3 or 4 who are entirely sympathetic. As for the men, some of them seem to be very nice types. But there aren't many of them in the shop where I work, apart from the machine-setters, who are not real comrades. I hope to be moved to another shop after a time, so as to enlarge my experience. [...]

Well, au revoir. Write soon.

S.W. (Weil, 1965)

She was paid at a piece-rate and found that however hard she worked, she could not make enough to be properly nourished. The speed at which she worked was considerably too slow since she could not train her mind to stop thinking. This in turn brought about anxiety and fear of not reaching the prescribed rate to be kept on and she lived from day to day in the constant apprehension of being sacked for not reaching the required quotas. The work was extremely hard and during the next year she was to suffer burns, cuts and abscesses to accompany the headaches which had never abated. She describes the reification of the individual in the factory as one of the worst aspects of industrial life and the arbitrariness with which the employee is hired, fired and manipulated. Under these conditions the smallest act of kindness, a sympathetic smile, for example, comes to represent an indescribable favour. Inevitably, despite certain allowances which her foreman made for inexperience, she found herself eventually laid off. There followed a period in which she went from factory to factory, frequently exhausted from walking after not having had enough to eat, looking for work. By this time she did at least have a work permit, which had been initially difficult to obtain. She describes the feeling of comradeship which she felt with some others whom she met at this period who were also looking for work as 'miraculous'. Her journal reads:

Wednesday – (divine weather) with 2 fitters. One aged 18. The other 58. *Very* interesting, but extremely reserved. But obviously a real man. Living alone (wife left him). His big interest is his hobby, photography. 'They killed the cinema with the Talkies, instead of letting it be what it really is, the most perfect development of photography.' [...] Affects a certain cynicism. But obviously a man of heart.

Conversation between the 3 of us the whole morning, extraordinarily free, easy, on a level above the petty miseries of life which are the over-riding preoccupation of slaves, especially women. What a relief, after Alsthom!

The young one is interesting too. As we were going along by Saint-Cloud he said: 'If I were in form (he isn't, alas, because he's hungry) I should draw – Everyone has something that interests him.' 'For me', says the other one, 'it's photography.' The young one asks me: 'And you, what is your passion?' Embarrassed, I answer: 'Reading.' And he; 'Yes, I can imagine that. But not novels. More philosophic, wouldn't it be?' Then we talk about Zola, and Jack London.

Clearly, both of them have revolutionary tendencies (but that's quite the wrong word – no, say rather that they have class awareness and the spirit of free men). But when we get on to national defence we no longer agree. However, I don't insist.

Complete comradeship. For the first time in my life, really. No barrier, either in class difference (because it has been eliminated), or in sex. Miraculous. (Weil, 1956)

She found work in the Basse-Indre Forges where, much to her relief, she was not assigned to the conveyor belt. The next day she wrote to a friend:

Dear Boris,
I force myself to write you a few lines, because otherwise I should not have the courage to leave any written trace of the first impressions of my new experience. The self-styled sympathetic little establishment proved to be in the first place, a fairly large establishment and then, above all, a foul, a very foul establishment. And in that foul establishment there is one particularly loathsome workshop: it is mine. I hasten to add, for your reassurance, that I was moved out at the end of the morning and put in a quiet little corner where I have a good chance of remaining all next week and where I am not on a machine.

Yesterday I was on the same job the whole day (stamping press). I worked until 4 o'clock at the rate of 400 pieces an hour (note that the job was by the hour, at 3 frs. an hour) and I felt I was working hard. At 4 o'clock the foreman came and said that if I didn't do 800 he would get rid of me: 'If you do 800 tomorrow, *perhaps I'll consent* to keep you.' They make a favour, you see, of allowing us to kill ourselves, and we have to say thank you. By straining my utmost I got up to 600 an hour. Nevertheless, they let me start again this morning (they are short of women because the place is so bad that the personnel are always leaving; and they have urgent orders for armaments). I was at the same job for an hour and by making even greater efforts I got up to just over 650. Then I was given various other jobs, always with the same instructions, namely, to go at full speed. For 9 hours a day (because the mid-day break ends at 1, not 1.15 as I told you) the women work like this, literally without a moment's respite. If you are changing from one job to another, or looking for a container, it is always at the double.

All the same, perhaps I should have given way if I had been kept in their infernal shop. Where I now I am with workers who take things equably. I should never have believed there could be such differences between two corners of the same place.

Well, that's enough for today. I am almost sorry I've written. You have enough troubles without my telling you more sad stories.

Affectionately,
S.W. (Weil, 1965)

None of the conditions under which she and the other employees worked allowed for the essential conditions she believed indispensable for dignity in labour. Among these prerequisites were the possibility for thought, for invention and for the exercise of judgement. After only three weeks in the Alsthom factory she had come to see herself as a slave and was constantly amazed, outside the factory to perceive that she was in fact like everyone else: 'How is it that I, a slave, can get on this bus, use it by paying my twelve sous like anybody else? What an extraordinary favour. If they had brutally forced me off . . . I think it would have seemed perfectly natural to me.' (Weil, 1951a) Again she was sacked and after another period of unemployment worked at the Renault factory in Boulogne-Billancourt. The over-riding impression she gained from this experience was of the pliability of human beings and the speed with which all feelings of anger or revolt against inhumane conditions was changed to total submission. She felt exactly like a beast of burden. To Albertine again she wrote:

Dear Albertine.

It did me good to hear from you. There are some things, it seems to me, in which only you and I understand one another. You are still alive; you can't imagine how happy that makes me. [...]

You certainly deserved to get free. Any progress in life is always dearly bought. Almost always at the price of intolerable pain. [...]

Do you know, an idea has suddenly struck me. I see you and me, in the holidays, with some sous in our pockets and rucksacks on our backs, tramping the roads and paths and fields. We'd sleep in barns now and then. And sometimes we'd do some harvesting in exchange for a meal. [...] What do you say? [...]

What you wrote about the factory went straight to my heart. I felt the same as you, ever since I was a child. That is why I had to go there in the end, and you can never know how it made me suffer before, until I went. But once you get there, how different it is! As a result, I now see the social problem in this way: What a factory ought to be is something like what you felt that day at Saint-Chamond, and what I have so often felt – a place where one makes a hard and painful, but nevertheless joyful, contact with real life. Not the gloomy place it is where people only obey orders, and have all their humanity broken down, and become degraded lower than the machines.

On one occasion I experienced fully the thing that I had glimpsed, like you, from outside. It was at my first place. Imagine me in front of a great furnace which vomits flames and scorching heat full in my face. The fire comes from five or six openings at the bottom of the furnace. I stand right in front of it to insert about thirty large metal bobbins, which are made by an Italian woman with a brave and open countenance who is just alongside me. These bobbins are for the trams and metros. I have to take great care that they don't fall into the open holes, because they would melt. Therefore I must stand close up to the furnace and not make any clumsy movement, in spite of the scorching heat on my face and the fire on my arms (which still show the burns). I close the shutter and wait a few minutes; then I open it and draw the red-hot bobbins out with a hook. I must do it very quickly or else the last ones would begin to melt, and must take even greater care lest any of them fall into the open holes. And then I do it all over again. A welder with a serious expression and dark spectacles sits opposite me, working intently. Each time I wince from the furnace heat on my face, he looks at me with a sad smile of fraternal sympathy which does me untold good. On the other side, around some big tables, is a group of armature winders. They work together as a team, like brothers, carefully and without haste. They are highly skilled copper workers; they must calculate, and read very complicated drawings, and make use of descriptive geometry. Further on, a hefty youth is sledge-hammering some iron bars, raising a din to split your head. All this is going on in a corner at the far end of the workshop, where one feels at home, and where the overseer and foreman hardly ever come. I was there 4 times, for 2 or 3 hours (at 7 to 8 frs. an hour – which counts, you know!). The first time, after an hour and a half of the heat and effort and pain I lost control of my movements and couldn't close the shutter. One of the copper workers (all very nice types) immediately noticed and jumped to do it for me. I would go back to that little corner of the workshop this moment if I could (or at least as soon as I have recovered my strength). On those evenings I felt the joy of eating bread that one has earned.

But that experience stands out as unique in my factory life. What working in a factory meant for me personally was as follows. It meant that all the external reasons (which I had previously thought internal) upon which my sense of personal dignity, my self-respect, was based were radically destroyed within two or three weeks by the daily experience of brutal constraint. And don't imagine that this provoked in me any rebellious reaction. No, on the contrary; it produced the last thing I expected from myself – docility. The resigned docility of a beast of burden. It seemed to me that I was born to wait for, and receive, and carry out orders – that I had never done and never would do anything else. I am not proud of that confession. It is the kind of suffering no worker talks about: it is too painful even to think of it. When I was kept away from work by illness I became fully aware of the degradation into which I was falling, and I swore to myself that I would go on enduring the life until the day when I was able to pull myself together in spite of it. And I kept my word. Slowly and painfully, in and through slavery. I reconquered the sense of my human dignity – a sense which relied, this time, upon nothing outside myself and was accompanied always by the knowledge that I possessed no right to anything, and that any moment free from humiliation and suffering should be accepted as a favour, as merely a lucky chance.

There are two factors in this slavery: the necessity for speed, and passive obedience to orders. Speed: in order to 'make the grade' one has to repeat movement faster than one can think, so that not only reflection but even day-dreaming is impossible. In front of his machine, the worker has to annihilate his soul, his thought, his feelings, and everything, for eight hours a day. If he is irritated, or sad, or disgusted, he must swallow and completely suppress his irritation, sadness, or disgust; they would slow down his output. And the same with joy. Then orders: from the time he clocks in to the time he clocks out he may at any moment receive any order; and he must always obey without a word. The order may be an unpleasant or a dangerous or even an impracticable one; or two superiors may give contradictory orders; no matter, one submits in silence. To speak to a superior – even for something indispensable – is always to risk a snub, even though he may be a kindly man (the kindest men have spells of bad temper); and one must take the snub too in silence. As for one's own fits of irritation or bad humour, one must swallow them; they can have no outlet either in word or gesture. All one's movements are determined all the time by the work. In this situation, thought shrivels up and withdraws, as the flesh flinches from a lancet. One *cannot* be 'conscious'.

In all this I am speaking of unskilled work, of course (and especially the women's work).

And in the midst of it all a smile, a word of kindness, a moment of human contact, have more value than the most devoted friendships among the priviliged, both great and small. It is only there that one knows what human brotherhood is. But there is little of it, very little. Most often, relations between comrades reflect the harshness which dominates everything there.

Now I have chattered enough. I could write volumes about it all.

I wanted also to say this: I feel that the change from that hard life to my present one is corrupting me. I know now what it's like when a worker gets a 'permanent billet'. But I try to resist. If I let myself go I should forget it all and settle down among my privileges without wishing to think of them as such. But don't worry, I'm not letting myself go. Moreover, I said farewell to my gaiety in that life; it has left an indelible bitterness in my heart. Yet all the same I am glad to have experienced it.

Keep this letter – perhaps I'll ask you for it one day, if I want to

collect all my memories of that time. Not so as to publish
something about it (at least I think not), but to prevent myself
from forgetting. It is difficult not to forget when one changes
one's way of life so radically.

S.W. (Weil, 1965)

In her life as a worker she became strongly aware of two
things. First that she no longer felt as though she had any
rights and second that the idea of time was unbearable. The
reason for the latter was that workers live in fear of what is
to come, in the form of orders. Human beings crave warmth
and fellow feeling at work. In the factory what they experience is 'icy pandemonium.' Her experience was to leave an
indelible impression on her spirit. She was as she put it
branded like so many others with the mark of a slave. What
had remained of her belief in revolution disappeared completely. She came to believe instead that the workers' capacity for action, let alone for revolution was seriously over-
estimated by the theorists of the day. She believed that no
new technique, no re-adaptation of machines to their opera-
tors and no technical innovation would effectively alleviate
the suffering which comes from the humiliation of being
treated as an object. Not religion, but revolution, she said,
was the opium of the people.

Simone Weil had become very weak and ill during the
time she spent in the factories. Shattered in mind and body
she recognized her sufferings as 'biological and not social'.
Her parents went with her to Portugal for a holiday. Leaving them, she went by herself to a small fishing village
where the first of 'three contacts with Christianity that have
really counted' took place.

As I worked in the factory, indistinguishable to all eyes, including
my own, from the anonymous mass, the affliction of others
entered into my flesh and my soul. Nothing separated me from it
for I had really forgotten my past and I looked forward to no
future, finding it difficult to imagine the possibility of surviving
all the fatigue. What I went through there marked me in so lasting
a manner that still to-day when any human being, whoever he

may be and in whatever circumstances, speaks to me without brutality, I cannot help having the impression that there must be a mistake and that unfortunately the mistake will in all probability disappear. There I received for ever the mark of a slave, like the branding of the red-hot iron which the Romans put on the foreheads of their most despised slaves. Since then I have always regarded myself as a slave.

In this state of mind then, and in a wretched condition physically, I entered the little Portuguese village, which, alas, was very wretched too, on the very day of its patronal festival. I was alone. It was the evening and there was a full moon. It was by the sea. The wives of the fishermen were going in procession to make a tour of all the ships, carrying candles and singing what must certainly be very ancient hymns of a heart-rending sadness. Nothing can give any idea of it. I have never heard anything so poignant unless it were the song of the boatmen on the Volga. There the conviction was suddenly borne in upon me that Christianity is pre-eminently the religion of slaves, that slaves cannot help belonging to it, and I among others. (Weil, 1951b)

On her return, she was appointed to teach philosophy at the lycée of Bourges where she continued her investigations into the nature of industrial labour. There she was fortunate enough to meet an engineer, M. Bernard, who was also the technical manager of a factory at Rosières, not far away. Through him, she was able to put into operation an idea she had long cherished. This was to recount a selection of the great works of Greek literature, of which she believed the workers were the most appropriate readership. She believed that this literature would go straight to the hearts of the workers, indeed that their true message could be understood by none better.

It is in respect of one thing only that human nature can bear for the soul's desire to be directed not towards what might be or what will be but towards what is and that is in respect of beauty. Everything beautiful is the object of desire but one desires that it be not otherwise, that it be unchanged, that it be exactly what it

is. One looks with desire at a clear starry night and one desires
exactly the sight before one's eyes. Since the people are forced to
direct all their desires towards what they already possess, beauty
is made for them and they for it. For other social classes, poetry is
a luxury but the people need poetry as they need bread. . . .
(Weil, 1951a)

Works such as these could act as what she termed *metaxu* or
bridges between the world of the good and the world of the
necessary. She began with Sophocles' *Antigone*, followed by
Electra and they were published in the factory house
magazine Bernard had started, *Entre Nous*.

For almost a year, Bernard and Simone Weil corre-
sponded. He was anxious to learn from her experiences and
do as much as he could for her and the workers under his
control. He was generous and hospitable to her suggestions
and relations between them were good. However, as news
of sit-in strikes in Paris reached her, Simone Weil could
not conceal her delight. Demonstrating a singular insensi-
tivity in the circumstances, she decided to send him a
letter expressing her 'unspeakable joy and relief', which
wounded him greatly. Although he could understand her
having those feelings, he could not accept her gratuitous
expression of them to him. Sadly, what could have grown
into a fruitful collaboration between representatives of top
and bottom of the factory ceased abruptly in consequence.

This was the period of the Popular Front in both France
and Spain, and a large part of the political writing of
Simone Weil, that is, a large part of the work which she
actually intended for publication (as opposed to that which
appeared after her death) was accomplished during this
time. She became increasingly interested, for example, in
the colonial question and wrote movingly and ironically on
the reaction of France to the attempted German occupation
of Morocco. Increasingly,the concepts of state and nationhood became distasteful and meaningless to her, and she
wrote now about the fictitious or imaginary character of
each.

In August and September of 1936 she went to fight in the Spanish Civil War and was for a while attached to a group of anarchists under Durutti, the main leader of the Catalan anarchists. An accident in which her foot was burned with boiling oil meant she had to be removed from the Aragon front to Sitges, with her illusions about the war equally badly damaged.

My own feeling was that when once a certain class of people has been placed by the temporal and spiritual authorities outside the ranks of those whose life has value, then nothing comes more naturally to men than murder. As soon as men know that they can kill without fear of punishment or blame, they kill; or at least they encourage killers with approving smiles. If anyone happens to feel a slight distaste to begin with, he keeps quiet and he soon begins to suppress it for fear of seeming unmanly. People get carried away by a sort of intoxication which is irresistible without a fortitude of soul which I am bound to consider exceptional since I have met with it nowhere. ... (Weil, 1965)

In the spring of 1937 she travelled again, this time in Italy. No one reading the letters written during this period could doubt the generous and exuberant love of life that was in her.

In Spain she had met a young student, Jean Posternak, who had told her about Italy. To him she wrote:

Cher ami,
Your directions for the *Maggio musicale* were in line with my own inclination, so I complied with them. I had never heard *Figaro*, apart from excerpts, and as Bruno Walter's conducting was beyond all praise you can easily imagine the impression it made on me. And yet the impression paled beside the *Incoronazione di Poppaea*, played in the Boboli garden amphitheatre under the stars with the Pitti palace for background. I bitterly regretted your absence, because it was a marvel you would really have appreciated, a marvel to be remembered all one's life. But I like to believe you will hear it one day. The public was cool (pack of brutes!). Luckily, however, my enjoyment was enough to fill a whole amphitheatre. Music of such simplicity, serenity, and

sweetness, of such dancing movement. . . . You remember my reaction when you put anything at all on the gramophone after Bach? Well, there are melodies of Monteverdi which I would admire even after the famous andante.

This return to Florence has been a delight. If the first contact with Florence is delightful, how much more so to return to it as to a home after a short journey! And that is exactly the impression I had. Definitely, I shall not go to Venice this time. It is certain that I shall love it (if only from deference to you) if I ever see it; but it is equally certain that it will never be so close to my heart as Florence. The beauties of Florence are of a kind which d'Annunzio could never celebrate, or so I imagine. I say this in praise of Florence, because I am far from sharing your sympathy for the *Fuoco*, which you advised me in one of your letters to read. It is a way of understanding art and life which horrifies me, and I am convinced the man will soon be in profound and justified oblivion.

I shall have collected in a short time at Florence a certain number of pure joys. Fiesole (whence I descended just to listen to Mozart . . .), San Miniato (where I returned twice, Florence's most beautiful church in my opinion), the old sacristy of San Lorenzo, the bas-reliefs of the Campanile, the Giotto frescoes at Santa Croce, Giorgione's Concert, David, the Dawn and the Night . . . and mingled with them some verses of Dante, Petrarch, Michelangelo, and Lorenzo the Magnificent. (Do you know his poems? I didn't know till I came here that he wrote any; some of them are lovely:

> *Quant' e bella giovinezza*
> *Che si sfugge tuttavia . . .*)

Rossini, Mozart, Monteverdi, Galico – for I have just purchased his complete works and spent some luminous hours one afternoon perusing his extraordinary original insights about uniformly accelerated motion. That is as aesthetically pleasing as anything, especially when one reads it here. And Machiavelli, etc., etc. How I wish I knew and understood the underlying connection between all these flowers of the Italian genius, instead of merely enjoying them on the surface . . . I have also made a mental collection of a great many Florentine 'fiaschetterie' (charming word!) because I almost always eat in them (pasta al sugo, 70c. to 1 lira) and always at a different one. Near the Carmine (with the beautiful Masaccio frescoes) there is one which is always full of young workmen and little old pensioners who enjoy themselves by making up songs, both words and music! How I pity the unfortunates who have plenty of money and eat in restaurants at 8 or 10 lire.

And just conceive that in addition to this I also frequent the House of the Fascio, in a delightful old palace where I was taken by one of the founders of the Florence Fascio – a railwayman by profession and a former trade unionist (this was our common subject) with whom I got into conversation at a cafe terrace in the Piazza Vittorio Emmanuele. In the Casa del Fascio there is an information bureau for foreigners, in the charge of a young intellectual – sincere, intelligent and, of course, attractive (they are chosen for that). In his office I met a marquis of one of the oldest Florentine families – very rich, very fascist, very interesting. Among the things he told me (I did not hide my own opinions) some were sympathetic, others less so. It would take too long to relate. At the Dopolavoro office I was given a collection of stories written by workers. Lamentable, compared to those in the papers I read (do you remember?). The fatuousness of paternalism in all its horror. To me, this is significant.

At this point I must tell you about my meeting with your friend A. I would be very interested to know what he said about it, if he has written to you . . . I think that if you could have been there behind a screen you'd have had a good laugh. For my part, I have wanted very much for a long time to have a frank conversation with exactly the sort of young man he is – that is to say, holding the opinions you know and at the same time possessing intelligence and personality, so that he is not a mere echo. He seemed to me to be like that; with one of those characters which always interest me, full of repressed ardour and unavowed ambitions. So I am grateful to you for the introduction; but I doubt if he has any such feeling. I fairly made him gasp. And yet I didn't do it on purpose.

He thinks that my legitimate and normal place in society is in the depths of a salt-mine. (He would send me there, I think, if he is consistent, as soon as his people govern France.) And I quite agree with him. If I had any choice in the matter I would prefer hardship and starvation in a salt-mine to living with the narrow and limited horizon of these young people. I should feel the mine less suffocating than that atmosphere – the nationalistic obsession the adoration of power in its most brutal form, namely the collectivity (see Plato's 'great beast', *Republic*, Book VI), the camouflaged deification of death. By contrast, what you wrote to me about Toscanini (you know what I mean) seemed like a great breath of fresh air. There are still men in the world who feel themselves compatriots of all men, in the noble tradition of Marcus Aurelius and Goethe.

Thank heaven, the people who are obsessed by all these myths are not the only people in this country; there are also men and women of the people, and young fellows in blue overalls, whose faces and manners have visibly been moulded only by daily contact with problems of real life. .... (Weil, 1965)

She is brimming over with joy in everything that surrounds her, finds in Stresa, Milan, Florence, Bologna, all that is charming and delightful. She listens to Rossini, Verdi, Donizetti, eats and drinks with gusto, looks at paintings, frescoes, sculpture, goes to theatres and puppet shows, and finally makes her way to Assisi, where 'something stronger than I was compelled me for the first time in my life to go down on my knees.' (Weil, 1951b)

Returning to France, this time to teach both philosophy and Greek at the lycée of Saint Quentin in Picardy she continued her prolific writing, arguing more and more strenuously against offensive operation in war and in favour of defensive guerrilla warfare which she considered both more morally acceptable and generally more effective. Her already poor health was beginning to deteriorate and in January 1938 she was granted six months' sick leave. She went to Solesmes, to the Benedictine monastery famous for the plain-chant of which she was particularly fond. During this short but significant period in her life, while she was listening to the music, when as she said, each sound as it entered her head felt like a blow, the thought of the passion of Christ entered into her once and for all. Here too, she met a young Englishman whose radiant face after having taken communion made such an extraordinary impression upon her. They met and he introduced her to the meta-physical poets of the seventeenth century, notably to Donne, Crashaw and most importantly to George Herbert's poem 'Love'. This poem was to have great significance in her life since:

> I used to think I was merely
> reciting it as a beautiful poem,
> but without my knowing it the recitation
> had the virtue of a prayer. It was during
> one of those recitations that, as I told
> you, Christ himself came down and took
> possession of me. (Weil, 1951b)

The events that had taken place in Portugal, in Assisi and in Solesmes provided her spirit with a new certainty and her private writing with a new language. In her vocabulary was now included the word God. Her public writing at this time reflects secular preoccupations and it was during this period, from 1938 to 1940 that some of her most powerful essays were written, among them 'The *Iliad* or the Poem of Force', and 'Some Reflections on the Origins of Hitlerism'. They compare the latter totalitarianism with the Roman civilization whose influence she considered to be at the root of many of the ills of modern society. A devoted Hellenist, she attributed much of what was worth preserving in the latter to ideas which the Greeks had held, and which had gradually been discredited. Chief of these is the idea of balance, the importance of which in all spheres of human activity she was at pains to emphasize.

It was at about this time that she also began a series of notebooks subsequently entrusted to a friend, in which she would record her daily thoughts. In them is revealed her extraordinarily wide erudition; her familiarity with and love of all forms of folklore from all countries of the world, including the Scandinavian, Welsh, Eskimo, German; Sanskrit and the Upanishads, of Japanese and Chinese literature and culture, of mathematics, her real passion, and of physics and science of all kinds. She also wrote a play,

Venise Sauvée whose theme of rootedness and uprooting
was to occupy her till the end of her life. *Venise Sauvée*
concerns the attempted rape of the beautiful city of Venice
by a group of conspirators as in Thomas Otway's seventeenth century *Venice Preserv'd* or *A Plot Discovered*. One
of the conspirators is eventually so touched by the beauty of
the city as to betray the plot to the authorities, on condition
that his co-plotters be spared. Venice is spared therefore,
but Jaffier, the hero, sees the evil which he attempted to
avoid being thrust back upon himself. He himself is betrayed by the Ten, the guardians of the city, who refuse to
keep their promise of clemency to the conspirators, among
them his best friend. As Jacques Cabaud has pointed out,
the decisive factor is never mentioned in the play (Cabaud,
1964). It is not only the vision and memory of the eternal
beauty of the city, with its canals and palaces, which would
shortly see devastation, rape and pillage, but the beauty of
the city as a kind of repository, which finally prompts the
hero to betray the plot. The unforgivable crime that the
conspirators would be committing was not the particular
murder or robbery of this or that individual only, but the
crime of uprooting. They would be robbing the Venetians
of their *enracinement*. Later, while Simone Weil was
working in London for the Free French she was to write
elaborating this theme and defining in detail the charge
against the conspirators. Simone Weil's interest in the
'miracle' of Catharism centres on the fact that:

around Toulouse in the twelfth century the highest thought dwelt
within a whole human environment and not only in the minds of a
certain number of individuals. That, it seems to me, is the sole
difference between philosophy and religion, so long as religion is
something not dogmatic.

No thought attains to its fullest existence unless it is incarnated
in a human environment, and by environment I mean something
open to the world around, something which is steeped in the
surrounding society and is in contact with the whole of it, and not
simply a closed circle of disciples, around a master. For the lack
of such an environment in which to breathe, a superior mind

makes a philosophy for itself; but that is a second best and it produces thought of a lesser degree of reality. Probably there was an environment for the Pythagoreans, but this is a subject about which we have practically no knowledge. In Plato's time there was no longer anything of the sort; and one feels continually in his work his regret for the absence of such an environment, a nostalgic regret. (Weil, 1965)

Meanwhile, around her there was a very real conspiracy not to capture one city alone, but whole nations and a whole race. On 10 May 1940, the Germans began to move towards Paris. Under the Vichy regime, the rights of French Jews were being systematically restricted and gradually reduced by statutory regulations published periodically in the newspapers. Simone Weil's reaction to their appearance in the press was to write a letter of enquiry to the Minister of Education. In this letter she asked whether she might be given a reason for the Minister's failure to reply to a previous letter of hers requesting a teaching post in Algeria. In fact, one of the many statutory regulations expressly forbade Jews to teach. This prohibition was in part, she said, the reason for her writing. She stated that she had read the statutes but was unable to discover whom exactly was referred to by the term Jew. In the most civil terms she explained that this was a point never touched upon in her studies and about which she felt an uncertainty the Minister would, she hoped, be kind enough to dispel. The crux of the letter lies in its implication that such statutory regulations had no legal worth whatsoever. She pointed out that it was useless to refer back to grandparents for definition as the regulations required, for, without knowing what constituted Jewishness one was incapable of knowing if one had three Jewish grandparents. She added that she did not seriously consider herself connected intimately with a tribe inhabiting Palestine two thousand years ago. Personally she regarded herself as belonging to the French nation and the French tradition. Her letter was never answered.

On 13 June Paris was declared an open city. The Germans

arrived that night. In the afternoon, her parents persuaded her, much against her will, to accompany them as far as Nevers and from there to Vichy and Marseille. Once having left Paris, which she had always hoped would be defended, she planned to join those in London who were continuing the fight there. This could only be done by going through another country. Her brother managed to get to the United States without too much difficulty and she wrote to him later saying she must above all avoid going over there to live. She would do so, she continued, only on one condition – that he convey to her the absolute certainty that she would be able to realize her project of going from there to England. She wanted from him the most solemn promise that official authorization for this last leg of the journey would be granted. It was at about this time, during the first year of the war, that Simone Weil began to read the *Bhagavad Gita* and to read her own position into that of Arjuna. The *Bhagavad* addressed questions which were relevant to her concerns at the time, the purity of motive and of action in war. Now also was the time she began the study of gnosticism and the history of religion which was to form an important part of her thinking in the remaining years.

In Marseille she joined the Resistance network and her time there was spent initially writing for the war effort (including 'Sur les Responsabilités de la Littérature') and helping those whom she saw as unjustly treated. In this case they were, among others, the Indonesians and other nationals living in France who had been rounded up and put into camps. She was questioned several times by the police but continued her writing, publishing for the *Cahiers du Sud* and attempting to place another project concerning the creation of a front-line nursing squad. Simone Weil believed that one of the main reasons for Hitler's success so far was that his troops, trained not only for much longer than the French and Allied forces, but for offensive rather than defensive initiatives, and lived a kind of ersatz religion. Hitler had created special groups, like the young, fanaticized S.S., ready and eager to demonstrate suicidal daring, the source of which, she believed was extreme brutality. Her front-line nursing squad would similarly capture the imagination by its great courage (casualties would almost certainly be bound to occur). The symbolic presence of women in the front-line would be incalculably powerful. For the French and Allied soldiers there would be before their very eyes reminders of the values for which they were fighting and of the homes which they were defending. The Germans had the advantage of almost a decade's preparation for aggression and the inestimably valuable psychological advantage of progressing towards an objective. The French and Allied troops could only feel they were guarding the status quo.

Simultaneously, suspecting that she might not have much time left in the country, she wanted very much to know at first-hand the lives of agricultural workers. Through a friend, she met a man who helped her to find such work. This was Father Perrin, a Dominican monk then working with the many refugees who had poured into Marseille during this time. She liked him enormously even at their first meeting and soon arranged to meet him regularly and to discuss not only the possibility of work but more importantly, religious questions with which she was becoming increasingly concerned. Before long, discussion centred on the question of baptism. The burning question in her mind at the time, mentioned with apparent casualness to friends and priests was whether the Church admitted salvation outside the Church. These concerns were to her of cardinal importance but very few people even suspected their existence within her at the time. During part of the time she was in Marseille, Perrin was sent to Montpellier. Some of her most beautiful letters were written as a result and an entire spiritual biography, an account of her life hitherto, survives from this period.

Father Perrin did find her work of the kind which she had requested, where she expected to witness, as before, the extinction of her own intelligence through fatigue. With some reservations he wrote to his friend Gustave Thibon, a farmer in the Ardèche whom she promised to teach Greek in the evenings after her day's work in the fields. Thibon was sceptical of the idea:

... I am a little suspicious of graduates in philosophy, and as for intellectuals who want to return to the land I am well enough acquainted with them to know that, with a few rare exceptions they belong to that order of cranks whose undertakings generally come to a bad end. ...

Soon, however, he changed his mind and:

gradually discovered that the side of her character which I found so impossible, far from revealing her real deep nature, showed only her exterior and social self. In her case the respective positions of being and appearing were reversed: unlike most people she gained immeasurably in an atmosphere of close intimacy; with alarming spontaneity she displayed all that was most unpleasing in her nature, but it needed much time and affection, and a great deal of reserve had to be overcome, before she showed what was best in her. She was just then beginning to open with all her soul to Christianity, a limpid mysticism emanated from her; in no other human being have I come across such familiarity with religious mysteries; never have I felt the word *supernatural* to be more charged with reality than when in contact with her.

Such mysticism had nothing in common with those religious speculations divorced from any personal commitment which are all too frequently the only testimony of intellectuals who apply themselves to the things of God. She actually experienced in its heart-breaking reality the distance between 'knowing' and 'knowing with all one's soul', and the one object of her life was to abolish that distance. (Weil, 1952a)

In teaching she used the Greek text of the Pater, which she already knew well. This time, however, having resolved to learn it by heart, when she recited it a similar experience as when saying the Herbert poem overwhelmed her. She found the effect of the words themselves totally enchanting: 'the infinite sweetness of the Greek text so took hold of me that for several days I could not prevent myself from repeating them over and over again.' (Weil, 1951b) From that time on she began to say it every morning with absolute attention.

At times the very first words tear my thoughts from my body and transport them to a place outside space where there is neither perspective nor point of view. Space opens up. The infinity of the ordinary expanses of perception is replaced by an infinity to the second or sometimes to the third degree. At the same time, filling every part of this infinity, there is a silence, a silence that is not an absence of sound but that is the object of a positive sensation more positive than that of sound. Noises, if there are any, only reach me after crossing that silence. . . . Sometimes, also, during this recitation or at other moments, Christ is present with me in person, but his presence is infinitely more real, more poignant and clearer than on that first occasion when he took possession of me. (Weil, 1951b)

She and Thibon read Plato together; she did this with such educative genius that her teaching was as living as an original creation. Thibon gave her to read some of his own unpublished work and from his farm she went to work on the grape harvest. She worked eight hours a day, every day for four weeks. When she returned to Marseille, the period that followed was one of the most productive in her career. From this time dates the essay on the future of science, including 'Reflections on the Quantum Theory', several poems, and the first of the well-known letters to Father Perrin. The latter had by this time made no secret of the fact that he wanted to give her baptism. She moved closer to the Church than she had ever hitherto been. She attended Mass regularly, chiefly in the mornings, Father Perrin noticed, so as to listen to the living silence of the church. She spoke long and often with priests. Writing to Perrin, she said that she was at this time more ready to die for the Church, however, than to enter it.

I should like to draw your attention to one point. It is that there is an absolutely insurmountable obstacle to the incarnation of Christianity. It is the use of the two little words *anathema sit*. I remain with all those things that cannot enter the Church, the universal repository, because of those two little words. I remain with them all the more because my own intelligence is numbered with them. . . . The proper function of the intelligence demands total freedom. . . . In order that the present attitude of the Church might be effective and that she might really penetrate like a wedge into social existence, she would have to say openly that she had changed or wished to change. . . . After the fall of the Roman Empire, which had been totalitarian, it was the Church that was the first to establish a rough sort of totalitarianism in Europe in the thirteenth century, after the war with the Albigensians. . . . And the motive power of this totalitarianism was the use of those two little words *anathema sit*. (Weil, 1951b)

For obvious reasons Simone Weil had been unable to persuade her parents to settle down in a village in the South of France and cultivate their garden. Writing to a friend just before their departure, she said that she could not refuse to accompany them. She had hoped that their efforts to get to the US would not be successful since she still had no assurance from her brother that she would be able to get from there to England. She now considered Father Perrin a close friend and writing to him soon before her departure she was bold enough to chide him with possessing an imperfection, that of attachment. In his case it was to the Church, which she claimed he thought of as a home. She apologized for continuing to trouble him, saying she believed that within her were thoughts that were worth much more than she herself.

The fact that they happen to be in me prevents people from paying attention to them. I see no one but you whom I can implore to give them attention. I should like you to transfer the charity you have so generously bestowed on me to that which I bear within me.

She left with anguish, having decided that to remain would be an act of personal will. She was guided by the hope that in doing so she would be in a better position to promote the front-line nursing squad plan and to be included in their number. It seemed, she said, as though something were telling her to go.

P.S. – You know that for me there is no question in this departure of an escape from suffering and danger. My anguish comes precisely from the fear that in spite of myself, and unwittingly, by going I shall be doing what I want above everything else not to do – that is to say running away. Up till now we have lived here very peacefully. If this peace is destroyed just after I have gone away, it will be frightful for me. If I were sure it was going to be like that, I think that I should stay. If you know anything which might throw any light on what is going to happen, I count on you to tell me. (Weil, 1951b)

She also wrote to Gustave Thibon, virtually giving away all her notes and telling him that she would be happy if they were transmuted by his thoughts into something which he might like to publish.

You tell me that in my notebooks you have found, besides things which you yourself had thought, others you had not thought but for which you were waiting; so now they belong to you, and I hope that after having been transmuted within you they will one day come out in one of your works. For it is certainly far better for an idea to be associated with your fortunes than with mine. I have a feeling that my own fortunes will never be good in this world (it is not that I count on their being better elsewhere; I cannot think that will be so). I am not a person with whom it is advisable to link one's fate. Human beings have always more or less sensed this; but, I do not know for what mysterious reason, ideas seem to have less discernment. I wish nothing better for those which have come in my direction than that they should have a good establishment, and I should be very happy for them to find a lodging beneath your pen, whilst changing their form so as to reflect your likeness. (Weil, 1952a)

She and her parents sailed on 14 May for Casablanca, and from there reached New York on 6 July 1942.

Once they had arrived in New York, she found that everyone believed it would be impossible for her to get to England. She used every contact and every possible means to get herself a job in England, imploring her old classmate Maurice Schumann to intercede, and pestering any and all those capable of helping her to achieve her ends. To Schumann she wrote:

Cher ami,
Any really useful work, not requiring technical expertise but involving a high degree of hardship and danger, would suit me perfectly.

Hardship and danger are essential because of my particular mentality. Luckily, it is not universal, because it would make all organized activities impossible, but as far as I am concerned I cannot change it; I know this by experience.

The suffering all over the world obsesses and overwhelms me to the point of annihilating my faculties and the only way I can revive them and release myself from the obsession is by getting for myself a large share of danger and hardship. That is a necessary condition before I can exert my capacity for work.

I beseech you to get for me, if you can, the amount of hardship and danger which can save me from being wasted by sterile chagrin. In my present situation I cannot live. It very nearly makes me despair.

I cannot believe it is impossible to give me what I need. It is unlikely there is so much demand for painful and dangerous jobs that not one is available. And even if that is so, it would be easy to make one. For there is plenty to be done; you know it as well as I do.

I have much to say about this; but by word of mouth, not by letter.

It seems to me, then, that the best thing would be to assign me to some provisional work, which you could easily choose for me yourself, you know me well enough for that, so as to get me to London quickly, as quickly as possible; and then I could be transferred to whatever seemed the most suitable operation, after full discussion. I would accept any provisional work anywhere – propaganda or press, for example, or anything else. But if it was a job not involving a high degree of hardship and danger I could only accept it provisionally; otherwise I should be consumed by the same chagrin in London as in New York, and it would paralyse me. It is unfortunate to have that sort of character; but that is really how I am, and I can do nothing about it; it is something too essential in me to be modified. The more so because it is not, I am certain, a question of character only, but of vocation.

In this respect, the project I sent you would have satisfied my needs perfectly, and I am very distressed that A.Ph. [André

Philip, Commissioner of the Interior and Labour in the National Committee of the Free French Movement] thinks it impracticable. I confess, however, that I have not yet lost all hope of its realization some day; I am, and have long been, so convinced that it is a thing that ought to be done.

In my case, there is other more urgent work at the present time, and I am hungry to take part in it without delay.

Only arrange for me to come. I know it is difficult just now. But I also know that people do manage it, including women. I very much hope you'll be able to help. If A.Ph. could take me in his luggage, as secretary or something when he returns from here. . . .

Anyway, I thank you very, very much.

Kindest wishes,
Simone Weil

I will very gladly do you an article, of course. You'll receive it soon. (Weil, 1965)

She eventually succeeded in getting authorization to join the provisional French government in London.

She was still haunted by the question of whether or not her ideas were compatible with membership of the Church and before she left she urged her brother to make sure he baptized both his children so that they would never experience similar wretchedness.

On her arrival she loved London and found the British full of humour and kindness. Addressing her parents in English as 'Darlings' from then on, she now wrote to New York very much the same kind of letters as on her first trip to Italy, rejoicing in the English spring, apple trees in blossom, gooseberry fools in the summer. She found digs in Notting Hill and became good friends of the family that lived there. She coached the boys, despite the long hours she worked at the offices of the Free French. There she was given the job of editing and collating material and writing reports on political documents emanating from France.

In the event, to her permanent and fatal chagrin, no one gave serious consideration to her request to be sent back behind enemy lines. Having read her nursing squad plan de

Gaulle said simply she was mad. From this period, December 1942 to August 1943, dates not only the book by which she is best known, *The Need for Roots*, but also over a dozen major papers, translations of extracts from the *Upanishads* and notes on Greek philosophers. Not all that she wrote while she was in London has even now been published and it is clear that she must have been writing day and night for over a year.

Only gradually did it become apparent that she would only be given work of an intellectual nature and that her requests to play a more immediately practical role in the war effort would be disregarded. When one of her colleagues was chosen to return to France, even though the mission was later cancelled, Simone Weil began to feel the disappointment, the remorse and finally the despair which was to weaken her spirit and eventually her will to live. She continued to write to her parents in New York the most cheerful letters, hiding from them the truth that she was gradually losing heart.

Darlings,
Your description in your last letter of your stay at Bethlehem gave me a lot of pain and pleasure at the same time. A lot of pain, because of the heat and other discomforts, and I do so want you to have nothing but well-being in every way! At the same time I am very glad you don't put on rose-coloured spectacles when you write. If the colours are mixed one knows one is getting the truth and letters can bring you really close.

Naturally, it was the parts about Sylvie [Simone Weil's young niece] that gave me pleasure. You can never tell me too much about her; I am insatiable. You cannot imagine what it is for me. It makes me happy both to think of her and to think of the brief but unalloyed happiness she has given you. I only wish she had somewhere to walk where there are no crocodiles of little schoolgirls.

There seems to be nothing in her circumstances at present which could make her grow up as a 'Mary in tar'.[1]

I am delighted, too, that the A.'s and the Reverends[2] are nice

---

[1] Presumably a reference to the Grimm story 'Mother Holle'.
[2] An American clergyman and his wife who lived on the same floor as Simone Weil's parents [Richard Rees].

and sympathetic neighbours. Remember me to all. And tell the young one that I think of her and do not forget her, and that I very fervently hope the spiritual good she desires will come to her one day *authentically*.

Darling M. you think that I have something to give. That is the wrong way to put it. But I too have a sort of growing inner certainty that there is within me a deposit of pure gold which must be handed on. Only I become more and more convinced, by experience and by observing my contemporaries, that there is no one to receive it.

It is indivisible, and whatever is added to it becomes part of it. And as it grows it becomes more compact. I cannot distribute it piecemeal.

To receive it calls for an effort. And effort is fatiguing!

Some people feel in a confused way that there is something. But once they have made a few polite remarks about my intelligence their conscience is clear. After which, they listen to me or read me with the same hurried attention which they give to everything, making up their minds definitely about each separate little hint of an idea as soon as it appears: 'I agree with this', 'I don't agree with that', 'this is marvellous', 'that is completely idiotic' (the latter antithesis comes from my chief). In the end they say: 'Very interesting', and pass on to something else. They have avoided fatigue.

What else can one expect? I am convinced that the most fervent Christians among them don't concentrate their attention much more when they are praying or reading the Gospel.

Why imagine it is better elsewhere? I have seen some of those elsewheres.

As for posterity, before there is a generation with muscle and power of thought the books and manuscripts of our day will surely have disappeared.

This does not distress me at all. The mine of gold is inexhaustible.

As for the practical uselessness of my writing effort – since they refused to give me the job I wanted, that or something . . . (but I cannot conceive the possibility for myself of anything else).

There it is.

The chance of your seeing Antonio[1] is what chiefly interests me

---

[1] That is to say: I hope you will soon get to Algiers.

now. But don't count on it too much, for fear of disappointment. I am still without any information on the subject.

> Au revoir, darlings. A thousand kisses.
>
> Simone (Weil, 1965)

After a year of superhuman mental exertion she was found one April morning, unconscious on the floor of her lodgings. She was in a very pitiable state. Tuberculosis was diagnosed at the Middlesex Hospital and she was taken for treatment to the country, to a sanatorium in Ashford, Kent. From there she wrote to her brother:

My dear brother,

... I have told our parents that I love London; but the truth is only that I would love it passionately if the state of the world allowed me any freedom of mind. As things are, I cannot enjoy anything.

Every day, I am more and more cruelly torn by regret and remorse for having been so weak as to follow your advice last year.

As for you, if you now had favourable conditions for mathematical work I would certainly advise you to devote yourself entirely to mathematics, for good and all if possible, until the day of your death.

Take good note, however, that I myself feel thankful every day for having crossed the sea again.

But in the event of your coming over to us, in the moral sense, I have no idea at all what they would do with you. Not make you a soldier, certainly, as things are; or more exactly, a soldier with special duties. But what? I don't know. And where? I've no idea. ...

The B.'s are charming. Unfortunately I have only seen them once.

I have work and, as usual, I am too tired to go about. The journey from my room to the office and back is enough. (N.B. – Better not let your parents read this, although it's their custom. So take precautions.)

Love to Eveline [Simone Weil's sister-in-law], Alain, and my niece. I hope she still goes into peals of laughter.

> Salut,
> S.W. (Weil, 1965)

No one will ever know what was the cause of her death on 24 August of that year. There were numerous very obviously contributory physical factors; the habitually weak state of her health, the unremitting headaches, massive over-exertion, heavy smoking, and her disinclination to take nourishment. Richard Rees writes:

her selfless idealism and her extraordinary capacity for sympathy and pity and self-sacrificing kindness stand out conspicuously in everything that is known about her life. And as for her death, whatever explanation one may give of it will amount in the end to saying that she died of love. (Rees, 1962)

After her death, as her writing began to appear and receive critical acclaim, debate inevitably arose over whether she had committed suicide and whether she had finally entered the Catholic Church. On the first question; according to the doctor who attended her, death was due to 'cardiac failure due to degeneration through starvation and not through pulmonary tuberculosis'. (Pétrement, 1977) Simone Weil had shown ever greater reluctance to eat as her sadness and fatigue increased and while she thought of the severe restrictions imposed upon those living in France. She knew that she was considered odd in this as in much else. Deprived of the capacity to act, thoughts and ideas were now the most important to her; having already conveyed them into the safe hands of Thibon and Father Perrin, it is possible that her own personal survival had by this time become a matter of indifference to her.

In the operation of writing, the hand which holds the pen, and the body and soul which are attached to it, with all their social environment, are things of infinitesimal importance for those who love the truth. They are infinitely small in the order of nothingness. That at any rate is the measure of importance I attach in this operation not only to my own personality but to yours and to that of any other writer I respect. Only the personality of those whom I more or less despise matters to me in such a domain. . . . (Weil, 1952a)

On the second question she had always maintained that by entering the Church, she would be cut off, as she refused to be, from the 'immense, unfortunate mass of unbelievers'. While yearning for the sacraments, she would consider herself permanently deprived of them unless and until a time should come when she was no longer able to work with her intellect. In Ashford, according to the medical report, she maintained total mental lucidity; her eyes kept their brilliance and she could read and write.

She often quoted admiringly the reply given by a young seaman who, having performed an act of almost unbelievable bravery, was asked how he had managed to do it. 'Had to' was the answer and in it is also the essence of Simone Weil's philosophy. It is difficult not to see in her tragically early death the unity and integrity she herself saw in the world. All energy, she claimed, comes from desire. When she was finally obliged to extinguish forever the only desire left in her, the energy required to live diminished till none was left to sustain her.

Her spiritual and social legacy is incalculable. She demonstrates that it is possible to address questions of both ethics and metaphysics in the language and logic of materialism and politics. She shows the intimate connection between various disciplines, the beauty and power of mathematics, the relevance of the classics, and the absolute necessity for intellectual work to be grounded in the physical. She found ways to live, think and write which have touched all our concerns. Her work is the expression of respect for the human being and for the 'inarticulate, anonymous mass which has vanished'. She gives new and vital meaning to the phrase 'another world'. For her it means the world inhabited by individuals dead or unborn. She strips the phrase of old connotation and stresses the personal and social importance of being rooted in another world. Her influence as a teacher is profound not only through her striking powers of synthesis, imagery and analogy, but because of her definition of the purpose of education itself. It is to train the attention, to teach the attitude of intellectual waiting and to develop the capacity of the self to disappear. Thinking personally is to commit the sin of pride in 'forgetting one is God'.

According to Father Perrin, the last sentence she wrote in her notebook before her death was: 'The most important part of education – to teach the meaning of "to know" (in the scientific sense).'

Possibly her greatest influence has been in, as it were, demythologizing mysticism. She believed that the truths she glimpsed in her mystical experiences were simple truths, open to all, which had been deformed over time (since the thirteenth century in particular) by a certain patriotic and partisan spirit in the Church. The meaning of those experiences was as clear as 'the love that irradiates the tenderest smile of somebody one loves'. Their reality is seized through what she termed the decreation of the personality.

Decreation is based on the idea of a voluntary, unsolicited, unreasonable, unnecessary and absurd act. This act is an imitation of what she calls the abdication of a God who is entirely absent from the universe. The world is defined by necessity, within whose physical laws human beings are obliged to live and knowledge of whose causes and effects can be acquired. The attempt to acquire knowledge of its ends and purposes, however, leads to a cul-de-sac of contradiction which may be seized through the perception of beauty and of affliction. Instead of looking for a purpose in the existence of the world she focuses her attention instead on the reality of her love for it. In the context of her own death, the following takes on special significance:

Losing somebody: one suffers because the person who has died, the absent one has become imaginary, false. But the desire one has for him is not imaginary. Must go to the depths of oneself to where desire which is not imaginary lives. Hunger: one imagines foods, but the hunger itself is real: seize it. The presence of the person lost is imaginary, but the absence is real enough; it is from now on that person's way of appearing. (Weil, 1952a)

There is an absurdity in the act of decreation, of ridding oneself of the personal and of all that is named 'I', and to Simone Weil the universe is viewed as a kind of absurdity. 'As a child, for a joke, hides behind an armchair from his mother, God plays at separating himself from God through creation. We are this joke of God's.' (Weil, 1950) In order to achieve the impersonal, a humility is required which is not an attribute. It is not the opposite of arrogance for example, and can never be included in an opinion of one's self in comparison with a personal ideal. For Simone Weil there could not exist a personal ideal since what is ideal is *ipso facto* impersonal. Humility, she claims, is not a poor opinion of one's own person in comparison with others. It is a radically poor opinion of one's person in relation to what is impersonal in one's self. God or the Good, in refraining from intervening, by remaining supernatural and refusing to affect the necessary and natural order of things is power-less. The imitation of this powerlessness on the part of human beings is a similar refusal to intervene in areas into which they are not irresistibly impelled and provided none of their actions is done 'for God' or 'for' anything. 'God should not be put in the dative.' (Weil, 1956) In decreation, human beings perform only those actions which they can in no way refrain from performing and these in turn are limited by the quality of attention bestowed upon them.

This part of Simone Weil's work is the most easily mis-construed. Critics have seen in it either an authoritarianism or a *laissez-faire* attitude denying human responsibility for the condition of the world. Her notion of decreation, how-ever, calls for an even more urgent sense of responsibility in human affairs than if God were present. This is no quietist doctrine. It is not a question of concentrating attention on a given phenomenon and then allowing other wills to impose themselves. On the contrary. She says, when God is 'emp-tied of his divinity', involvement with the world is as great, if not greater than before; only the relation to it is different. One must be committed without the use of will-power and highly conscious without being self-conscious.

There is nothing which comes closer to true humility than the intelligence. It is impossible to feel pride in one's intelligence at the moment when one really and truly exercises it. And when one does so exercise it one is not attached to it. For one knows that, even if one were to become an idiot the very next moment and remain so for the rest of one's life, truth goes on existing. (Weil, 1956)

One can be conscious of having used one's intelligence, or of going to use it but never that one is in the process of using it, and the sort of detachment to which she aspires is very similar to the intelligence. The image she uses to convey the impersonal instrumentality achieved through decreation is that of a blind man's stick. 'May the whole universe, in relation to my body be to me what to a blind man his stick is in relation to his hand. His sensitivity is no longer really in his hand but at the end of the stick.' 'May the whole universe become like a second body to me.' The object is to 'obliterate from one's self one's point of view, to regard one's self as part of a chain of mutual compensations of energy'. Of the absent God who refuses to falsify by intervention she says 'He loves not as I love but as an emerald is green ... I too, if I were in a state of perfection, I would love as an emerald is green ... I would be an impersonal person.' (Weil, 1950) It is impossible to love God if one regards God as responsible for everything. Those who have attempted to do so and have revolted against God have been unwilling to appreciate the absurdity and the subtlety of the act of creation. They have set human happiness as the ideal, measured against it the misery of their lives or the lives of other people and in a straight-forward condemnation, blamed God for his obvious lack of success. It is as though angry shareholders had censured management for failure to reap their anticipated dividends.

So as to limit actions to those one is 'irresistibly impelled to perform', Simone Weil advocates a radical reassessment of the validity of current methods of social communication and exchange. She believed that every person is an accretion of attributes centred around a 'childlike belief that good and not evil will be done to him or her'. This belief continues, in the teeth of all the evidence to the contrary, and respect for its existence in others is, according to her, one of the bases of authentic exchange. One of the main reasons that have prevented the survival in the world of the sort of exchange she describes (and which was present in societies that did not revere size or magnitude, in particular the Languedocian civilization) is that human societies model-led on or influenced by the Romans have substituted in their daily lives words that in essence have no meaning for those that do. The development of the society in which she found herself living in France in the 1920s and 30s had come about with more regard for speed than for meaning. It had substituted what she calls 'salaries' for realities. A 'salary' is anything by which a person can be made to believe that the future is not made out of exactly the same components as the present.

This is not to say she had no hope for improvement in human affairs or that there is not an urgent need for human beings to have faith in the effectiveness of their efforts directed towards whatever ends. What she held was that 'belief in' this cause or that should not be a substitute for the object itself as it nearly always becomes. 'As when one writes, one makes the shape of letters on paper with a view not to the shape but to the idea one wants to express.' Often, too, the cause or belief can turn into deadening habit, stifling the life out of its object. When people begin to talk *as* exponents, adherents, members, of particular move-ments, schools, races, nationalities, the impersonal in them is deformed and communication becomes impossible. Belief in the family, in love, in friendship, in revolution, in the future, and particularly in progress can become hindrances that interfere with authentic exchange.

If it can be agreed that there is no absolute good, that God is absent, then so too is absolute evil and the imaginary battle between two fictitious forces waged throughout history in one form or other is equally without meaning. The objects of our efforts, she claims, ought to be not to seek to do good (for that can never be done intentionally) but to throw weight and support behind whichever side has be-come the lighter or the weaker. The idea of counter-balance is crucial to her thought and underlies all aspects of it.

Balance, for Simone Weil, represents a demonstrable truth which can be acknowledged by all. Philosophical truths, like all others, she believed were those which could be demonstrated as clearly and indisputably as the laws of mathematics and of geometry in particular. 'The ideas of limit, measure, degree, proportion, relation, comparison, contingency, interdependence and interrelation of means and ends ... all the elementary principles of rational thought' were missing from the social sphere which she saw as 'peopled by myths and monsters ... absolutes and abstract entities'. (Weil, 1962) She warns against the misuse of language in obscuring these clearly demonstrable principles. She believed that those who use language in their professional lives – journalists, writers, politicians and lawyers – have a greater responsibility than most to use language with care and regard for the truth. In her plan for the reorganization of the French nation after the war, the proposed penalties for deliberate distortion of language for the purpose of propaganda are severe.

Most people in the world are what is called uneducated. Those who are literate and claim thereby to be able to exchange knowledge with one another through language have a special obligation to those who use different methods. To illustrate this she often uses the image of a prisoner in a dock, stammering answers while the men of the law keep up a flow of witticisms. Writ large, this is also an image of the state of most of the populations of the world in relation to the so-called developed nations. She wished those who use both speech and written language to be aware of the dual nature of language and to beware of its obfuscating potential.

It is a theme which runs throughout her historical and political papers and finds an echo in her religious thought where she emphasizes that Christ specified 'where two or three are gathered in my name'. He did not say where two hundred, or fifty, or ten are gathered in my name there am I in the midst of them. 'Everybody knows' she says 'that really intimate conversation can only take place between two or three. Even if there are only six or seven present, collective language begins to dominate.' (Weil, 1951b) Very often communication is most effective through a silence as at the centre of music. 'The central point of music is the silence which separates a rising from a descending movement.' (Weil, 1956) She compares it to a wave whose shape is perfect just at the moment when it begins to disintegrate. The act of creation and of authentic exchange makes clear the nothingness from which it comes. It is as much a stripping off as a putting on. The nothingness governed by change from which it emanates, the absurdity which produces it and which denies it permanence, is often unbearable. Contemplation of this emptiness of meaning is most often avoided by use of the imagination. Decreation is the act of allowing moments, empty of meaning, to remain 'unfilled'.

The imagination 'filler of voids' realm of the private, personal and partial is Plato's cavern, home of illusion and a safe bolt-hole from the light of shared knowledge. What is dangerous about the imagination is its power to prevent the mind from encountering head-on the notion of limit. The imagination tends to consecrate, sanctify and privatize experience. We speak of capturing the imagination and the idea of possession is always present in it. Reciprocally we say that a work of art has 'captured the spirit' of something. This is because the painter has imposed upon imagination the idea of limit which is provided by work. Left unbridled, the imagination leads *away* from the truth. It brings out old thoughts, old grievances to mull over or new fantasies to play with and in returning to them, desires to dominate them. This is always a false solution, she says. 'Not to think of something – supreme faculty.' (Weil, 1952a) Balance, or perfect equilibrium in the moral as well as the aesthetic sphere is achieved when no attempt is made to alter the distance between desire and its object and when the notion of limit is unchanged.

In the last months of her life, Simone Weil wrote a paper entitled 'Reflections on the Rebellion'. This was apparently the only work of hers that de Gaulle could be persuaded to read *in toto*. It is interesting to speculate what would have happened if he had taken into account others of her proposals for the rebuilding of France after the war. Her plan for the creation of a Supreme Council of the Rebellion is alleged to have influenced the creation in France of the National Council of the Resistance. There was a very large difference, however, between hers and the plan put into operation. Hers was an international and European council, rather than a national one. It also called for the abolition of the old political parties whereas de Gaulle's council resurrected them. Historically, political parties have always laid greater stress on the rights of man than on obligations. Simone Weil reverses this position and analyses the extent to which the idea of rights, including as it does an emphasis on the personal, prevents human beings from seeking the impersonal in themselves which alone enables them to see the needs of others as clearly as their own.

One of the most important needs of a new France if she was not any longer to be seen as a cold State, 'hitherto courted and flattered and finally calumnied and betrayed' was recognition of the need for roots. Of the work which she wrote on this subject Camus was later to say it seemed to him impossible to imagine the rebirth of Europe without taking into consideration the suggestions outlined in it by Simone Weil. De Gaulle was less impressed. This is hardly surprising considering that on one occasion during her work for him she had also suggested that it might be 'dangerous to hold a plebiscite concerning a constitution drafted by a national committee appointed by de Gaulle at a time when de Gaulle is in power'. She always recommended the strictest controls on all powers, including should he be disavowed, the death penalty for any President of the Republic.

In *The Need for Roots*, she defines the crime of uprooting which, whether it be in seventeenth century Italy or twentieth century South Africa, consists in the destruction of physical links with the past and dissolution of the community. She claims that loss of the past in this way is the equivalent of loss of the supernatural, i.e. that through which it is demonstrable that the good is different from necessity and whereby the dead can speak with an authentic voice to the living.

The Need for Roots is the most complete expression of her social thought. In it she compares and contrasts the two principal aspects under which she views society. The first is as 'the Great Beast' of Plato and the second as the repository of cultural values that symbolizes respect for the past and aspiration for the future. Each collectivity is unique. There is an obligation to preserve its roots in the past to the extent that it provides sustenance for a certain number of people. But if the collectivities themselves are not nourishing, if instead, they devour souls, there is no such obligation. Writing in the context of a defeated and humiliated France, she maintains it is the urgent duty of government to discover what the needs are of the souls within that collectivity and draws up a list of those which seem to her essential.

One of the major factors of the 'uprooting' of workers in France is the fact that their social condition is 'an absolute and perpetual dependence on money'. In the claims of the workers, what should be looked for are the 'signs and tokens of their suffering'. Often money is shorthand for the needs that workers have not been educated to express.

The resolution of this problem which is essentially the technical one of judging and analysing the effect of machines upon the moral well-being of workers, is less difficult than finding the willingness to implement the necessary reforms. This is because since Richelieu, 'it is only the nation that has assumed the main responsibility of the collectivity to the human individual, that of maintaining throughout the present, the links with the past and the future.' In an indictment of patriotism, she argues that workers have always recognized the idiocy of taking the State for an object of fidelity. Workers, she says, have always been shocked by it, since their sense of justice is strong. She is undaunted by the enormity of the task facing the next government of France, namely to inspire a people.

The problem of a method for breathing an inspiration into a people is quite a new one. Plato alludes to it in his *Politics* and elsewhere; doubtless there were precepts on this subject among the secret stores of knowledge accumulated in pre-Roman antiquity, of which no trace has been left. Possibly this problem and others akin to it continued to be discussed in such circles as those of the Templars and early freemasons. Montesquieu, unless I am mistaken, was unaware of it. Rousseau, with his powerful mind, clearly recognized its existence, but didn't go any further. The men of 1789 do not appear to have had any inkling of it. In 1793, without people having gone to the trouble of raising the problem, still less of investigating it, hasty solutions were improvised, such as festivals in honour of the Supreme Being, of the Goddess of Reason, which were just ridiculous and odious. In the nineteenth century, the level of general intelligence had descended very far below the point at which such questions are raised.

In our own day, people have investigated and penetrated deeply into the problem of propaganda. Hitler, in particular, has made lasting contributions on this subject to the store of human knowledge. But it is an altogether different problem. Propaganda is not directed towards creating an inspiration: it closes, seals up all the openings through which an inspiration might pass; it fills the whole spirit with fanaticism. Its measures cannot be suitable for obtaining a contrary objective. Nor is it just a question of adopting reverse measures: the causal connection is not so simple.

It must not be thought either that the inspiring of a people is a mystery reserved to God alone, and for which, consequently, no method exists. The supreme and perfect state of mystical contemplation is something that is infinitely more mysterious still, and yet St. John of the Cross wrote treatises on the method of attaining to such a state, which, by their scientific precision, are far and away superior to anything produced by the psychologists or professors of our own time. If he felt called upon to do this, he was doubtless right, for he was certainly competent; the beauty of his writings is a sufficiently clear indication of their authenticity. Actually, from remote antiquity, long before Christianity, right up to the latter half of the Renaissance, it was always universally recognized that there is a method to be followed in spiritual matters and in everything connected with the soul's welfare. The ever greater methodical control which men have exercised over matter since the sixteenth century has led them to believe, by way of contrast, that the things of the soul are either arbitrary or else bound up with some form of magic, with the immediate efficacy of intentions and words.

Such is not the case. Everything in creation is dependent on method, including the points of intersection between this world and the next. That is what the word *Logos* indicates, signifying connection even more than word. The method merely differs according to the different sphere. The higher one goes, the more rigorous and precise it becomes. It would be strange, indeed, if the order of material things were to reflect more of divine wisdom than that of spiritual things. The contrary is true.

It is unfortunate for us that this problem, in regard to which, unless I am wrong, we have nothing we can look to for guidance, should be precisely the one that requires today the most urgent solution on our part, under pain not so much of disappearing altogether as of never having really existed. (Weil, 1952b)

Never since the Renaissance have public activities been visualized as other than a means of establishing a particular form of power regarded as desirable for one reason or another. But, she says, power is not an end. 'By nature, in essence and by definition, it constitutes a means. It is to politics what a piano is to musical composition ... we had confused the manufacture of a piano with the composition of a sonata.' She asks who would be willing to implement new solutions and who would set the idea of greatness high enough aims in the new France. What had hitherto held sway was a false notion of greatness which did not differ fundamentally from that of Hitler. What is necessary is to give up the adulation of force.

Two phenomena had contributed to the disaster befalling France. The first was the power of the idea of force and the second was the post-sixteenth century conception of science. Science teaches that force controls everything, yet we know from experience that justice is not unreal. There is only one possible choice to be made. Either we must perceive in the universe, alongside force, a principle of a different kind or else we must recognize force as being the unique and sovereign ruler over human relations. Since we know that justice is 'real enough in the hearts of men' it must be the modern conception of science that is wrong. It is wrong, she suggests, because science is no longer regarded as a religious subject 'as physical labour was regarded as sacred' by the Greeks.

For the Greeks, physical labour was the direct expression of religious faith. Their science was rooted in the idea that one must not look for the unlimited in what is limited. Modern science, however, expanding towards space, and not recognizing a merely global responsibility, was cut off from that root four hundred years ago. She argues for a return to it and a recognition of the sacred nature of physical labour. This recognition is at the core of the new society she wishes to help form.

Physical labour is a daily death. To labour is to place one's own being, body and soul, in the circuit of inert matter, turn it into an intermediary between one state and another of a fragment of matter, make of it an instrument. The labourer turns his body and soul into an appendix of the tool which he handles. The movements of the body and the concentration of the mind are a function of the requirements of the tool, which itself is adapted to the matter being worked upon. Death and labour are things of necessity and not choice. The world only gives itself to man in the form of food and warmth if man gives himself to the world in the form of labour. But death and labour can be submitted to either in an attitude of revolt or in one of consent. They can be submitted to either in their naked truth or else wrapped around with lies. . . . (Weil, 1952b)

'Analysis of Oppression', part of a very long article entitled 'Reflections on the Causes of Liberty and Social Oppression' was begun ten years before *The Need for Roots* when Simone Weil was in her early twenties. There is a story attached to it which shows again that somewhat surprising characteristic which made her appear either naive or unfeeling. She herself was only too aware of it. From Marseille in 1940, she wrote to her friend Simone Pétrement asking what had happened to some verses and other literature left behind in the Weils' hurried escape from Paris.

Aware of its importance and believing herself to have the only copy of the *Reflections on the Causes of Freedom and Social Oppression*, of which the essay reproduced here forms only a quarter, Simone Pétrement wrote out by hand the entire work. When she saw Simone Weil a year later, she mentioned having made a copy in case something should happen in those dangerous times to the original. Simone Weil replied that it would have been better if Pétrement had used the time for her own work.

In the article she claims that Marxism, while unifying efforts to validate the scientific method and throw off oppression does not adequately explain the instability of power and the reasons why, as human beings come increasingly through technical progress to dominate nature, they remain incapable of dominating forces of control. Her conclusion is that subjection is the natural condition of human beings in a world where the idea of servitude has become confused with that of servility, and where the inquisitive and acquisitive take precedence in human affairs over the contemplative. The faculty of consent has less meaning, if any, than the faculty of control and has come to be held in contempt. By exercising the faculty of consent and remaining *disponible* what she is advocating is not the forelock-touching servility that bows to superior strength, and certainly not a cowardly obedience to the mechanics of capitalism but an informed and mature stoicism, an *amor fati* that considers all human endeavour and behaviour as subject to laws to the same extent as matter. The nature and character of the laws are variable but subjection to them remains constant and invariable. She suggests that Marxism provides an analysis of a specific force but allows this particular one to overshadow the notion of subjection itself, which she considers more important.

'The *Iliad* or the Poem of Force' is about this very idea. It is a seminal essay of Simone Weil's published in December 1940 and January 1941 under the rough anagram, Emile Novis, of her name. In 1945, when Simone Weil was still virtually unknown in the English speaking world, Mary

McCarthy wrote the beautiful translation of it which is reproduced here. It is the most powerful argument 'not to admire force, not to hate the enemy and not to scorn the unfortunate'. This is close to the spirit of Greenham and Comiso and other women's peace camps throughout the world.

Once the experience of war makes visible the possibility of death that lies locked up in each moment, our thoughts cannot travel from one day to the next without meeting death's face. The mind is then strung up to a pitch it can stand for only a short time; but each new dawn reintroduces the same necessity; and days piled on days make years. On each one of these days the soul suffers violence. Regularly, every morning, the soul castrates itself of aspiration, for thought cannot journey through time without meeting death on the way. Thus war effaces all conceptions of purpose or goal, including even its own 'war aims'. It effaces the very notion of war's being brought to an end. (Weil, 1945)

The beauty of the *Iliad*, however, lies not only in not glamorizing society which makes man make war, but in painting the nature of force itself, to which society too is subject. The author of the *Iliad* speaks of the petrifactive power of force, of its power to turn people into stone and make them into things. Simone Weil comments that it is difficult to tell whether the author is a Greek or a Trojan. Her great message is that it is a matter of urgency to discover why such poetry comes into being so rarely and how the spirit which informs it and recognizes so clearly the identical nature of the subjection to force of both victor and loser, master and slave, may be restored.

If the *Iliad* is a stark portrayal of the powerlessness of human nature in relation to force, what has come to be celebrated, mistakenly in her view, in later centuries is the collective power of society against it. This is what human beings have come eventually in the shape of the nation or the state, to worship. In the essay 'Human Personality', she examines the idea of justice, and concludes that the 'subordination of the person to the collectivity is in the nature of things, like the inferiority of a gram to a kilogram on the

scales. But there can be a scales on which the gram outweighs the kilogram. It is only necessary for one arm to be
more than a thousand times as long as the other. The law of
equilibrium easily overcomes an inequality of weight. . . .'
(Weil, 1962) Safeguarding of the 'person' is only possible
when *'Je est un autre'*. This is the link between her social
and religious thought. When we know that everything we
mean by 'I' is other than it seems to us, then a balance is
produced between others, whose limits are identical, and
ourselves. Equal weight attaches to each, and a point established upon which social justice may be based. This the
'realm of the real', where as she put it, one can breathe. In a
letter to Joë Bousquet, a poet and crippled veteran of the
First World War, she wrote:

Cher ami,
First of all, thank you for what you have just done for me. If your
letter is effective, as I hope, you will have done it, not for me but
for others through me, for your younger brothers who should be
infinitely dear to you since the same fate has struck them. Perhaps
some of them will owe to you, just before the moment of death,
the solace of an exchange of sympathy.

   You are specially privileged in that the present state of the
world is a reality for you. Perhaps even more so than for those
who at this moment are killing and dying, wounding and being
wounded, because they are taken unawares, without knowing
where they are or what is happening to them; and, like you in
your time, they are unable to think thoughts appropriate to their
situation. As for the others, the people here for example, what is
happening is a confused nightmare for some of them, though very
few, and for the majority it is a vague background like a theatrical
drop-scene. In either case it is unreal.

   But you, on the other hand, for twenty years you have been
repeating in thought that destiny which seized and then released
so many men, but which seized you permanently; and which now
returns again to seize millions of men. You, I repeat, are now
really equipped to think it. Or if you are still not quite ready – as I
think you are not – you have at least only a thin shell to break
before emerging from the darkness inside the egg into the light of
truth. It is a very ancient image. The egg is this world we see.
The bird in it is Love, the Love which is God himself and which

lives in the depths of every man, though at first as an invisible seed. When the shell is broken and the being is released, it still has this same world before it. But it is no longer inside. Space is opened and torn apart. The spirit, leaving the miserable body in some corner, is transported to a point outside space, which is not a point of view, which has no perspective, but from which this world is seen as it is, unconfused by perspective. Compared to what it is inside the egg, space has become an infinity to the second or rather the third power. The moment stands still. The whole of space is filled, even though sounds can be heard, with a dense silence which is not an absence of sound but is a positive object of sensation; it is the secret word, the word of Love who holds us in his arms from the beginning. (Weil, 1965)

There has always been in the popular literature which surrounds her name in this country a tendency to make of Simone Weil a latter-day saint, an absurd absolutist or to impose upon her stereotypes with which every woman is familiar. Many of the articles written about her reflect in their titles ('Passions of the Red Virgin', 'Bluestocking or Saint?', 'Sergeant-Major Angel') the sexism she endured during her lifetime. Many of her most ardent champions have bestowed upon her the ultimate accolade ('Donna Quixote', *Brave Men*) of honorary male status. Many, emphasizing the most negative aspects of her work, have placed her sorrowfully in the category of a 'dolorosa'. 'It is all too easy,' as her first English biographer wrote, 'to dramatize Simone Weil as a sort of Saint Joan of the Workshops or to sentimentalize her as an up-to-date blend of Hypatia and the Little Flower.' (Rees, 1966) This kind of marginalizing is deadly. It kills the very thing it purports to celebrate. Simone Weil's courage and endurance against the temptation of 'loving only in the imagination' was not so much a matter of saintliness as of attention. Simone Pétrement, herself a graduate of the Ecole Normale, a contemporary of Simone Weil's there and one of her greatest friends, writes of the way people tended to regard her during her lifetime. They had the impression

that some element of common humanity was missing in her – the very thickness of nature so to speak.

Indeed one senses that many of her old classmates, when they finally read her writings, were surprised to discover that she was so human. I myself was astonished by the incredible sensitivity she revealed. Certainly, when it came to generosity, a concern and pity for others, nobody has ever denied that she had these qualities, and in the highest, most selfless forms. In this sense she was more human than anyone else. But what was hard to believe was that she had the ordinary human frailties. One might even think that she didn't have the same needs or the same desires as others, that she was not wounded or hurt by the same things. She forbade herself all weakness with such firm determination that one could mistake for a peculiarity of her nature what was in truth a product of her will.

As for the plans she had already formed, her whole conception of what she wanted to do with her life, it was . . . as she herself later said . . . a great misfortune to have been born a female. So she decided to reduce this obstacle as much as possible by disregarding it, that is to say, by giving up any desire to think of herself as a woman or to be regarded as such by others, at least for a set period of time. It was perhaps this that made many people consider her in some way inhuman. (Pétrement, 1977)

Absence of weakness and frailty do not always indicate that 'some element of common humanity' is missing in a person. Yet curiosity is still expressed over her apparent asexuality or by the absence in her adult life, at least, of any important emotional or sexual relationship. Writing to a student who had asked for her advice about love, she refers to the 'terrifying risk, if one is the object of deep love, of becoming the arbiter of another human existence'. Just as she had advised her students not to seek truths, she advised her not to avoid love but not to seek it either. Her passion for justice, her love and respect for the individual and the fear, through attachment, of adversely affecting the life of another account for Simone Weil's determination not to express the very deep emotional life that was so obviously within her. Her disregard for conventional dress, behaviour, manner and appearance made her conspicuous and she felt it keenly. The great misfortune is that she should have believed that outside her family she was never loved, nor should be. She was indeed much loved, as countless testaments after her death amply show. Wittily summing up her refusal of the martyr's crown, Thibon, one of the many whose lives were profoundly and permanently affected by her, writes:

In the great volume of the universe, as she read it, her ego was like a word which she had succeeded, perhaps, in *erasing*, but it was still *underlined*.

LOVE

Love bade me welcome: yet my soul drew back,
    Guiltie of dust and sinne.
But quick-ey'd Love, observing me grow slack
    From my first entrance in,
Drew nearer to me, sweetly questioning
    If I lack'd any thing.

A guest, I answer'd, worthy to be here:
    Love said, You shall be he.
I the unkinde, ungratefull? Ah my deare,
    I cannot look on thee.
Love took my hand, and smiling did reply,
    Who made the eyes but I?

Truth Lord, but I have marred them: let my shame
    Go where it doth deserve.
And know you not, sayes Love, who bore the blame?
    My deare, then I will serve.'
You must sit downe, sayes Love, and taste my meat:
    So I did sit and eat.

                George Herbert

REFERENCES

Cabaud, J. (1964), *Simone Weil: A Fellowship in Love,* Harvill, London; Channel Press, New York, 1965. Originally published as *L'Expérience Vécue de Simone Weil avec de nombreux inédits,* Plon, Paris, 1957.

Eliot, T. S. (1952), 'Preface' in Simone Weil, *The Need for Roots: Prelude to a Declaration of Duties towards Mankind*, translated by A. F.

Wills, Routledge and Kegan Paul, London; Putnam's Sons, New York, 1953.

Pétrement, S. (1977), *Simone Weil: A Life*, translated by R. Rosenthal, Mowbrays, London and Oxford (English translation Random House, Inc., New York, 1976). Originally published as *La Vie de Simone Weil*, Fayard, Paris, 1973.

Price, H. (1978), 'Translator's Preface' in Simone Weil, *Lectures on Philosophy*, translated by H. Price, Cambridge University Press, Cambridge, 1978. Originally published as *Leçons de philosophie*, Plon, Paris, 1959.

Rees, R. (1962), 'Introduction' in *Simone Weil: Selected Essays 1934–43*, translated by R. Rees, Oxford University Press, London, 1962.

— (1966), *Simone Weil: A Sketch for a Portrait*, Oxford University Press, London, 1966.

Reynaud-Guérithault, A. (1978), 'Introduction' in Simone Weil, *Lectures on Philosophy*, translated by H. Price, Cambridge University Press, Cambridge, 1978. Originally published as *Leçons de philosophie*, Plon, Paris, 1959.

Weil, S. (1945), 'The *Iliad* or the Poem of Force', translated by Mary McCarthy, in *Politics*, New York, November 1945. Originally published as *'L'Iliade* ou le poème de la force' [signed Emile Novis], *Cahiers du Sud*, XIX, 230, December 1940–January 1941.

— (1950), *La Connaissance surnaturelle*, Gallimard, Paris, 1950.

— (1951a), *La Condition ouvrière,* Gallimard, Paris, 1951.

— (1951b), *Waiting on God*, translated by Emma Craufurd, Routledge and Kegan Paul. Originally published as *L'Attente de Dieu*, La Colombe, Paris, 1950.

— (1952a), *Gravity and Grace*, translated by Emma Craufurd, Routledge and Kegan Paul, London. Originally published as *La Pesanteur et la Grâce*, Plon, Paris, 1947.

— (1952b), *The Need for Roots: Prelude to a Declaration of Duties towards Mankind*, translated by A. F. Wills, Routledge and Kegan Paul: Putnam's Sons, New York, 1953. Originally published as *L'Enracinement: Prélude à une déclaration des devoirs envers l'être humain*, Gallimard, Paris, 1949.

— (1956), *The Notebooks of Simone Weil*, translated by A. F. Wills, 2 vols, Routledge and Kegan Paul, London: Putnam's Sons, New York, 1956. Originally published as *Cahiers I*, Plon, Paris, 1953; *Cahiers II*, Plon, Paris, 1956.

— (1962), 'Human Personality' in *Selected Essays 1934–43 by Simone Weil*, chosen and translated by R. Rees, Oxford University Press, London. Originally published as 'La Personne et le sacré' in *Ecrits de Londres et dernières lettres*, Gallimard, Paris, 1957.

— (1965), *Simone Weil: Seventy Letters*, translated and arranged by R. Rees, Oxford University Press, London.

HUMAN PERSONALITY

———————— ⊙ ————————

This essay, one of Simone Weil's most powerful and beautiful, was written during the last year of her brief life, in the late winter and early spring of 1942–3. The title on the manuscript reads 'Collectivity. Person. Impersonal. Right. Justice.' She had recently arrived in England from New York where she had finally left her parents after their flight from Vichy France. As the following letter shows, she had no idea how her work would be received by her superiors in the Free French organization. Nevertheless England enchanted her and she writes reassuringly:

'Darlings,
I received the letter addressed to Mme R's. I am so glad you say you are happy, although I daren't believe it....The spring is here, and there are trees of pink blossom in the London squares. London is full of delicious little squares. But I don't see much of London because work absorbs me. Not that I'm overworking at all. I am automatically stopped from time to time by fatigue, which forces me to rest until my energy revives; but I don't go out much at those times either. You say you are certain that my work is successful; but the truth is, I haven't the slightest idea if what I am doing is likely to be effective. That depends upon far too many unknown factors. But I cannot go into details. My companions are as nice as

*possible. You can tell A. that some of the things I was told when I
was with you about the groups here were completely untrue. . . .'*

*Nevertheless reaction from her Free French colleagues to
this work, as to much else she wrote at the time, was im-
patient. They wanted her to write on 'something concrete,
like trade-union problems'. She was in fact doing precisely
that, though her approach was radically different from what
they had expected.*

'You do not interest me.'[1] No man can say these words to
another without committing a cruelty and offending against
justice.

'Your person[2] does not interest me.' These words can be
used in an affectionate conversation between close friends,
without jarring upon even the tenderest nerve of their
friendship.

In the same way, one can say without degrading oneself,
'My person does not count', but not 'I do not count'.

This proves that something is amiss with the vocabulary
of the modern trend of thought known as Personalism. And
in this domain, where there is a grave error of vocabulary it
is almost certainly the sign of a grave error of thought.

There is something sacred in every man, but it is not his
person. Nor yet is it the human personality. It is this man;
no more and no less.

I see a passer-by in the street. He has long arms, blue
eyes, and a mind whose thoughts I do not know, but perhaps they are commonplace.

It is neither his person, nor the human personality in
him, which is sacred to me. It is he. The whole of him. The

---

[1] This essay appeared in *La Table Ronde* (December 1950) with the title 'La
Personnalité humaine, le juste et l'injuste' and in *Ecrits de Londres* with the title
'La Personne et le sacré' [R. Rees].

[2] The implications of the French *personne* cannot be conveyed completely by a
single word in English. What Simone Weil meant by 'person' in this context will
become clearer as the essay proceeds, as also will the pejorative sense in which
she uses the word 'personality'.

arms, the eyes, the thoughts, everything. Not without infinite scruple would I touch anything of this.

If it were the human personality in him that was sacred to me, I could easily put out his eyes. As a blind man he would be exactly as much a human personality as before. I should not have touched the person in him at all. I should have destroyed nothing but his eyes.

It is impossible to define what is meant by respect for human personality. It is not just that it cannot be defined in words. That can be said of many perfectly clear ideas. But this one cannot be conceived either; it cannot be defined nor isolated by the silent operation of the mind.

To set up as a standard of public morality a notion which can neither be defined nor conceived is to open the door to every kind of tyranny.

The notion of rights, which was launched into the world in 1789, has proved unable, because of its intrinsic inadequacy, to fulfil the role assigned to it.

To combine two inadequate notions, by talking about the rights of human personality, will not bring us any further.

What is it, exactly, that prevents me from putting that man's eyes out if I am allowed to do so and if it takes my fancy?

Although it is the whole of him that is sacred to me, he is not sacred in all respects and from every point of view. He is not sacred in as much as he happens to have long arms, blue eyes, or possibly commonplace thoughts. Nor as a duke, if he is one; nor as a dustman, if that is what he is. Nothing of all this would stay my hand.

What would stay it is the knowledge that if someone were to put out his eyes, his soul would be lacerated by the thought that harm was being done to him.

At the bottom of the heart of every human being, from earliest infancy until the tomb, there is something that goes on indomitably expecting, in the teeth of all experience of crimes committed, suffered, and witnessed, that good and not evil will be done to him. It is this above all that is sacred in every human being.

The good is the only source of the sacred. There is nothing sacred except the good and what pertains to it.

This profound and childlike and unchanging expectation of good in the heart is not what is involved when we agitate for our rights. The motive which prompts a little boy to watch jealously to see if his brother has a slightly larger piece of cake arises from a much more superficial level of the soul. The word justice means two very different things according to whether it refers to the one or the other level. It is only the former one that matters.

Every time that there arises from the depths of a human heart the childish cry which Christ himself could not restrain, 'Why am I being hurt?', then there is certainly injustice. For if, as often happens, it is only the result of a misunderstanding, then the injustice consists in the inadequacy of the explanation.

Those people who inflict the blows which provoke this cry are prompted by different motives according to temperament or occasion. There are some people who get a positive pleasure from the cry; and many others simply do not hear it. For it is a silent cry, which sounds only in the secret heart.

These two states of mind are closer than they appear to be. The second is only a weaker mode of the first; its deafness is complacently cultivated because it is agreeable and it offers a positive satisfaction of its own. There are no other restraints upon our will than material necessity and the existence of other human beings around us. Any imaginary extension of these limits is seductive, so there is a seduction in whatever helps us to forget the reality of the obstacles. That is why upheavals like war and civil war are so intoxicating; they empty human lives of their reality and seem to turn people into puppets. That is also why slavery is so pleasant to the masters.

In those who have suffered too many blows, in slaves for example, that place in the heart from which the infliction of evil evokes a cry of surprise may seem to be dead. But it is never quite dead; it is simply unable to cry out any more. It has sunk into a state of dumb and ceaseless lamentation.

And even in those who still have the power to cry out, the cry hardly ever expresses itself, either inwardly or outwardly, in coherent language. Usually, the words through which it seeks expression are quite irrelevant.

That is all the more inevitable because those who most often have occasion to feel that evil is being done to them are those who are least trained in the art of speech. Nothing, for example, is more frightful than to see some poor wretch in the police court stammering before a magistrate who keeps up an elegant flow of witticisms.

Apart from the intelligence, the only human faculty which has an interest in public freedom of expression is that point in the heart which cries out against evil. But as it cannot express itself, freedom is of little use to it. What is first needed is a system of public education capable of providing it, so far as possible, with means of expression; and next, a regime in which the public freedom of expression is characterized not so much by freedom as by an attentive silence in which this faint and inept cry can make itself heard; and finally, institutions are needed of a sort which will, so far as possible, put power into the hands of men who are able and anxious to hear and understand it.

Clearly, a political party busily seeking, or maintaining itself in power can discern nothing in these cries except a noise. Its reaction will be different according to whether the noise interferes with or contributes to that of its own propaganda. But it can never be capable of the tender and sensitive attention which is needed to understand its meaning.

The same is true to a lesser degree of organizations contaminated by party influences; in other words, when public life is dominated by a party system, it is true of all organizations, including, for example, trade unions and even churches.

Naturally, too, parties and similar organizations are equally insensitive to intellectual scruples.

So when freedom of expression means in fact no more than freedom of propaganda for organizations of this kind, there is in fact no free expression for the only parts of the human soul that deserve it. Or if there is any, it is infinitesimal; hardly more than in a totalitarian system.

And this is how it is in a democracy where the party system controls the distribution of power; which is what we call democracy in France, for up to now we have known no other. We must therefore invent something different.

Applying the same criterion in the same way to any public institution we can reach equally obvious conclusions.

It is not the person which provides this criterion. When the infliction of evil provokes a cry of sorrowful surprise from the depth of the soul, it is not a personal thing. Injury to the personality and its desires is not sufficient to evoke it, but only and always the sense of contact with injustice through pain. It is always, in the last of men as in Christ himself, an impersonal protest.

There are also many cries of personal protest, but they are unimportant; you may provoke as many of them as you wish without violating anything sacred.

★

So far from its being his person, what is sacred in a human being is the impersonal in him.

Everything which is impersonal in man is sacred, and nothing else.

In our days, when writers and scientists have so oddly usurped the place of priests, the public acknowledges, with a totally unjustified docility, that the artistic and scientific faculties are sacred. This is generally held to be self-evident, though it is very far from being so. If any reason is felt to be called for, people allege that the free play of these faculties is one of the highest manifestations of the human personality.

Often it is, indeed, no more than that. In which case it is easy to see how much it is worth and what can be expected from it.

One of its results is the sort of attitude which is summed up in Blake's horrible saying: 'Sooner murder an infant in its cradle than nurse unacted desires',[1] or the attitude which breeds the idea of the 'gratuitous act'. Another result is a science in which every possible standard, criterion, and value is recognized except truth.

Gregorian chant, Romanesque architecture, the *Iliad*, the invention of geometry were not, for the people through whom they were brought into being and made available to us, occasions for the manifestation of personality.

When science, art, literature, and philosophy are simply the manifestation of personality they are on a level where glorious and dazzling achievements are possible, which can make a man's name live for thousands of years. But above this level, far above, separated by an abyss, is the level where the highest things are achieved. These things are essentially anonymous.

It is pure chance whether the names of those who reach this level are preserved or lost; even when they are remembered they have become anonymous. Their personality has vanished.

Truth and beauty dwell on this level of the impersonal and the anonymous. This is the realm of the sacred; on the other level nothing is sacred, except in the sense that we might say this of a touch of colour in a picture if it represented the Eucharist.

What is sacred in science is truth; what is sacred in art is beauty. Truth and beauty are impersonal. All this is too obvious.

If a child is doing a sum and does it wrong, the mistake bears the stamp of his personality. If he does the sum exactly right, his personality does not enter into it at all.

Perfection is impersonal. Our personality is the part of us which belongs to error and sin. The whole effort of the mystic has always been to become such that there is no part left in his soul to say 'I'.

---

[1] It seems possible that Simone Weil took Blake to mean: *If you desire to murder an infant you should do so,* instead of: *If you stifle your desires, you are doing something similar to murdering an infant.* But her point does not depend upon this illustration [R. Rees].

But the part of the soul which says 'We' is infinitely more dangerous still.

★

Impersonality is only reached by the practice of a form of attention which is rare in itself and impossible except in solitude; and not only physical but mental solitude. This is never achieved by a man who thinks of himself as a member of a collectivity, as part of something which says 'We'.

Men as parts of a collectivity are debarred from even the lower forms of the impersonal. A group of human beings cannot even add two and two. Working out a sum takes place in a mind temporarily oblivious of the existence of any other minds.

Although the personal and the impersonal are opposed, there is a way from the one to the other. But there is no way from the collective to the impersonal. A collectivity must dissolve into separate persons before the impersonal can be reached.

This is the only sense in which the person has more of the sacred than the collectivity.

The collectivity is not only alien to the sacred, but it deludes us with a false imitation of it.

Idolatry is the name of the error which attributes a sacred character to the collectivity; and it is the commonest of crimes, at all times, at all places. The man for whom the development of personality is all that counts has totally lost all sense of the sacred; and it is hard to know which of these errors is the worst. They are often found combined, in various proportions, in the same mind. But the second error is much less powerful and enduring than the first.

Spiritually, the struggle between Germany and France in 1940 was in the main not a struggle between barbarism and civilization or between evil and good, but between the first of these two errors and the second. The victory of the former is not surprising; it is by nature the stronger.

There is nothing scandalous in the subordination of the person to the collectivity; it is a mechanical fact of the same order as the inferiority of a gram to a kilogram on the scales. The person is in fact always subordinate to the collectivity, even in its so-called free expression.

For example, it is precisely those artists and writers who are most inclined to think of their art as the manifestation of their personality who are in fact the most in bondage to public taste. Hugo had no difficulty in reconciling the cult of the self with his role of 'resounding echo'; and examples like Wilde, Gide, and the Surrealists are even more obvious. Scientists of the same class are equally enslaved by fashion, which rules over science even more despotically than over the shape of hats. For these men the collective opinion of specialists is practically a dictatorship.

The person, being subordinate to the collective both in fact and by the nature of things, enjoys no natural rights which can be appealed to on its behalf.

It is said, quite correctly, that in antiquity there existed no notion of respect for the person. The ancients thought far too clearly to entertain such a confused idea.

The human being can only escape from the collective by raising himself above the personal and entering into the impersonal. The moment he does this, there is something in him, a small portion of his soul, upon which nothing of the collective can get a hold. If he can root himself in the impersonal good so as to be able to draw energy from it, then he is in a condition, whenever he feels the obligation to do so, to bring to bear without any outside help, against any collectivity, a small but real force.

There are occasions when an almost infinitesimal force can be decisive. A collectivity is much stronger than a single man; but every collectivity depends for its existence upon operations, of which simple addition is the elementary example, which can only be performed by a mind in a state of solitude.

This dependence suggests a method of giving the impersonal a hold on the collective, if only we could find out how to use it.

Every man who has once touched the level of the impersonal is charged with a responsibility towards all human beings; to safeguard, not their persons, but whatever frail potentialities are hidden within them for passing over to the impersonal.

It is primarily to these men that the appeal to respect the sacredness of the human being should be addressed. For such an appeal can have no reality unless it is addressed to someone capable of understanding it.

It is useless to explain to a collectivity that there is something in each of the units composing it which it ought not to violate. To begin with, a collectivity is not someone, except by a fiction; it has only an abstract existence and can only be spoken to fictitiously. And, moreover, if it were someone it would be someone who was not disposed to respect anything except himself.

Further, the chief danger does not lie in the collectivity's tendency to circumscribe the person, but in the person's tendency to immolate himself in the collective. Or perhaps the first danger is only a superficial and deceptive aspect of the second.

Just as it is useless to tell the collectivity that the person is sacred, it is also useless to tell the person so. The person cannot believe it. It does not feel sacred. The reason that prevents the person from feeling sacred is that actually it is not.

If there are some people who feel differently, who feel something sacred in their own persons and believe they can generalize and attribute it to every person, they are under a double illusion.

What they feel is not the authentic sense of the sacred but its false imitation engendered by the collective; and if they feel it in respect of their own person it is because it participates in collective prestige through the social consideration bestowed upon it.

So they are mistaken in thinking they can generalize from their own case. Their motive is generous, but it cannot have enough force to make them really see the mass of people as anything but mere anonymous human matter. But it is hard for them to find this out, because they have no contact with the mass of people.

The person in man is a thing in distress; it feels cold and is always looking for a warm shelter.

But those in whom it is, in fact or in expectation, warmly wrapped in social consideration are unaware of this.

That is why it was not in popular circles that the philosophy of personalism originated and developed, but among writers, for whom it is part of their profession to have or hope to acquire a name and a reputation.

Relations between the collectivity and the person should be arranged with the sole purpose of removing whatever is detrimental to the growth and mysterious germination of the impersonal element in the soul.

This means, on the one hand, that for every person there should be enough room, enough freedom to plan the use of one's time, the opportunity to reach ever higher levels of attention, some solitude, some silence. At the same time the person needs warmth, lest it be driven by distress to submerge itself in the collective.

If this is the good, then modern societies, even democratic ones, seem to go about as far as it is possible to go in the direction of evil. In particular, a modern factory reaches perhaps almost the limit of horror. Everybody in it is constantly harassed and kept on edge by the interference of extraneous wills while the soul is left in cold and desolate misery. What man needs is silence and warmth; what he is given is an icy pandemonium.

Physical labour may be painful, but it is not degrading as such. It is not art; it is not science; it is something else, possessing an exactly equal value with art and science, for it provides an equal opportunity to reach the impersonal stage of attention.

To take a youth who has a vocation for this kind of work and employ him at a conveyor-belt or as a piece-work machinist is no less a crime than to put out the eyes of the young Watteau and make him turn a grindstone. But the painter's vocation can be discerned and the other cannot.

Exactly to the same extent as art and science, though in a different way, physical labour is a certain contact with the reality, the truth, and the beauty of this universe and with the eternal wisdom which is the order in it.

For this reason it is sacrilege to degrade labour in exactly the same sense that it is sacrilege to trample upon the Eucharist.

If the workers felt this, if they felt that by being the victim they are in a certain sense the accomplice of sacrilege, their resistance would have a very different force from what is provided by the consideration of personal rights. It would not be an economic demand but an impulse from the depth of their being, fierce and desperate like that of a young girl who is being forced into a brothel; and at the same time it would be a cry of hope from the depth of their heart.

This feeling, which surely enough exists in them, is so inarticulate as to be indiscernible even to themselves; and it is not the professionals of speech who can express it for them.

Usually, when addressing them on their conditions, the selected topic is wages; and for men burdened with a fatigue that makes any effort of attention painful it is a relief to contemplate the unproblematic clarity of figures.

In this way, they forget that the subject of the bargain, which they complain they are being forced to sell cheap and for less than the just price, is nothing other than their soul.

Suppose the devil were bargaining for the soul of some poor wretch and someone, moved by pity, should step in and say to the devil: 'It is a shame for you to bid so low; the commodity is worth at least twice as much.'

Such is the sinister farce which has been played by the working-class movement, its trade unions, its political parties, its leftist intellectuals.

This bargaining spirit was already implicit in the notion of rights which the men of 1789 so unwisely made the keynote of their deliberate challenge to the world. By so doing, they ensured its inefficacy in advance.

★

The notion of rights is linked with the notion of sharing out, of exchange, of measured quantity. It has a commercial flavour, essentially evocative of legal claims and arguments. Rights are always asserted in a tone of contention; and when this tone is adopted, it must rely upon force in the background, or else it will be laughed at.

There is a number of other notions, all in the same category, which are themselves entirely alien to the supernatural but nevertheless a little superior to brute force. All of them relate to the behaviour of the collective animal, to use Plato's language, while it still exhibits a few traces of the training imposed on it by the supernatural working of grace. If they are not continually revived by a renewal of this working, if they are merely survivals of it, they become necessarily subject to the animal's caprice.

To this category belong the notion of rights, and of personality, and of democracy. As Bernanos had the courage to point out, democracy offers no defence against dictatorship. By the nature of things, the person is subdued to the collectivity, and rights are dependent upon force. The lies and misconceptions which obscure this truth are extremely dangerous because they prevent us from appealing to the only thing which is immune to force and can preserve us from it: namely, that other force which is the radiance of the spirit. It is only in plants, by virtue of the sun's energy caught up by the green leaves and operating in the sap, that inert matter can find its way upward against the law of gravity. A plant deprived of light is gradually but inexorably overcome by gravity and death.

Among the lies in question is the eighteenth-century materialists' notion of natural right. We do not owe this to Rousseau, whose lucid and powerful spirit was of genuinely Christian inspiration, but to Diderot and the Encyclopédistes.

It was from Rome that we inherited the notion of rights, and like everything else that comes from ancient Rome, who is the woman full of the names of blasphemy in the Apocalypse, it is pagan and unbaptizable. The Romans, like Hitler, understood that power is not fully efficacious unless clothed in a few ideas, and to this end they made use of the idea of rights, which is admirably suited to it. Modern Germany has been accused of flouting the idea; but she invoked it *ad nauseam* in her role of deprived, proletarian nation. It is true, of course, that she allows only one right to her victims: obedience. Ancient Rome did the same.

It is singularly monstrous that ancient Rome should be praised for having bequeathed to us the notion of rights. If we examine Roman law in its cradle, to see what species it belongs to, we discover that property was defined by the *jus utendi et abutendi*. And in fact the things which the property owner had the right to use or abuse at will were for the most part human beings.

The Greeks had no conception of rights. They had no words to express it. They were content with the name of justice.

It is extraordinary that Antigone's unwritten law should have been confused with the idea of natural right. In Creon's eyes there was absolutely nothing that was natural in Antigone's behaviour. He thought she was mad.

And we should be the last people to disagree with him; we who at this moment are thinking, talking, and behaving exactly as he did. One has only to consult the text.

Antigone says to Creon: 'It was not Zeus who published that edict; it was not Justice, companion of the gods in the other world, who set such laws among men.'[1] Creon tries to convince her that his orders were just; he accuses her of having outraged one of her brothers by honouring the other, so that the same honour has been paid to the impious and the loyal, to the one who died in the attempt to destroy his own country and the one who died defending it.

She answers: 'Nevertheless the other world demands equal laws.' To which he sensibly objects: 'There can be no equal sharing between a brave man and a traitor', and she has only the absurd reply: 'Who knows whether this holds in the other world?'

---

[1] We have translated the author's own versions of the Greek [R. Rees].

Creon's comment is perfectly reasonable: 'A foe is never a friend, not even in death.' And the little simpleton can only reply: 'I was born to share, not hate, but love.'

To which Creon, ever more reasonable: 'Pass, then, to the other world, and if thou must love, love those who dwell there.'

And, truly, this was the right place for her. For the unwritten law which this little girl obeyed had nothing whatsoever in common with rights, or with the natural; it was the same love, extreme and absurd, which led Christ to the Cross.

It was Justice, companion of the gods in the other world, who dictated this surfeit of love, and not any right at all. Rights have no direct connection with love.

Just as the notion of rights is alien to the Greek mind, so also it is alien to the Christian inspiration whenever it is pure and uncontaminated by the Roman, Hebraic, or Aristotelian heritage. One cannot imagine St Francis of Assisi talking about rights.

If you say to someone who has ears to hear: 'What you are doing to me is not just', you may touch and awaken at its source the spirit of attention and love. But it is not the same with words like 'I have the right . . .' or 'you have no right to. . . .' They evoke a latent war and awaken the spirit of contention. To place the notion of rights at the centre of social conflicts is to inhibit any possible impulse of charity on both sides.

Relying almost exclusively on this notion, it becomes impossible to keep one's eyes on the real problem. If someone tries to browbeat a farmer to sell his eggs at a moderate price, the farmer can say: 'I have the right to keep my eggs if I don't get a good enough price.' But if a young girl is being forced into a brothel she will not talk about her rights. In such a situation the word would sound ludicrously inadequate.

Thus it is that the social drama, which corresponds to the latter situation, is falsely assimilated, by the use of the word 'rights', to the former one.

Thanks to this word, what should have been a cry of protest from the depth of the heart has been turned into a shrill nagging of claims and counter-claims, which is both impure and unpractical.

★

The notion of rights, by its very mediocrity, leads on naturally to that of the person, for rights are related to personal things. They are on that level.

It is much worse still if the word 'personal' is added to the word 'rights', thus implying the rights of the personality to what is called full expression. In that case the tone that colours the cry of the oppressed would be even meaner than bargaining. It would be the tone of envy.

For the full expression of personality depends upon its being inflated by social prestige; it is a social privilege. No one mentions this to the masses when haranguing them about personal rights. They are told the opposite; and their minds have not enough analytic power to perceive this truth clearly for themselves. But they feel it; their everyday experience makes them certain of it.

However, this is not a reason for them to reject the slogan. To the dimmed understanding of our age there seems nothing odd in claiming an equal share of privilege for everybody – an equal share in things whose essence is privilege. The claim is both absurd and base; absurd because privilege is, by definition, inequality; and base because it is not worth claiming.

But the category of men who formulate claims, and everything else, the men who have the monopoly of language, is a category of privileged people. They are not the ones to say that privilege is unworthy to be desired. They don't think so and, in any case, it would be indecent for them to say it.

Many indispensable truths, which could save men, go unspoken for reasons of this kind; those who could utter them cannot formulate them and those who could formulate them cannot utter them. If politics were taken seriously, finding a remedy for this would be one of its more urgent problems.

In an unstable society the privileged have a bad conscience. Some of them hide it behind a defiant air and say to the masses: 'It is quite appropriate that I should possess privileges which you are denied.' Others benevolently profess: 'I claim for all of you an equal share in the privileges I enjoy.'

The first attitude is odious. The second is silly, and also too easy.

Both of them equally encourage the people down the road of evil, away from their true and unique good, which they do not possess, but to which, in a sense, they are so close. They are far closer than those who bestow pity on them to an authentic good, which could be a source of beauty and truth and joy and fulfilment. But since they have not reached it and do not know how to, this good might as well be infinitely far away. Those who speak for the people and to them are incapable of understanding either their distress or what an overflowing good is almost within their reach. And, for the people, it is indispensable to be understood.

Affliction is by its nature inarticulate. The afflicted silently beseech to be given the words to express themselves. There are times when they are given none; but there are also times when they are given words, but ill-chosen ones, because those who choose them know nothing of the affliction they would interpret.

Usually, they are far removed from it by the circumstances of their life; but even if they are in close contact with it or have recently experienced it themselves, they are still remote from it because they put it at a distance at the first possible moment.

Thought revolts from contemplating affliction, to the same degree that living flesh recoils from death. A stag advancing voluntarily step by step to offer itself to the teeth of a pack of hounds is about as probable as an act of attention directed towards a real affliction, which is close at hand, on the part of a mind which is free to avoid it.

But that which is indispensable to the good and is impossible naturally is always possible supernaturally.

★

Supernatural good is not a sort of supplement to natural good, as we are told, with support from Aristotle, for our greater comfort. It would be nice if this were true, but it is not. In all the crucial problems of human existence the only choice is between supernatural good on the one hand and evil on the other.

To put into the mouth of the afflicted words from the vocabulary of middle values, such as democracy, rights, personality, is to offer them something which can bring them no good and will inevitably do them much harm.

These notions do not dwell in heaven; they hang in the middle air, and for this very reason they cannot root themselves in earth.

It is the light falling continually from heaven which alone gives a tree the energy to send powerful roots deep into the earth. The tree is really rooted in the sky.

It is only what comes from heaven that can make a real impress on the earth.

In order to provide an armour for the afflicted, one must put into their mouths only those words whose rightful abode is in heaven, beyond heaven, in the other world. There is no fear of its being impossible. Affliction disposes the soul to welcome and avidly drink in everything which comes from there. For these products it is not consumers but producers who are in short supply.

The test for suitable words is easily recognized and applied. The afflicted are overwhelmed with evil and starving for good. The only words suitable for them are those which express nothing but good, in its pure state. It is easy to discriminate. Words which can be associated with something signifying an evil are alien to pure good. We are criticizing a man when we say: 'He puts his person forward; therefore the person is alien to good. We can speak of an abuse of democracy; therefore democracy is alien to good. To possess a right implies the possibility of making good or bad use of it; therefore rights are alien to good. On the other hand, it is always and everywhere good to fulfil an obligation. Truth, beauty, justice, compassion are always and everywhere good.

For the aspirations of the afflicted, if we wish to be sure of using the right words, all that is necessary is to confine ourselves to those words and phrases which always, everywhere, in all circumstances express only the good.

This is one of the only two services which can be rendered to the afflicted with words. The other is to find the words which express the truth of their affliction, the words which can give resonance, through the crust of external circumstances, to the cry which is always inaudible: 'Why am I being hurt?'

For this, they cannot count upon men of talent, personality, celebrity, or even genius in the sense in which the word is usually employed, which assimilates it to talent. They can count only upon men of the very highest genius: the poet of the *Iliad*, Aeschylus, Sophocles, Shakespeare as he was when he wrote *Lear*, or Racine when he wrote *Phèdre*. There are not very many of them.

But there are many human beings only poorly or moderately endowed by nature, who seem infinitely inferior not merely to Homer, Aeschylus, Sophocles, Shakespeare, and Racine but also to Virgil, Corneille, and Hugo, but who nevertheless inhabit the realm of impersonal good where the latter poets never set foot.

A village idiot in the literal sense of the word, if he really loves truth, is infinitely superior to Aristotle in his thought, even though he never utters anything but inarticulate murmurs. He is infinitely closer to Plato than Aristotle ever was. He has genius, while only the word talent applies to Aristotle. If a fairy offered to change his destiny for one resembling Aristotle's he would be wise to refuse unhesitatingly. But he does not know this. And nobody tells him. Everybody tells him the contrary. But he must be told. Idiots, men without talent, men whose talent is average or only a little more, must be encouraged if they possess genius. We need not be afraid of making them proud, because love of truth is always accompanied by humility. Real genius is nothing else but the supernatural virtue of humility in the domain of thought.

What is needed is to cherish the growth of genius, with a warm and tender respect, and not, as the men of 1789 proposed, to encourage the flowering of talents. For it is only heroes of real purity, the saints and geniuses, who can help the afflicted. But the help is obstructed by a screen which is formed between the two by the men of talent, intelligence, energy, character, or strong personality. The screen must not be damaged, but put aside as gently and imperceptibly as possible. The far more dangerous screen of the collective must be broken by abolishing every part of our institutions and customs which harbours the party spirit in any form whatsoever. Neither a personality nor a party is ever responsive either to truth or to affliction.

★

There is a natural alliance between truth and affliction, because both of them are mute suppliants, eternally condemned to stand speechless in our presence.

Just as a vagrant accused of stealing a carrot from a field stands before a comfortably seated judge who keeps up an elegant flow of queries, comments and witticisms while the accused is unable to stammer a word, so truth stands before an intelligence which is concerned with the elegant manipulation of opinions.

It is always language that formulates opinions, even when there are no words spoken. The natural faculty called intelligence is concerned with opinion and language. Language expresses relations; but it expresses only a few, because its operation needs time. When it is confused and vague, without precision or order, when the speaker or listener is deficient in the power of holding a thought in his mind, then language is empty or almost empty of any real relational content. When it is perfectly clear, precise, rigorous, ordered, when it is addressed to a mind which is capable of keeping a thought present while it adds another to it and of keeping them both present while it adds a third, and so on, then in such a case language can hold a fairly rich content of relations. But like all wealth, this relative wealth is abject poverty compared with the perfection which alone is desirable.

At the very best, a mind enclosed in language is in prison. It is limited to the number of relations which words can make simultaneously present to it; and remains in ignorance of thoughts which involve the combination of a greater number. These thoughts are outside language, they are unformulable, although they are perfectly rigorous and clear and although every one of the relations they involve is capable of precise expression in words. So the mind moves in a closed space of partial truth, which may be larger or smaller, without ever being able so much as to glance at what is outside.

If a captive mind is unaware of being in prison, it is living in error. If it has recognized the fact, even for the tenth of a second, and then quickly forgotten it in order to avoid suffering, it is living in falsehood. Men of the most brilliant intelligence can be born, live, and die in error and falsehood. In them, intelligence is neither a good, nor even an asset. The difference between more or less intelligent men is like the difference between criminals condemned to life imprisonment in smaller or larger cells. The intelligent man who is proud of his intelligence is like a condemned man who is proud of his large cell.

A man whose mind feels that it is captive would prefer to blind himself to the fact. But if he hates falsehood, he will not do so; and in that case he will have to suffer a lot. He will beat his head against the wall until he faints. He will come to again and look with terror at the wall, until one day he begins afresh to beat his head against it; and once again he will faint. And so on endlessly and without hope. One day he will wake up on the other side of the wall.

Perhaps he is still in a prison, although a larger one. No matter. He has found the key; he knows the secret which breaks down every wall. He has passed beyond what men call intelligence, into the beginning of wisdom.

The mind which is enclosed within language can possess only opinions. The mind which has learned to grasp thoughts which are inexpressible because of the number of relations they combine, although they are more rigorous and clearer than anything that can be expressed in the most precise language, such a mind has reached the point where it already dwells in truth. It possesses certainty and unclouded faith. And it matters little whether its original intelligence was great or small, whether its prison cell was narrow or wide. All that matters is that it has come to the end of its intelligence, such as it was, and has passed beyond it. A village idiot is as close to truth as a child prodigy. The one and the other are separated from it only by a wall. But the only way into truth is through one's own annihilation; through dwelling a long time in a state of extreme and total humiliation.

It is the same barrier which keeps us from understanding affliction. Just as truth is a different thing from opinion, so affliction is a different thing from suffering. Affliction is a device for pulverizing the soul; the man who falls into it is like a workman who gets caught up in a machine. He is no longer a man but a torn and bloody rag on the teeth of a cog-wheel.

The degree and type of suffering which constitutes affliction in the strict sense of the word varies greatly with different people. It depends chiefly upon the amount of vitality they start with and upon their attitude towards suffering.

Human thought is unable to acknowledge the reality of affliction. To acknowledge the reality of affliction means saying to oneself: 'I may lose at any moment, through the play of circumstances over which I have no control, anything whatsoever that I possess, including those things which are so intimately mine that I consider them as being myself. There is nothing that I might not lose. It could happen at any moment that what I am might be abolished and replaced by anything whatsoever of the filthiest and most contemptible sort.'

To be aware of this in the depth of one's soul is to experience non-being. It is the state of extreme and total humiliation which is also the condition for passing over into truth. It is a death of the soul. This is why the naked spectacle of affliction makes the soul shudder as the flesh shudders at the proximity of death.

We think piously of the dead when we evoke them in memory, or when we walk among graves, or when we see them decently laid out on a bed. But the sight of corpses lying about as on a battlefield can sometimes be both sinister and grotesque. It arouses horror. At the stark sight of death, the flesh recoils.

When affliction is seen vaguely from a distance, either physical or mental, so that it can be confused with simple suffering, it inspires in generous souls a tender feeling of pity. But if by chance it is suddenly revealed to them in all its nakedness as a corrosive force, a mutilation or leprosy of the soul, then people shiver and recoil. The afflicted themselves feel the same shock of horror at their own condition.

To listen to someone is to put oneself in his place while he is speaking. To put oneself in the place of someone whose soul is corroded by affliction, or in near danger of it, is to annihilate oneself. It is more difficult than suicide would be for a happy child. Therefore the afflicted are not listened to. They are like someone whose tongue has been cut out and who occasionally forgets the fact. When they move their lips no ear perceives any sound. And they themselves soon sink into impotence in the use of language, because of the certainty of not being heard.

That is why there is no hope for the vagrant as he stands before the magistrate. Even if, through his stammerings, he should utter a cry to pierce the soul, neither the magistrate nor the public will hear it. His cry is mute. And the afflicted are nearly always equally deaf to one another; and each of them, constrained by the general indifference, strives by means of self-delusion or forgetfulness to become deaf to his own self.

Only by the supernatural working of grace can a soul pass through its own annihilation to the place where alone it can get the sort of attention which can attend to truth and to affliction. It is the same attention which listens to both of them. The name of this intense, pure, disinterested, gratuitous, generous attention is love.

Because affliction and truth need the same kind of attention before they can be heard, the spirit of justice and the spirit of truth are one. The spirit of justice and truth is nothing else but a certain kind of attention, which is pure love.

Thanks to an eternal and providential decree, everything produced by a man in every sphere, when he is ruled by the spirit of justice and truth, is endowed with the radiance of beauty.

Beauty is the supreme mystery of this world. It is a gleam which attracts the attention and yet does nothing to sustain it. Beauty always promises, but never gives anything; it stimulates hunger but has no nourishment for the part of the soul which looks in this world for sustenance. It feeds only the part of the soul that gazes. While exciting desire, it makes clear that there is nothing in it to be desired, because the one thing we want is that it should not change. If one does not seek means to evade the exquisite anguish it inflicts, then desire is gradually transformed into love; and one begins to acquire the faculty of pure and disinterested attention.

In proportion to the hideousness of affliction is the supreme beauty of its true representation. Even in recent times one can point to *Phèdre, L'Ecole des femmes, Lear*, and the poems of Villon; but far better examples are the plays of Aeschylus and Sophocles, and far better still, the *Iliad*, the book of Job and certain folk poems; and far beyond these again are the accounts of the Passion in the Gospels. The radiance of beauty illumines affliction with the light of the spirit of justice and love, which is the only light by which human thought can confront affliction and report the truth of it.

And it sometimes happens that a fragment of inexpressible truth is reflected in words which, although they cannot hold the truth that inspired them, have nevertheless so perfect a formal correspondence with it that every mind seeking that truth finds support in them. Whenever this happens a gleam of beauty illumines the words.

Everything which originates from pure love is lit with the radiance of beauty.

Beauty can be perceived, though very dimly and mixed with many false substitutes, within the cell where all human thought is at first imprisoned. And upon her rest all the hopes of truth and justice, with tongue cut out. She, too, has no language; she does not speak; she says nothing. But she has a voice to cry out. She cries out and points to truth and justice who are dumb, like a dog who barks to bring people to his master lying unconscious in the snow.

Justice, truth, and beauty are sisters and comrades. With three such beautiful words we have no need to look for any others.

★

Justice consists in seeing that no harm is done to men. Whenever a man cries inwardly: 'Why am I being hurt?' harm is being done to him. He is often mistaken when he tries to define the harm, and why and by whom it is being inflicted on him. But the cry itself is infallible.

The other cry, which we hear so often: 'Why has somebody else got more than I have?', refers to rights. We must learn to distinguish between the two cries and to do all that is possible, as gently as possible, to hush the second one, with the help of a code of justice, regular tribunals, and the police. Minds capable of solving problems of this kind can be formed in a law school.

But the cry 'Why am I being hurt?' raises quite different problems, for which the spirit of truth, justice, and love is indispensable.

In every soul the cry to be delivered from evil is incessant. The Lord's Prayer addresses it to God. But God has power to deliver from evil only the eternal part of the soul of those who have made real and direct contact with him. The rest of the soul, and the entire soul of whoever has not received the grace of real and direct contact with God, is at the mercy of men's caprice and the hazards of circumstance.

Therefore it is for men to see that men are preserved from harm.

When harm is done to a man, real evil enters into him; not merely pain and suffering, but the actual horror of evil. Just as men have the power of transmitting good to one another, so they have the power to transmit evil. One may transmit evil to a human being by flattering him or giving him comforts and pleasures; but most often men transmit evil to other men by doing them harm.

Nevertheless, eternal wisdom does not abandon the soul entirely to the mercy of chance and men's caprice. The harm inflicted on a man by a wound from outside sharpens his thirst for the good and thus there automatically arises the possibility of a cure. If the wound is deep, the thirst is for good in its purest form. The part of the soul which cries 'Why am I being hurt?' is on the deepest level and even in the most corrupt of men it remains from earliest infancy perfectly intact and totally innocent.

To maintain justice and preserve men from all harm means first of all to prevent harm being done to them. For those to whom harm has been done, it means to efface the material consequences by putting them in a place where the wound, if it is not too deep, may be cured naturally by a spell of well-being. But for those in whom the wound is a laceration of the soul it means further, and above all, to offer them good in its purest form to assuage their thirst.

Sometimes it may be necessary to inflict harm in order to stimulate this thirst before assuaging it, and that is what punishment is for. Men who are so estranged from the good that they seek to spread evil everywhere can only be reintegrated with the good by having harm inflicted upon them. This must be done until the completely innocent part of their soul awakens with the surprised cry 'Why am I being hurt?' The innocent part of the criminal's soul must then be fed to make it grow until it becomes able to judge and condemn his past crimes and at last, by the help of grace, to forgive them. With this the punishment is completed; the criminal has been reintegrated with the good and should be publicly and solemnly reintegrated with society.

That is what punishment is. Even capital punishment, although it excludes reintegration with society in the literal sense, should be the same thing. Punishment is solely a method of procuring pure good for men who do not desire it. The art of punishing is the art of awakening in a criminal, by pain or even death, the desire for pure good.

★

But we have lost all idea of what punishment is. We are not aware that its purpose is to procure good for a man. For us it stops short with the infliction of harm. That is why there is one, and only one, thing in modern society more hideous than crime – namely, repressive justice.

To make the idea of repressive justice the main motive of war or revolt is inconceivably dangerous. It is necessary to use fear as a deterrent against the criminal activity of cowards; but that repressive justice, as we ignorantly conceive it today, should be made the motive of heroes is appalling.

All talk of chastisement, punishment, retribution or punitive justice nowadays always refers solely to the basest kind of revenge.

The treasure of suffering and violent death, which Christ chose for himself and which he so often offers to those he loves, means so little to us that we throw it to those whom we least esteem, knowing that they will make nothing of it and having no intention of helping them to discover its value.

For criminals, true punishment; for those whom affliction has bitten deep into the soul, such help as may bring them to quench their thirst at the supernatural springs; for everyone else, some well-being, a great deal of beauty, and protection from those who would harm him; in every sphere, a strict curb upon the chatter of lies, propaganda, and opinion, and the encouragement of a silence in which truth can germinate and grow; this is what is due to men.

To ensure that they get it, we can only count upon those who have passed beyond a certain barrier, and it may be objected that they are too few in number. Probably there are not many of them, but they are no object for statistics, because most of them are hidden. Pure good from heaven only reaches the earth in imperceptible quantities, whether in the individual soul or in society. The grain of mustard seed is 'the least of all seeds'. Persephone ate only one grain of the pomegranate. A pearl buried deep in a field is not visible; neither is the yeast in dough.

But just as the catalysts or bacteria, such as yeast, operate by their mere presence in chemical reactions, so in human affairs the invisible seed of pure good is decisive when it is put in the right place.

How is it to be put there?

Much could be done by those whose function it is to advise the public what to praise, what to admire, what to hope and strive and seek for. It would be a great advance if even a few of these makers of opinion were to resolve in their hearts to eschew absolutely and without exception everything that is not pure good, perfection, truth, justice, love.

It would be an even greater advance if the majority of those who possess today some fragments of spiritual authority were aware of their obligation never to hold up for human aspiration anything but the real good in its perfect purity.

★

By the power of words we always mean their power of illusion and error. But, thanks to a providential arrangement, there are certain words which possess, in themselves, when properly used, a virtue which illumines and lifts up towards the good. These are the words which refer to an absolute perfection which we cannot conceive. Since the proper use of these words involves not trying to make them fit any conception, it is in the words themselves, as words, that the power to enlighten and draw upward resides. What they express is beyond our conception.

God and *truth* are such words; also *justice, love,* and *good*.

It is dangerous to use words of this kind. They are like an ordeal. To use them legitimately one must avoid referring them to anything humanly conceivable and at the same time one must associate with them ideas and actions which are derived solely and directly from the light which they shed. Otherwise, everyone quickly recognizes them for lies.

They are uncomfortable companions. Words like *right, democracy* and *person* are more accommodating and are therefore naturally preferred by even the best intentioned of those who assume public functions. Public functions have no other meaning except the possibility of doing good to men, and those who assume them with good intentions do in fact want to procure good for their contemporaries; but they usually make the mistake of thinking they can begin by getting it at bargain prices.

Words of the middle region, such as *right, democracy, person,* are valid in their own region, which is that of ordinary institutions. But for the sustaining inspiration of which all institutions are, as it were, the projection, a different language is needed.

The subordination of the person to the collectivity is in the nature of things, like the inferiority of a gram to a kilogram on the scales. But there can be a scales on which the gram outweighs the kilogram. It is only necessary for one arm to be more than a thousand times as long as the other. The law of equilibrium easily overcomes an inequality of weight. But the lesser will never outweigh the greater unless the relation between them is regulated by the law of equilibrium.

In the same way, there is no guarantee for democracy, or for the protection of the person against the collectivity, without a disposition of public life relating it to the higher good which is impersonal and unrelated to any political form.

It is true that the word person is often applied to God. But in the passage where Christ offers God himself as an example to men of the perfection which they are told to achieve, he uses not only the image of a person but also, above all, that of an impersonal order: 'That ye may be like the children of your Father which is in heaven; for he maketh his sun to rise on the evil and on the good, and sendeth rain on the just and on the unjust.'

Justice, truth, and beauty are the image in our world of this impersonal and divine order of the universe. Nothing inferior to them is worthy to be the inspiration of men who accept the fact of death.

Above those institutions which are concerned with protecting rights and persons and democratic freedoms, others must be invented for the purpose of exposing and abolishing everything in contemporary life which buries the soul under injustice, lies, and ugliness.

They must be invented, for they are unknown, and it is impossible to doubt that they are indispensable.

From *Selected Essays 1934–43 by Simone Weil*, chosen and translated by Richard Rees, Oxford University Press, London, 1962. Originally published as 'La Personne et le sacré' in *Ecrits de Londres et dernières lettres*, Gallimard, Paris, 1957.

THE SELF

─────────── ◎ ───────────

We possess nothing in the world – a mere chance can strip us of everything – except the power to say 'I'. That is what we have to give to God – in other words, to destroy. There is absolutely no other free act which it is given us to accomplish – only the destruction of the 'I'.

Offering: We cannot offer anything but the 'I', and all we call an offering is merely a label attached to a compensatory assertion of the 'I'.

Nothing in the world can rob us of the power to say 'I'. Nothing except extreme affliction. Nothing is worse than extreme affliction which destroys the 'I' from outside, because after that we can no longer destroy it ourselves. What happens to those whose 'I' has been destroyed from outside by affliction? It is not possible to imagine anything for them but annihilation according to the atheistic or materialistic conception.

Though they may have lost their 'I', it does not mean that they have no more egoism. Quite the reverse. To be sure, this may occasionally happen when a dog-like devotion is brought about, but at other times the being is reduced to naked, vegetative egoism. An egoism without an 'I'.

So long as we ourselves have begun the process of destroying the 'I', we can prevent any affliction from causing harm. For the 'I' is not destroyed by external pressure without a violent revolt. If for the love of God we refuse to give ourselves over to this revolt, the destruction does not take place from outside but from within.

Redemptive suffering. If a human being who is in a state of perfection and has through grace completely destroyed the 'I' in himself, falls into that degree of affliction which corresponds for him to the destruction of the 'I' from outside – we have there the cross in its fullness. Affliction can no longer destroy the 'I' in him for the 'I' in him no longer exists, having completely disappeared and left the place to God. But affliction produces an effect which is equivalent, on the plane of perfection, to the exterior destruction of the 'I'. It produces the absence of God. 'My God, why hast Thou forsaken me?'

What is this absence of God produced by extreme affliction within the perfect soul? What is the value which is attached to it and which is known as redemptive suffering?

Redemptive suffering is that by which evil really has fullness of being to the utmost extent of its capacity.

By redemptive suffering, God is present in extreme evil. For the absence of God is the mode of divine presence which corresponds to evil – absence which is felt. He who has not God within himself cannot feel his presence.

It is the purity, the perfection, the plenitude, the abyss of evil. Whereas hell is a false abyss (cf. Thibon). Hell is superficial. Hell is a nothingness which has the pretension and gives the illusion of being.

Purely external destruction of the 'I' is quasi-infernal suffering. External destruction with which the soul associates itself through love is expiatory suffering. The bringing about of the absence of God in a soul completely emptied of self through love is redemptive suffering.

In affliction, the vital instinct survives all the attachments

which have been torn away, and blindly fastens itself to
everything which can provide it with support, like a plant
fastens its tendrils. Gratitude (except in a base form) and
justice are not conceivable in this state. Slavery. There is no
longer the extra amount of energy required to support free-
will by which man takes the measure of things. Affliction,
from this point of view, is hideous as life in its nakedness
always is, like an amputated stump, like the swarming of
insects. Life without form. Survival is then the only
attachment. That is where extreme affliction begins – when
all other attachments are replaced by that of survival.
Attachment appears then in its nakedness without any other
object but itself – Hell.

It is by this mechanism that to those in affliction life
appears as the one thing desirable, at the very time when
their life is in no way preferable to death.

In this state, to accept death is total detachment.

Quasi-hell on earth. Complete uprooting in affliction.

Human injustice as a general rule produces not martyrs
but quasi-damned souls. Beings who have fallen into this
quasi-hell are like someone stripped and wounded by
robbers. They have lost the clothing of character.

The greatest suffering which allows any of a man's roots
to remain is at an infinite distance from this quasi-hell.

When we do a service to beings thus uprooted and we
receive in exchange discourtesy, ingratitude, betrayal, we
are merely enduring a small share of their affliction. It is
our duty to expose ourselves to it in a limited measure just
as it is our duty to expose ourselves to affliction. When it
comes we should endure it as we endure affliction, without
referring it back to particular people, for it cannot be
referred back to anything. There is something impersonal
in quasi-infernal affliction as there is in perfection.

For those whose 'I' is dead we can do nothing, absolutely
nothing. We never know, however, whether in a particular
person the 'I' is quite dead or only inanimate. If it is not

quite dead, love can reanimate it as though by an injection, but it must be love which is utterly pure without the slightest trace of condescension, for the least shade of contempt drives towards death.

When the 'I' is wounded from outside it starts by revolting in the most extreme and bitter manner like an animal at bay. But as soon as the 'I' is half dead, it wants to be finished off and allows itself to sink into unconsciousness. If it is then awakened by a touch of love, there is sharp pain which results in anger and sometimes hatred for whoever has provoked this pain. Hence the apparently inexplicable vindictiveness of the fallen towards their benefactors.

It can also happen that the love of the benefactor is not pure. Then, in the 'I', awakened by love but immediately wounded afresh by contempt, there surges up the bitterest of hatreds, a hatred which is legitimate.

He, on the contrary, in whom the 'I' is quite dead is in no way embarrassed by the love which is shown him. He takes what comes just as dogs and cats receive food, warmth and caresses, and, like them, he is eager to obtain as much as possible. As the case may be, he either attaches himself like a dog or accepts what comes to him with a certain indifference like a cat. Without the slightest scruple he absorbs all the energy of whoever tries to help him.

Unfortunately in every charitable work there is a danger lest the majority of its clients should be composed of people with no scruples, and above all, of people in whom the 'I' has been killed.

The weaker the character of him who endures affliction, the more quickly is the 'I' destroyed. To be more exact, the limit of the affliction which destroys the 'I' is situated at a greater or lesser distance according to the quality of the character, and the further it is the more the character is said to be strong.

The position of this limit, whether near or far, is probably a fact of nature in the same way as a gift for mathematics, and he who, without having any faith, is proud of preserving his morale in difficult circumstances, has no more reason to be so than the youth who is conceited because mathematics come easily to him. He who believes in God is in danger of a still greater illusion – that of attributing to grace what is simply an essentially mechanical effect of nature.

The agony of extreme affliction is the destruction of the 'I' *from outside*: Arnolphe, Phèdre, Lycaon. We are right to fall on our knees, to make abject supplication when that violent death which is going to strike us down threatens to kill the 'I' from outside even before life is destroyed.

'Niobe also, of the beautiful hair, thought of eating.' That is sublime, in the same way as space in Giotto's frescoes.

A humiliation which forces us to renounce even despair.

The sin in me says 'I'.

I am all. But this particular 'I' is God. And it is not an 'I'.

Evil makes distinctions, it prevents God from being equivalent to all.

It is because of my wretchedness that I am 'I'. It is on account of the wretchedness of the universe that, in a sense, God is 'I' (that is to say a person).

The Pharisees were people who relied on their own strength to be virtuous.

Humility consists in knowing that in what we call 'I' there is no source of energy by which we can rise.

Everything without exception which is of value in me comes from somewhere other than myself, not as a gift but as a loan which must be ceaselessly renewed. Everything without exception which is in me is absolutely valueless; and, among the gifts which have come to me from elsewhere, everything which I appropriate becomes valueless immediately I do so.

Perfect joy excludes even the very feeling of joy, for in the soul filled by the object no corner is left for saying 'I'.

We cannot imagine such joys when they are absent, thus the incentive for seeking them is lacking.

From *Gravity and Grace*, translated by Emma Craufurd, Routledge and Kegan Paul, London, 1952. Originally published as *La Pesanteur et La Grâce*, Plon, Paris, 1947.

THE NEEDS OF THE SOUL

———————— ⊚ ————————

This excerpt forms the first part of The Need for Roots. *Written during 1942–3 and possibly after she was admitted to hospital, it is by this work that Simone Weil is probably best-known. Its appearance in 1949 influenced a generation of thinkers and writers both in and outside France. Camus, who was one of the first to recognize her genius, said he could not imagine a rebirth of Europe which did not take into account the analysis and proposals for social reform she drew up in this work. Quoting two of her phrases, 'Official history is believing the murderers at their word' and 'Who can admire Alexander with all his soul if he doesn't have a base soul?', he pointed out in his preface how isolated a spirit the writer of those words had been in inter-war France.*

Subsequently and ironically, the philosophy of existential engagement Simone Weil so amply exemplified with her life was popularized in intellectual circles by Sartre and others.

In the second part of the book, 'Uprootedness and Nationhood', she argues that in order for 'France' to possess any proper meaning to its citizens, it would be necessary for them to be able to recognize and attach themselves to both what was smaller than France, that's to say the région, *and what was larger, that's to say Europe.*

In the third and final section, 'The Growing of Roots', she

*defines physical labour as the spiritual core of well-ordered
social life. In his introduction to the English version of the
work which came out in 1952, T. S. Eliot described it as the
work of one who was 'more truly a lover of order and
hierarchy than most of those who call themselves Conser-
vative and more truly a lover of the people than most of
those who call themselves Socialist.' (Eliot, 1952)*

The notion of obligations comes before that of rights, which
is subordinate and relative to the former. A right is not
effectual by itself, but only in relation to the obligation to
which it corresponds, the effective exercise of a right
springing not from the individual who possesses it, but
from other men who consider themselves as being under a
certain obligation towards him. Recognition of an obligation makes it effectual. An obligation which goes unrecognized by anybody loses none of the full force of its existence.
A right which goes unrecognized by anybody is not worth
very much.

It makes nonsense to say that men have, on the one hand,
rights, and on the other hand, obligations. Such words only
express differences in point of view. The actual relationship
between the two is as between object and subject. A man,
considered in isolation, only has duties, amongst which are
certain duties towards himself. Other men, seen from his
point of view, only have rights. He, in his turn, has rights,
when seen from the point of view of other men, who recognize that they have obligations towards him. A man left
alone in the universe would have no rights whatever, but he
would have obligations.

The notion of rights, being of an objective order, is
inseparable from the notions of existence and reality. This
becomes apparent when the obligation descends to the
realm of fact; consequently, it always involves to a certain
extent the taking into account of actual given states and
particular situations. Rights are always found to be related
to certain conditions. Obligations alone remain independent

of conditions. They belong to a realm situated above all conditions, because it is situated above this world.

The men of 1789 did not recognize the existence of such a realm. All they recognized was the one on the human plane. That is why they started off with the idea of rights. But at the same time they wanted to postulate absolute principles. This contradiction caused them to tumble into a confusion of language and ideas which is largely responsible for the present political and social confusion. The realm of what is eternal, universal, unconditioned is other than the one conditioned by facts, and different ideas hold sway there, ones which are related to the most secret recesses of the human soul.

Obligations are only binding on human beings. There are no obligations for collectivities, as such. But they exist for all human beings who constitute, serve, command or represent a collectivity, in that part of their existence which is related to the collectivity as in that part which is independent of it.

All human beings are bound by identical obligations, although these are performed in different ways according to particular circumstances. No human being, whoever he may be, under whatever circumstances, can escape them without being guilty of crime; save where there are two genuine obligations which are in fact incompatible, and a man is forced to sacrifice one of them.

The imperfections of a social order can be measured by the number of situations of this kind it harbours within itself.

But even in such a case, a crime is committed if the obligation so sacrificed is not merely sacrificed in fact, but its existence denied into the bargain.

The object of any obligation, in the realm of human affairs, is always the human being as such. There exists an obligation towards every human being for the sole reason that he or she *is* a human being, without any other condition requiring to be fulfilled, and even without any recognition of such obligation on the part of the individual concerned.

This obligation is not based upon any *de facto* situation, nor upon jurisprudence, customs, social structure, relative state of forces, historical heritage, or presumed historical orientation; for no *de facto* situation is able to create an obligation.

This obligation is not based upon any convention; for all conventions are liable to be modified according to the wishes of the contracting parties, whereas in this case no change in the mind and will of Man can modify anything whatsoever.

This obligation is an eternal one. It is coextensive with the eternal destiny of human beings. Only human beings have an eternal destiny. Human collectivities have not got one. Nor are there, in regard to the latter, any direct obligations of an eternal nature. Duty towards the human being as such – that alone is eternal.

This obligation is an unconditional one. If it is founded on something, that something, whatever it is, does not form part of our world. In our world, it is not founded on anything at all. It is the one and only obligation in connection with human affairs that is not subject to any condition.

This obligation has no foundation, but only a verification in the common consent accorded by the universal conscience. It finds expression in some of the oldest written texts which have come down to us. It is recognized by everybody without exception in every single case where it is not attacked as a result of interest or passion. And it is in relation to it that we measure our progress.

The recognition of this obligation is expressed in a confused and imperfect form, that is, more or less imperfect according to the particular case, by what are called positive rights. To the extent to which positive rights are in contradiction with it, to that precise extent is their origin an illegitimate one.

Although this eternal obligation is coextensive with the eternal destiny of the human being, this destiny is not its direct motive. A human being's eternal destiny cannot be the motive of any obligation, for it is not subordinate to external actions.

The fact that a human being possesses an eternal destiny imposes only one obligation: respect. The obligation is only performed if the respect is effectively expressed in a real, not a fictitious, way; and this can only be done through the medium of Man's earthly needs.

On this point, the human conscience has never varied. Thousands of years ago, the Egyptians believed that no soul could justify itself after death unless it could say: 'I have never let anyone suffer from hunger.' All Christians know they are liable to hear Christ himself say to them one day: 'I was an hungered, and ye gave me no meat.' Everyone looks on progress as being, in the first place, a transition to a state of human society in which people will not suffer from hunger. To no matter whom the question may be put in general terms, nobody is of the opinion that any man is innocent if, possessing food himself in abundance and finding someone on his doorstep three parts dead from hunger, he brushes past without giving him anything.

So it is an eternal obligation towards the human being not to let him suffer from hunger when one has the chance of coming to his assistance. This obligation being the most obvious of all, it can serve as a model on which to draw up the list of eternal duties towards each human being. In order to be absolutely correctly made out, this list ought to proceed from the example just given by way of analogy.

Consequently, the list of obligations towards the human being should correspond to the list of such human needs as are vital, analogous to hunger.

Among such needs, there are some which are physical, like hunger itself. They are fairly easy to enumerate. They are concerned with protection against violence, housing, clothing, heating, hygiene and medical attention in case of illness. There are others which have no connection with the physical side of life, but are concerned with its moral side. Like the former, however, they are earthly, and are not directly related, so far as our intelligence is able to perceive, to the eternal destiny of Man. They form, like our physical needs, a necessary condition of our life on this earth. Which means to say that if they are not satisfied, we fall little by little into a state more or less resembling death, more or less akin to a purely vegetative existence.

They are much more difficult to recognize and to enumerate than are the needs of the body. But everyone recognizes that they exist. All the different forms of cruelty which a conqueror can exercise over a subject population, such as massacre, mutilation, organized famine, enslavement or large-scale deportation, are generally considered to be measures of a like description, even though a man's liberty or his native land are not physical necessities. Everyone knows that there are forms of cruelty which can injure a man's life without injuring his body. They are such as deprive him of a certain form of food necessary to the life of the soul.

Obligations, whether unconditional or relative, eternal or changing, direct or indirect with regard to human affairs, all stem, without exception, from the vital needs of the human being. Those which do not directly concern this, that or the other specific human being all exist to serve requirements which, with respect to Man, play a role analogous to food.

We owe a cornfield respect, not because of itself, but because it is food for mankind.

In the same way, we owe our respect to a collectivity, of whatever kind – country, family, or any other – not for itself, but because it is food for a certain number of human souls.

Actually, this obligation makes different attitudes, actions necessary according to different situations. But, taken by itself, it is absolutely identical for everybody. More particularly is this so for all those outside such a collectivity.

The degree of respect owing to human collectivities is a very high one, for several reasons.

To start with, each is unique, and, if destroyed, cannot be replaced. One sack of corn can always be substituted for another sack of corn. The food which a collectivity supplies for the souls of those who form part of it has no equivalent in the entire universe.

Secondly, because of its continuity, a collectivity is already moving forward into the future. It contains food, not only for the souls of the living, but also for the souls of beings yet unborn which are to come into the world during the immediately succeeding centuries.

Lastly, due to this same continuity, a collectivity has its roots in the past. It constitutes the sole agency for preserving the spiritual treasures accumulated by the dead, the sole transmitting agency by means of which the dead can speak to the living. And the sole earthly reality which is directly connected with the eternal destiny of Man is the irradiating light of those who have managed to become fully conscious of this destiny, transmitted from generation to generation.

Because of all this, it may happen that the obligation towards a collectivity which is in danger reaches the point of entailing a total sacrifice. But it does not follow from this that collectivities are superior to human beings. It sometimes happens too, that the obligation to go to the help of a human being in distress makes a total sacrifice necessary, without that implying any superiority on the part of the individual so helped.

A peasant may, under certain circumstances, be under the necessity, in order to cultivate his land, of risking exhaustion, illness or even death. But all the time he will be conscious of the fact that it is solely a matter of bread.

Similarly, even when a total sacrifice is required, no more is owed to any collectivity whatever than a respect analogous to the one owed to food.

It very often happens that the roles are reversed. There are collectivities which, instead of serving as food, do just the opposite: they devour souls. In such cases, the social body is diseased, and the first duty is to attempt a cure; in certain circumstances, it may be necessary to have recourse to surgical methods.

With regard to this matter, too, the obligation for those inside as for those outside the collectivity is an identical one.

It also happens that a collectivity supplies insufficient food for the souls of those forming part of it. In that case, it has to be improved.

Finally, there are dead collectivities which, without devouring souls, don't nourish them either. If it is absolutely certain that they are well and truly dead, that it isn't just a question of a temporary lethargy, then and only then should they be destroyed.

The first thing to be investigated is what are those needs which are for the life of the soul what the needs in the way of food, sleep and warmth are for the life of the body. We must try to enumerate and define them.

They must never be confused with desires, whims, fancies and vices. We must also distinguish between what is fundamental and what is fortuitous. Man requires, not rice or potatoes, but food; not wood or coal, but heating. In the same way, for the needs of the soul, we must recognize the different, but equivalent, sorts of satisfaction which cater for the same requirements. We must also distinguish between the soul's foods and poisons which, for a time, can give the impression of occupying the place of the former.

The lack of any such investigation forces governments, even when their intentions are honest, to act sporadically and at random.

Below are offered a few indications.

ORDER

The first of the soul's needs, the one which touches most nearly its eternal destiny, is order; that is to say, a texture of social relationships such that no one is compelled to violate imperative obligations in order to carry out other ones. It is only where this, in fact, occurs that external circumstances have any power to inflict spiritual violence on the soul. For he for whom the threat of death or suffering is the one thing standing in the way of the performance of an obligation, can overcome this disability, and will only suffer in his body. But he who finds that circumstances, in fact, render the various acts necessitated by a series of strict obligations incompatible with one another is, without being able to offer any resistance thereto, made to suffer in his love of good.

At the present time, a very considerable amount of confusion and incompatibility exists between obligations.

Whoever acts in such a way as to increase this incompatibility is a trouble-maker. Whoever acts in such a way as to diminish it is an agent of order. Whoever, so as to simplify problems, denies the existence of certain obligations has, in his heart, made a compact with crime.

Unfortunately, we possess no method for diminishing this incompatibility. We cannot even be sure that the idea of an order in which all obligations would be compatible with one another isn't itself a fiction. When duty descends to the level of facts, so many independent relationships are brought into play that incompatibility seems far more likely than compatibility.

Nevertheless, we have every day before us the example of a universe in which an infinite number of independent mechanical actions concur so as to produce an order that, in the midst of variations, remains fixed. Furthermore, we love the beauty of the world, because we sense behind it the presence of something akin to that wisdom we should like to possess to slake our thirst for good.

In a minor degree, really beautiful works of art are examples of *ensembles* in which independent factors concur, in a manner impossible to understand, so as to form a unique thing of beauty.

Finally, a consciousness of the various obligations always proceeds from a desire for good which is unique, unchanging and identical with itself for every man, from the cradle to the grave. This desire, perpetually stirring in the depths of our being, makes it impossible for us ever to resign ourselves to situations in which obligations are incompatible with one another. Either we have recourse to lying in order to forget their existence, or we struggle blindly to extricate ourselves from them.

The contemplation of veritable works of art, and much more still that of the beauty of the world, and again much more that of the unrealized good to which we aspire, can sustain us in our efforts to think continually about that human order which should be the subject uppermost in our minds.

The great instigators of violence have encouraged themselves with the thought of how blind, mechanical force is sovereign throughout the whole universe.

By looking at the world with keener senses than theirs, we shall find a more powerful encouragement in the thought of how these innumerable blind forces are limited, made to balance one against the other, brought to form a united whole by something which we do not understand, but which we call beauty.

If we keep ever-present in our minds the idea of a veritable human order, if we think of it as of something to which a total sacrifice is due should the need arise, we shall be in a similar position to that of a man travelling, without a guide, through the night, but continually thinking of the direction he wishes to follow. Such a traveller's way is lit by a great hope.

Order is the first need of all; it even stands above all needs properly so-called. To be able to conceive it, we must know what the other needs are.

The first characteristic which distinguishes needs from desires, fancies or vices, and foods from gluttonous repasts or poisons, is that needs are limited, in exactly the same way as are the foods corresponding to them. A miser never has enough gold, but the time comes when any man provided with an unlimited supply of bread finds he has had enough. Food brings satiety. The same applies to the soul's foods.

The second characteristic, closely connected with the first, is that needs are arranged in antithetical pairs and have to combine together to form a balance. Man requires food, but also an interval between his meals; he requires warmth and coolness, rest and exercise. Likewise in the case of the soul's needs.

What is called the golden mean actually consists in satisfying neither the one nor the other of two contrary needs. It is a caricature of the genuinely balanced state in which contrary needs are each fully satisfied in turn.

LIBERTY

One of the indispensable foods of the human soul is liberty. Liberty, taking the word in its concrete sense, consists in the ability to choose. We must understand by that, of course, a real ability. Wherever men are living in community, rules imposed in the common interest must necessarily limit the possibilities of choice.

But a greater or lesser degree of liberty does not depend on whether the limits set are wider or narrower. Liberty attains its plenitude under conditions which are less easily gauged.

Rules should be sufficiently sensible and sufficiently straightforward so that anyone who so desires and is blessed with average powers of application may be able to understand, on the one hand the useful ends they serve, and on the other hand the actual necessities which have brought about their institution. They should emanate from a source of authority which is not looked upon as strange or hostile, but loved as something belonging to those placed under its direction. They should be sufficiently stable, general and limited in number for the mind to be able to grasp them once and for all, and not find itself brought up against them every time a decision has to be made.

Under these conditions, the liberty of men of goodwill, though limited in the sphere of action, is complete in that of conscience. For, having incorporated the rules into their own being, the prohibited possibilities no longer present themselves to the mind, and have not to be rejected. Just as the habit, formed by education, of not eating disgusting or dangerous things is not felt by the normal man to be any limitation of his liberty in the domain of food. Only a child feels such a limitation.

Those who are lacking in goodwill or who remain adolescent are never free under any form of society.

When the possibilities of choice are so wide as to injure the commonweal, men cease to enjoy liberty. For they must either seek refuge in irresponsibility, puerility and indifference – a refuge where the most they can find is boredom – or feel themselves weighed down by responsibility at all times for fear of causing harm to others. Under such circumstances, men, believing, wrongly, that they are in possession of liberty, and feeling that they get no enjoyment out of it, end up by thinking that liberty is not a good thing.

OBEDIENCE

Obedience is a vital need of the human soul. It is of two kinds: obedience to established rules and obedience to human beings looked upon as leaders. It presupposes consent, not in regard to every single order received, but the kind of consent that is given once and for all, with the sole reservation, in case of need, that the demands of conscience be satisfied.

It requires to be generally recognized, and above all by leaders themselves, that consent and not fear of punishment or hope of reward constitutes, in fact, the mainspring of obedience, so that submission may never be mistaken for servility. It should also be realized that those who command, obey in their turn, and the whole hierarchy should have its face set in the direction of a goal whose importance and even grandeur can be felt by all, from the highest to the lowest.

Obedience being a necessary food of the soul, whoever is definitely deprived of it is ill. Thus, any body politic governed by a sovereign ruler accountable to nobody is in the hands of a sick man.

That is why wherever a man is placed for life at the head of the social organism, he ought to be a symbol and not a ruler, as is the case with the king of England; etiquette ought also to restrict his freedom more narrowly than that of any single man of the people. In this way, the effective rulers, rulers though they be, have somebody over them; on the other hand, they are able to replace each other in un-broken continuity, and consequently to receive, each in his turn, that indispensable amount of obedience due to him.

Those who keep masses of men in subjection by exer-cising force and cruelty deprive them at once of two vital foods, liberty and obedience; for it is no longer within the power of such masses to accord their inner consent to the authority to which they are subjected. Those who encour-age a state of things in which the hope of gain is the principal motive take away from men their obedience, for consent which is its essence is not something which can be sold.

There are any number of signs showing that the men of our age have now for a long time been starved of obedience. But advantage has been taken of the fact to give them slavery.

RESPONSIBILITY

Initiative and responsibility, to feel one is useful and even indispensable, are vital needs of the human soul.

Complete privation from this point of view is the case of the unemployed person, even if he receives assistance to the extent of being able to feed, clothe and house himself. For he represents nothing at all in the economic life of his country, and the voting paper which represents his share in its political life doesn't hold any meaning for him.

The manual labourer is in a scarcely better position.

For this need to be satisfied it is necessary that a man should often have to take decisions in matters great or small, affecting interests that are distinct from his own, but in regard to which he feels a personal concern. He also re-quires to be continually called upon to supply fresh efforts. Finally, he requires to be able to encompass in thought the entire range of activity of the social organism to which he belongs, including branches in connection with which he has never to take a decision or offer any advice. For that, he must be made acquainted with it, be asked to interest himself in it, be brought to feel its value, its utility and, where necessary, its greatness, and be made fully aware of the part he plays in it.

Every social organism, of whatever kind it may be, which does not provide its members with these satisfactions, is diseased and must be restored to health.

In the case of every person of fairly strong character, the need to show initiative goes so far as the need to take command. A flourishing local and regional life, a host of educational activities and youth movements, ought to furnish whoever is able to take advantage of it with the opportunity to command at certain periods of his life.

EQUALITY

Equality is a vital need of the human soul. It consists in a recognition, at once public, general, effective and genuinely expressed in institutions and customs, that the same amount of respect and consideration is due to every human being because this respect is due to the human being as such and is not a matter of degree.

It follows that the inevitable differences among men ought never to imply any difference in the degree of respect. And so that these differences may not be felt to bear such an implication, a certain balance is necessary between equality and inequality.

A certain combination of equality and inequality is formed by equality of opportunity. If no matter who can attain the social rank corresponding to the function he is capable of filling, and if education is sufficiently generalized so that no one is prevented from developing any capacity simply on account of his birth, the prospects are the same for every child. In this way, the prospects for each man are the same as for any other man, both as regards himself when young, and as regards his children later on.

But when such a combination acts alone, and not as one

factor amongst other factors, it ceases to constitute a balance and contains great dangers.

To begin with, for a man who occupies an inferior position and suffers from it to know that his position is a result of his incapacity and that everybody is aware of the fact is not any consolation, but an additional motive of bitterness; according to the individual character, some men can thereby be thrown into a state of depression, while others can be encouraged to commit crime.

Then, in social life, a sort of aspirator towards the top is inevitably created. If a descending movement does not come to balance this ascending movement, the social body becomes sick. To the extent to which it is really possible for the son of a farm labourer to become one day a minister, to the same extent should it really be possible for the son of a minister to become one day a farm labourer. This second possibility could never assume any noticeable proportions without a very dangerous degree of social constraint.

This sort of equality, if allowed full play by itself, can make social life fluid to the point of decomposing it.

There are less clumsy methods of combining equality with differentiation. The first is by using proportion. Proportion can be defined as the combination of equality with inequality, and everywhere throughout the universe it is the sole factor making for balance.

Applied to the maintenance of social equilibrium, it would impose on each man burdens corresponding to the power and well-being he enjoys, and corresponding risks in cases of incapacity or neglect. For instance, an employer who is incapable or guilty of an offence against his workmen ought to be made to suffer far more, both in the spirit and in the flesh, than a workman who is incapable or guilty of an offence against his employer. Furthermore, all workmen ought to know that this is so. It would imply, on the one hand, a certain rearrangement with regard to risks, on the other hand, in criminal law, a conception of punishment in which social rank, as an aggravating circumstance, would necessarily play an important part in deciding what the penalty was to be. All the more reason, therefore, why the exercise of important public functions should carry with it serious personal risks.

Another way of rendering equality compatible with differentiation would be to take away as far as possible all quantitative character from differences. Where there is only a difference in kind, not in degree, there is no inequality at all.

By making money the sole, or almost the sole, motive of all actions, the sole, or almost the sole, measure of all things, the poison of inequality has been introduced everywhere. It is true that this inequality is mobile; it is not attached to persons, for money is made and lost; it is none the less real.

There are two sorts of inequality, each with its corresponding stimulant. A more or less stable inequality, like that of ancient France, produces an idolizing of superiors – not without a mixture of repressed hatred – and a submission to their commands. A mobile, fluid inequality produces a desire to better oneself. It is no nearer to equality than is stable inequality, and is every bit as unwholesome. The Revolution of 1789, in putting forward equality, only succeeded in reality in sanctioning the substitution of one form of inequality for another.

The more equality there is in a society, the smaller is the action of the two stimulants connected with the two forms of inequality, and hence other stimulants are necessary.

Equality is all the greater in proportion as different human conditions are regarded as being, not more nor less than one another, but simply as other. Let us look on the professions of miner and minister simply as two different vocations, like those of poet and mathematician. And let the material hardships attaching to the miner's condition be counted in honour of those who undergo them.

In wartime, if an army is filled with the right spirit, a soldier is proud and happy to be under fire instead of at headquarters; a general is proud and happy to think that the successful outcome of the battle depends on his forethought; and at the same time the soldier admires the general and the general the soldier.

Such a balance constitutes an equality. There would be equality in social conditions if this balance could be found therein. It would mean honouring each human condition with those marks of respect which are proper to it, and are not just a hollow pretence.

HIERARCHISM

Hierarchism is a vital need of the human soul. It is composed of a certain veneration, a certain devotion towards superiors, considered not as individuals, nor in relation to the powers they exercise, but as symbols. What they symbolize is that realm situated high above all men and whose expression in this world is made up of the obligations owed by each man to his fellow-men. A veritable hierarchy presupposes a consciousness on the part of the superiors of this symbolic function and a realization that it forms the only legitimate object of devotion among their subordinates. The effect of true hierarchism is to bring each one to fit himself morally into the place he occupies.

HONOUR

Honour is a vital need of the human soul. The respect due to every human being as such, even if effectively accorded, is not sufficient to satisfy this need, for it is identical for every one and unchanging; whereas honour has to do with a human being considered not simply as such, but from the point of view of his social surroundings. This need is fully satisfied where each of the social organisms to which a human being belongs allows him to share in a noble tradition enshrined in its past history and given public acknowledgement.

For example, for the need of honour to be satisfied in professional life, every profession requires to have some association really capable of keeping alive the memory of all the store of nobility, heroism, probity, generosity and genius spent in the exercise of that profession.

All oppression creates a famine in regard to the need of honour, for the noble traditions possessed by those suffering oppression go unrecognized, through lack of social prestige.

Conquest always has that effect. Vercingetorix was no hero to the Romans. Had France been conquered by the English in the fifteenth century, Joan of Arc would be well and truly forgotten, even to a great extent by us. We now talk about her to the Annamites and the Arabs; but they know very well that here in France we don't allow their heroes and saints to be talked about; therefore the state in which we keep them is an affront to their honour.

Social oppression has the same effects. Guynemer and Mermoz have become part of the public consciousness, thanks to the social prestige of aviation; the sometimes incredible heroism displayed by miners or fishermen barely awakes an echo among miners or fishermen themselves.

Deprivation of honour attains its extreme degree with that total deprivation of respect reserved for certain categories of human beings. In France, this affects, under various forms, prostitutes, ex-convicts, police agents and the sub-proletariat composed of colonial immigrants and natives. Categories of this kind ought not to exist.

Crime alone should place the individual who has committed it outside the social pale, and punishment should bring him back again inside it.

PUNISHMENT

Punishment is a vital need of the human soul. There are two kinds of punishment, disciplinary and penal. The former offers security against failings with which it would be too exhausting to struggle if there were no exterior support. But the most indispensable punishment for the soul is that inflicted for crime. By committing crime, a man places himself, of his own accord, outside the chain of eternal obligations which bind every human being to every other one. Punishment alone can weld him back again; fully so, if accompanied by consent on his part; otherwise only partially so. Just as the only way of showing respect for somebody suffering from hunger is to give him something to eat, so the only way of showing respect for somebody who has placed himself outside the law is to reinstate him inside the law by subjecting him to the punishment ordained by the law.

The need of punishment is not satisfied where, as is generally the case, the penal code is merely a method of exercising pressure through fear.

So that this need may be satisfied, it is above all necessary that everything connected with the penal law should wear a solemn and consecrated aspect; that the majesty of the law should make its presence felt by the court, the police, the accused, the guilty man – even when the case dealt with is of minor importance, provided it entails a possible loss of liberty. Punishment must be an honour. It must not only wipe out the stigma of the crime, but must be regarded as a supplementary form of education, compelling a higher devotion to the public good. The severity of the punishment must also be in keeping with the kind of obligation which has been violated, and not with the interests of public security.

The discredit attaching to the police, the irresponsible conduct of the judiciary, the prison system, the permanent social stigma cast upon ex-convicts, the scale of penalties which provides a much harsher punishment for ten acts of petty larceny than for one rape or certain types of murder, and which even provides punishments for ordinary misfortune – all this makes it impossible for there to exist among us, in France, anything that deserves the name of punishment.

For offences, as for crimes, the relative degree of immunity should increase, not as you go up, but as you go down the social scale. Otherwise the hardships inflicted will be felt to be in the nature of constraints or even abuses of power, and will no longer constitute punishments. Punishment only takes place where the hardship is accompanied at some time or another, even after it is over, and in retrospect, by a feeling of justice. Just as the musician awakens the sense of beauty in us by sounds, so the penal system should know how to awaken the sense of justice in the criminal by the infliction of pain, or even, if need be, of death. And in the same way as we can say of the apprentice who injures himself at his trade, that it is the trade which is getting into *him*, so punishment is a method for getting justice into the soul of the criminal by bodily suffering.

The question of the best means to employ to prevent a conspiracy from arising in high places with the object of obtaining immunity from the law, is one of the most difficult political problems to solve. It can only be solved if there are men whose duty it is to prevent such a conspiracy, and whose situation in life is such that they are not tempted to enter it themselves.

FREEDOM OF OPINION

Freedom of opinion and freedom of association are usually classed together. It is a mistake. Save in the case of natural groupings, association is not a need, but an expedient employed in the practical affairs of life.

On the other hand, complete, unlimited freedom of expression for every sort of opinion, without the least restriction or reserve, is an absolute need on the part of the intelligence. It follows from this that it is a need of the soul, for when the intelligence is ill-at-ease the whole soul is sick. The nature and limits of the satisfaction corresponding to this need are inscribed in the very structure of the various faculties of the soul. For the same thing can be at once limited and unlimited, just as one can produce the length of a rectangle indefinitely without it ceasing to be limited in width.

In the case of a human being, the intelligence can be exercised in three ways. It can work on technical problems, that is to say, discover means to achieve an already given objective. It can provide light when a choice lies before the will concerning the path to be followed. Finally, it can operate alone, separately from the other faculties, in a purely theoretical speculation where all question of action has been provisionally set aside.

When the soul is in a healthy condition, it is exercised in these three ways in turn, with different degrees of freedom. In the first function, it acts as a servant. In the second function, it acts destructively and requires to be reduced to silence immediately it begins to supply arguments to that part of the soul which, in the case of anyone not in a state of perfection, always places itself on the side of evil. But when it operates alone and separately, it must be in possession of sovereign liberty; otherwise something essential is wanting to the human being.

The same applies in a healthy society. That is why it would be desirable to create an absolutely free reserve in the field of publication, but in such a way as for it to be understood that the works found therein did not pledge their authors in any way and contained no direct advice for readers. There it would be possible to find, set out in their full force, all the arguments in favour of bad causes. It would be an excellent and salutary thing for them to be so displayed. Anybody could there sing the praises of what he most condemns. It would be publicly recognized that the object of such works was not to define their authors' attitudes *vis-à-vis* the problems of life, but to contribute, by preliminary researches, towards a complete and correct tabulation of data concerning each problem. The law would see to it that their publication did not involve any risk of whatever kind for the author.

On the other hand, publications destined to influence what is called opinion, that is to say, in effect, the conduct of life, constitute acts and ought to be subjected to the same restrictions as are all acts. In other words, they should not cause unlawful harm of any kind to any human being, and above all, should never contain any denial, explicit or implicit, of the eternal obligations towards the human being, once these obligations have been solemnly recognized by law.

The distinction between the two fields, the one which is outside action and the one which forms part of action, is impossible to express on paper in juridical terminology. But that doesn't prevent it from being a perfectly clear one. The separate existence of these two fields is not difficult to establish in fact, if only the will to do so is sufficiently strong.

It is obvious, for example, that the entire daily and weekly press comes within the second field; reviews also, for they all constitute, individually, a focus of radiation in regard to a particular way of thinking; only those which were to renounce this function would be able to lay claim to total liberty.

The same applies to literature. It would solve the argument which arose not long ago on the subject of literature and morals, and which was clouded over by the fact that all the talented people, through professional solidarity, were found on one side, and only fools and cowards on the other.

But the attitude of the fools and cowards was none the less, to a large extent, consistent with the demands of reason. Writers have an outrageous habit of playing a double game. Never so much as in our age have they claimed the role of directors of conscience and exercised it. Actually, during the years immediately preceding the war, no one challenged their right to it except the savants. The position formerly occupied by priests in the moral life of the country was held by physicists and novelists, which is sufficient to gauge the value of our progress. But if somebody called upon writers to render an account of the orientation set by their influence, they barricaded themselves indignantly behind the sacred privilege of art for art's sake.

There is not the least doubt, for example, that André Gide has always known that books like *Les Nourritures Terrestres* and *Les Caves du Vatican* have exercised an influence on the practical conduct of life of hundreds of young people, and he has been proud of the fact. There is, then, no reason for placing such books behind the inviolable barrier of art for art's sake, and sending to prison a young fellow who pushes somebody off a train in motion.[1] One might just as well claim the privileges of art for art's sake in support of crime. At one time the Surrealists came pretty close to doing so. All that has been repeated by so many idiots *ad nauseam* about the responsibility of our writers in the defeat of France in 1940 is, unfortunately, only too true.

If a writer, thanks to the complete freedom of expression accorded to pure intelligence, publishes written matter which goes contrary to the moral principals recognized by law, and if later on he becomes a notorious focus of influence, it is simple enough to ask him if he is prepared to state publicly that his writings do not express his personal attitude. If he is not prepared to do so, it is simple enough to punish him. If he lies, it is simple enough to discredit him. Moreover, it ought to be recognized that the moment a writer fills a role among the influences directing public opinion, he cannot claim to exercise unlimited freedom. Here again, a juridical definition is impossible; but the facts are not really difficult to discern. There is no reason at all why the sovereignty of the law should be limited to the field of what can be expressed in legal formulae, since that sovereignty is exercised just as well by judgments in equity.

Besides, the need of freedom itself, so essential to the intellect, calls for a corresponding protection against suggestion, propaganda, influence by means of obsession. These are methods of constraint, a special kind of constraint, not accompanied by fear or physical distress, but which is none the less a form of violence. Modern technique places extremely potent instruments at its service. This constraint is, by its very nature, collective, and human souls are its victims.

---

[1] *'d'emprisonner un garçon qui jette quelqu'un hors d'un train en marche'*: a reference to a gratuitous act performed by Lafcadio, hero of André Gide's *Caves du Vatican*, who pushes somebody off a train in Italy to prove to himself that he is capable of committing any act whatever, however motiveless, unrelated to preceding events [A. F. Wills].

Naturally, the State is guilty of crime if it makes use of such methods itself, save in cases where the public safety is absolutely at stake. But it should, furthermore, prevent their use. Publicity, for example, should be rigorously controlled by law and its volume very considerably reduced; it should also be severely prohibited from ever dealing with subjects which belong to the domain of thought.

Likewise, repression could be exercised against the press, radio broadcasts, or anything else of a similar kind, not only for offences against moral principles publicly recognized, but also for baseness of tone and thought, bad taste, vulgarity or a subtly corrupting moral atmosphere. This sort of repression could take place without in any way infringing on freedom of opinion. For instance, a newspaper could be suppressed without the members of its editorial staff losing the right to go on publishing wherever they liked, or even, in the less serious cases, remain associated to carry on the same paper under another name. Only, it would have been publicly branded with infamy and would run the risk of being so again. Freedom of opinion can be claimed solely – and even then with certain reservations – by the journalist, not by the paper; for it is only the journalist who is capable of forming an opinion.

Generally speaking, all problems to do with freedom of expression are clarified if it is posited that this freedom is a need of the intelligence, and that intelligence resides solely in the human being, individually considered. There is no such thing as a collective exercise of the intelligence. It follows that no group can legitimately claim freedom of expression, because no group has the slightest need of it.

In fact the opposite applies. Protection of freedom of thought requires that no group should be permitted by law to express an opinion. For when a group starts having opinions, it inevitably tends to impose them on its members. Sooner or later, these individuals find themselves debarred, with a greater or lesser degree of severity, and on a number of problems of greater or lesser importance, from expressing opinions opposed to those of the group, unless they care to leave it. But a break with any group to which one belongs always involves suffering – at any rate of a sentimental kind. And just as danger, exposure to suffering are healthy and necessary elements in the sphere of action, so are they unhealthy influences in the exercise of the intelligence. A fear, even a passing one, always provokes either a weakening or a tautening, depending on the degree of courage, and that is all that is required to damage the extremely delicate and fragile instrument of precision which constitutes our intelligence. Even friendship is, from this point of view, a great danger. The intelligence is defeated as soon as the expression of one's thoughts is preceded, explicitly or implicitly, by the little word 'we'. And when the light of the intelligence grows dim, it is not very long before the love of good becomes lost.

The immediate, practical solution would be the abolition of political parties. Party strife, as it existed under the Third Republic, is intolerable. The single party, which is, moreover, its inevitable outcome, is the worst evil of all. The only remaining possibility is a public life without parties. Nowadays, such an idea strikes us as a novel and daring proposition. All the better, since something novel is what is wanted. But, in point of fact, it is only going back to the tradition of 1789. In the eyes of the people of 1789, there was literally no other possibility. A public life like ours has been over the course of the last half-century would have seemed to them a hideous nightmare. They would never have believed it possible that a representative of the people should so divest himself of all personal dignity as to allow himself to become the docile member of a party.

Moreover, Rousseau had clearly demonstrated how party strife automatically destroys the Republic. He had foretold its effects. It would be a good thing just now to encourage the reading of the *Contrat Social*. Actually, at the present time, wherever there were political parties, democracy is dead. We all know that the parties in England have a certain tradition, spirit and function making it impossible to compare them to anything else. We all know, besides, that the rival teams in the United States are not political parties. A democracy where public life is made up of strife between political parties is incapable of preventing the formation of a party whose avowed aim is the overthrow of that democracy. If such a democracy brings in discriminatory laws, it cuts its own throat. If it doesn't, it is just as safe as a little bird in front of a snake.

A distinction ought to be drawn between two sorts of associations: those concerned with interests, where organization and discipline would be countenanced up to a certain point, and those concerned with ideas, where such things would be strictly forbidden. Under present conditions, it is a good thing to allow people to group themselves together to defend their interests, in other words, their wage receipts and so forth, and to leave these associations to act within very narrow limits and under the constant supervision of the authorities. But such associations should not be allowed to have anything to do with ideas. Associations in which ideas are being canvassed should be not so much associations as more or less fluid social mediums. When some action is contemplated within them, there is no reason why it need be put into execution by any persons other than those who approve of it.

In the working-class movement, for example, such a distinction would put an end to the present inextricable confusion. In the period before the war, the working-man's attention was being continually pulled in three directions at once. In the first place, by the struggle for higher wages; secondly, by what remained – growing ever feebler, but still showing some signs of life – of the old trade-union spirit of former days, idealist and more or less libertarian in character; and, lastly, by the political parties. Very often, when a strike was on, the workmen who struggled and suffered would have been quite incapable of deciding for themselves whether it was all a matter of wages, a revival of the old trade-union spirit, or a political manoeuvre conducted by a party; and nobody looking on from the outside was in any better position to judge.

That is an impossible state of affairs. When the war broke out, the French trade unions were dead or moribund, in spite of their millions of members – or because of them. They again took on some semblance of life, after a prolonged lethargy, when the Resistance against the invader got under way. That doesn't prove that they are viable. It is perfectly clear that they had been all but destroyed by two sorts of poison, each of which by itself is deadly.

Trade unions cannot flourish if at their meetings the workmen are obsessed by their earnings to the same extent as they are in the factory, when engaged in piece-work. To begin with, because the result is that sort of moral death always brought about by an obsession in regard to money. Next, because the trade union, having become, under present social conditions, a factor continually acting upon the economic life of the country, ends up inevitably by being transformed into a single, compulsory, professional organization, obliged to toe the line in public affairs. It has then been changed into the semblance of a corpse.

Besides, it is no less evident that trade unions cannot live in intimate contact with political parties. There is something resulting from the normal play of mechanical forces which makes such a thing quite impossible. For an analogous reason, moreover, the Socialist Party cannot live side by side with the Communist Party, because the latter's party character is, as it were, marked to a so much greater degree.

Furthermore, the obsession about wages strengthens Communist influence, because questions to do with money, however closely they may affect the majority of men, produce at the same time in all men a sensation of such deadly boredom that it requires to be compensated by the apocalyptic prospect of the Revolution, according to Communist tenets. If the middle classes haven't the same need of an apocalypse, it is because long rows of figures have a poetry, a prestige which tempers in some sort the boredom associated with money; whereas, when money is counted in sixpences, we have boredom in its pure, unadulterated state. Nevertheless, the taste shown by *bourgeois*, both great and small, for Fascism, indicates that, in spite of everything, they too can feel bored.

Under the Vichy Government, single and compulsory professional organizations for workmen have been created. It is a pity that they have been given, according to the modern fashion, the name of corporation, which denotes, in reality, something so very different and so beautiful. But it is a good thing that such dead organizations should be there to take over the dead part of trade-union activity. It would be dangerous to do away with them. It is far better to charge them with the day-to-day business of dealing with wages and what are called immediate demands. As for the political parties, if they were all strictly prohibited in a general atmosphere of liberty, it is to be hoped their underground existence would at any rate be made difficult for them.

In that event, the workmen's trade unions, if they still retain a spark of any real life, could become again, little by little, the expression of working-class thought, the instrument of working-class integrity. According to the traditions of the French working-class movement, which has always looked upon itself as responsible for the whole world, they would concern themselves with everything to do with justice – including, where necessary, questions about wages; but only at long intervals and to rescue human beings from poverty.

Naturally, they would have to be able to exert an influence on professional organizations, according to methods of procedure defined by law.

There would, perhaps, only be advantages to be gained by making it illegal for professional organizations to launch a strike, and allowing trade unions – with certain restrictions – to do so, while at the same time attaching risks to this responsibility, prohibiting any sort of coercion, and safeguarding the continuity of economic life.

As for the lock-out, there is no reason why it should not be entirely suppressed.

The authorized existence of associations for promoting ideas could be subject to two conditions. First, that excommunication may not be applied. Recruitment would be voluntary and as a result of personal affinity, without, however, making anybody liable to be invited to subscribe to a collection of assertions crystallized in written form. But once a member had been admitted, he could not be expelled except for some breach of integrity or undermining activities; which latter offence would, moreover, imply the existence of an illegal organization, and consequently expose the offender to a more severe punishment.

This would, in fact, amount to a measure of public safety, experience having shown that totalitarian States are set up by totalitarian parties, and that these totalitarian parties are formed by dint of expulsions for the crime of having an opinion of one's own.

The second condition could be that ideas must really be put into circulation, and tangible proof of such circulation given in the shape of pamphlets, reviews or typed bulletins in which problems of general interest were discussed. Too great a uniformity of opinion would render any such association suspect.

For the rest, all associations for promoting ideas would be authorized to act according as they thought fit, on condition that they didn't break the law or exert any sort of disciplinary pressure on their members.

As regards associations for promoting interests, their control would, in the first place, involve the making of a distinction, namely, that the word 'interest' sometimes expresses a need and at other times something quite different. In the case of a poor working-man, interest means food, lodging and heating. For an employer, it means something of a different kind. When the word is taken in its first sense, the action of the authorities should be mainly to stimulate, uphold and defend the interests concerned. When used in its second sense, the action of the authorities should be continually to supervise, limit and, whenever possible, curb the activities of the associations representing such interests. It goes without saying that the severest restrictions and the hardest punishments should be reserved for those which are, by their nature, the most powerful.

What has been called freedom of association has been, in fact, up to now, freedom for associations. But associations have not got to be free; they are instruments, they must be held in bondage. Only the human being is fit to be free.

As regards freedom of thought, it is very nearly true to say that without freedom there *is* no thought. But it is truer still to say that when thought is non-existent, it is non-free into the bargain. There has been a lot of freedom of thought over the past few years, but no thought. Rather like the case of a child who, not having any meat, asks for salt with which to season it.

SECURITY

Security is an essential need of the soul. Security means that the soul is not under the weight of fear or terror, except as the result of an accidental conjunction of circumstances and for brief and exceptional periods. Fear and terror, as permanent states of the soul, are wellnigh mortal poisons, whether they be caused by the threat of unemployment, police persecution, the presence of a foreign conqueror, the probability of invasion, or any other calamity which seems too much for human strength to bear.

The Roman masters used to place a whip in the hall within sight of their slaves, knowing that this spectacle reduced their hearts to that half-dead condition indispensable for slavery. On the other hand, according to the Egyptians, the just man should be able to say after death: 'I never caused anyone any fear'.

Even if permanent fear constitutes a latent state only, so that its painful effects are only rarely experienced directly, it remains always a disease. It is a semi-paralysis of the soul.

RISK

Risk is an essential need of the soul. The absence of risk produces a type of boredom which paralyses in a different way from fear, but almost as much. Moreover, there are certain situations which, involving as they do a diffused anguish without any clearly defined risks, spread the two kinds of disease at once.

Risk is a form of danger which provokes a deliberate reaction; that is to say, it doesn't go beyond the soul's resources to the point of crushing the soul beneath a load of fear. In some cases, there is a gambling aspect to it; in others, where some definite obligation forces a man to face it, it represents the finest possible stimulant.

The protection of mankind from fear and terror doesn't imply the abolition of risk; it implies, on the contrary, the permanent presence of a certain amount of risk in all aspects of social life; for the absence of risk weakens courage to the point of leaving the soul, if the need should arise, without the slightest inner protection against fear. All that is wanted is for risk to offer itself under such conditions that it is not transformed into a sensation of fatality.

PRIVATE PROPERTY

Private property is a vital need of the soul. The soul feels isolated, lost, if it is not surrounded by objects which seem to it like an extension of the bodily members. All men have an invincible inclination to appropriate in their own minds anything which over a long, uninterrupted period they have used for their work, pleasure or the necessities of life. Thus, a gardener, after a certain time, feels that the garden belongs to him. But where the feeling of appropriation doesn't coincide with any legally recognized proprietorship, men are continually exposed to extremely painful spiritual wrenches.

Once we recognize private property to be a need, this implies for everyone the possibility of possessing something more than the articles of ordinary consumption. The forms this need takes can vary considerably, depending on circumstances; but it is desirable that the majority of people should own their house and a little piece of land round it, and, whenever not technically impossible, the tools of their trade. Land and livestock figure among the tools necessary to the peasant's trade.

The principle of private property is violated where the land is worked by agricultural labourers and farm-hands under the orders of an estate-manager, and owned by townsmen who receive the profits. For of all those who are connected with that land, there is not one who, in one way or another, is not a stranger to it. It is wasted, not from the point of view of corn-production, but from that of the satisfaction of the property-need which it could procure.

Between this extreme case and that other one of the peasant who cultivates with his family the land he owns, there are a number of intermediate states where Man's need of appropriation is more or less unrecognized.

COLLECTIVE PROPERTY

Participation in collective possessions – a participation consisting not in any material enjoyment, but in a feeling of ownership – is a no less important need. It is more a question of a state of mind than of any legal formula. Where a real civic life exists, each one feels he has a personal ownership in the public monuments, gardens, ceremonial pomp and circumstance; and a display of sumptuousness, in which nearly all human beings seek fulfilment, is in this way placed within the reach of even the poorest. But it isn't just the State which ought to provide this satisfaction; it is every sort of collectivity in turn.

A great modern factory is a waste from the point of view of the need of property; for it is unable to provide either the workers, or the manager who is paid his salary by the board of directors, or the members of the board who never visit it, or the shareholders who are unaware of its existence, with the least satisfaction in connection with this need.

When methods of exchange and acquisition are such as to involve a waste of material and moral foods, it is time they were transformed.

There is no natural connection between property and money. The connection established nowadays is merely the result of a system which has made money the focus of all other possible motives. This system being an unhealthy one, we must bring about a dissociation in inverse order.

The true criterion in regard to property is that it is legitimate so long as it is real. Or, to be more precise, the laws concerning property are so much the better the more advantages they draw from the opportunities offered by the possessions of this world for the satisfaction of the property-need common to all men.

Consequently, the present modes of acquisition and possession require to be transformed in the name of the principle of property. Any form of possession which doesn't satisfy somebody's need of private or collective property can reasonably be regarded as useless.

That does not mean that it is necessary to transfer it to the State; but rather to try and turn it into some genuine form of property.

TRUTH

The need of truth is more sacred than any other need. Yet it is never mentioned. One feels afraid to read when once one has realized the quantity and the monstrousness of the material falsehoods shamelessly paraded, even in the books of the most reputable authors. Thereafter one reads as though one were drinking from a contaminated well.

There are men who work eight hours a day and make the immense effort of reading in the evenings so as to acquire knowledge. It is impossible for them to go and verify their sources in the big libraries. They have to take the book on trust. One has no right to give them spurious provender. What sense is there in pleading that authors act in good faith? *They* don't have to do physical labour for eight hours a day. Society provides for their sustenance so that they may have the leisure and give themselves the trouble to avoid error. A pointsman responsible for a train accident and pleading good faith would hardly be given a sympathetic hearing.

All the more reason why it is disgraceful to tolerate the

existence of newspapers on which, as everybody knows, not one of the collaborators would be able to stop, unless he were prepared from time to time to tamper knowingly with the truth.

The public is suspicious of newspapers, but its suspicions don't save it. Knowing, in a general way, that a newspaper contains both true and false statements, it divides the news up into these two categories, but in a rough-and-ready fashion, in accordance with its own predilections. It is thus delivered over to error.

We all know that when journalism becomes indistinguishable from organized lying, it constitutes a crime. But we think it is a crime impossible to punish. What is there to stop the punishment of activities once they are recognized to be criminal ones? Where does this strange notion of non-punishable crimes come from? It constitutes one of the most monstrous deformations of the judicial spirit.

Isn't it high time it were proclaimed that every discernible crime is a punishable one, and that we are resolved, if given the opportunity, to punish all crimes?

A few straightforward measures of public salubrity would protect the population from offences against the truth.

The first would be to set up, with such protection in view, special courts enjoying the highest prestige, composed of judges specially selected and trained. They would be responsible for publicly condemning any avoidable error, and would be able to sentence to prison or hard labour for repeated commission of the offence, aggravated by proven dishonesty of intention.

For instance, a lover of Ancient Greece, reading in one of Maritain's books: 'The greatest thinkers of antiquity had not thought of condemning slavery', would indict Maritain before one of these tribunals. He would take along with him the only important reference to slavery that has come down to us – the one from Aristotle. He would invite the judges to read the sentence: 'Some people assert that slavery is absolutely contrary to nature and reason.' He would observe that there is nothing to make us suppose these particular 'people' were not among the greatest thinkers of antiquity. The court would censure Maritain for having published – when it was so easy for him to avoid falling into such a mistake – a false assertion, and one constituting, however unintentionally, an outrageous calumny against an entire civilization. All the daily papers, weeklies and others; all the reviews and the radio would be obliged to bring the court's censure to the notice of the public, and, if need be, Maritain's answer. In this particular case, it seems most unlikely there could be one.

On the occasion when *Gringoire*[1] published *in extenso* a speech attributed to a Spanish anarchist, who had been announced as going to speak at a meeting in Paris, but who in fact, at the last minute, had been unable to leave Spain, a court of this kind would not have been out of place. Dishonesty being in such a case more patent than that two and two make four, no doubt prison or hard labour would not have been too severe a sentence.

Under this system, anybody, no matter who, discovering an avoidable error in a printed text or radio broadcast, would be entitled to bring an action before these courts.

The second measure would be to prohibit entirely all propaganda of whatever kind by the radio or daily press. These two instruments would only be allowed to be used for non-tendentious information.

The aforesaid courts would be there to see that the information supplied was not tendentious.

In the case of organs of information, they might have to pronounce judgment concerning not only erroneous assertions, but also intentional and tendentious omissions.

Circles in which ideas are discussed, and which desire to make them known, would only have a right to publish weekly, fortnightly or monthly journals. There is absolutely no need to appear more frequently in print, if one's object is to make people think instead of stupefying them.

[1] *Gringoire*: a pre-war weekly of a virulent turn and politically reactionary [A. F. Wills].

The propriety of the methods of persuasion used would be guaranteed, thanks to the control exercised by the above courts, which would be able to suppress any publication guilty of too frequent a distortion of the truth; though the editors would be allowed to let it reappear under another name.

Nothing in all this would involve the slightest attack on public liberty. It would only mean satisfaction of the human soul's most sacred need – protection against suggestion and falsehood.

But, it will be objected, how can we guarantee the impartiality of the judges? The only guarantee, apart from that of their complete independence, is that they should be drawn from very different social circles; be naturally gifted with a wide, clear and exact intelligence; and be trained in a school where they receive not just a legal education, but above all a spiritual one, and only secondarily an intellectual one. They must become accustomed to love truth.

There is no possible chance of satisfying a people's need of truth, unless men can be found for this purpose who love truth.

From *The Need for Roots: Prelude to a Declaration of Duties Towards Mankind*, translated by A. F. Wills, Routledge and Kegan Paul, London, 1952: Putnam's Sons, New York, 1953. Originally published as *L'Enracinement: Prélude à une déclaration des devoirs envers l'être humain*, Gallimard, Paris, 1949.

THE GREAT BEAST

———————— © ————————

The Great Beast[1] is the only object of idolatry, the only *ersatz* of God, the only imitation of something which is infinitely far from me and which is I myself.

If we could be egoistical it would be very pleasant. It would be a rest. But literally we cannot.

It is impossible for me to take myself as an end or, in consequence, my fellow man as an end, since he is my fellow. Nor can I take any material thing, because matter is still less capable of having finality conferred upon it than human beings are.

Only one thing can be taken as an end, for in relation to the human person it possesses a kind of transcendence: this is the collective. The collective is the object of all idolatry, this it is which chains us to the earth. In the case of avarice: gold is of the social order. In the case of ambition: power is of the social order. Science and art are full of the social element also. And love? Love is more or less of an exception: that is why we can go to God through love, not through avarice or ambition. Yet the social element is not

[1] On the origin of this myth cf. Plato, *Republic*, Book VI. To adore the 'Great Beast' is to think and act in conformity with the prejudices and reactions of the multitude to the detriment of all personal search for truth and goodness. [Gustav Thibon].

absent from love (passions excited by princes, celebrated people, all those who have prestige . . .).

There are two goods of the same denomination but radically different from each other: one which is the opposite of evil and one which is the absolute. The absolute has no opposite. The relative is not the opposite of the absolute; it is derived from it through a relationship which is not commutative. That which we want is the absolute good. That which is within our reach is the good which is correlated to evil. We betake ourselves to it by mistake, like the prince who starts to make love to the maid instead of the mistress. The error is due to the clothes. It is the social which throws the colour of the absolute over the relative. The remedy is in the idea of relationship. Relationship breaks its way out of the social. It is the monopoly of the individual. Society is the cave. The way out is solitude.

To relate belongs to the solitary spirit. No crowd can conceive relationship. 'This is good or bad in relation to . . .', 'in so far as . . .' That escapes the crowd. A crowd cannot add things together.

He who is above social life returns to it when he wishes, not so he who is below. It is the same with everything. A relationship which is not commutative between what is better and what is less good.

The vegetative and the social are the two realms where the good does not enter.

Christ redeemed the vegetative, not the social. He did not pray for the world.

The social order is irreducibly that of the prince of this world. Our only duty with regard to the social is to try to limit the evil of it. (Richelieu: the salvation of states lies only in this world.)

A society like the Church, which claims to be divine is perhaps more dangerous on account of the *ersatz* good which it contains than on account of the evil which sullies it.

Something of the social labelled divine: an intoxicating mixture which carries with it every sort of licence. Devil disguised.

Conscience is deceived by the social. Our supplementary energy (imaginative) is to a great extent taken up with the social. It has to be detached from it. That is the most difficult of detachments.

Meditation on the social mechanism is in this respect a purification of the first importance.

To contemplate the social is as good a way of detachment as to retire from the world. That is why I have not been wrong to rub shoulders with politics for so long.

It is only by entering the transcendental, the supernatural, the authentically spiritual order that man rises above the social. Until then, whatever he may do, the social is transcendent in relation to him.

On the non-supernatural plane, society is that which keeps evil (certain forms of it) away by forming as it were a barrier. A society of criminals or people given over to vice, even if only composed of a handful of men, destroys this barrier.

But what is it which impels people to enter such a society? Either necessity, or laxity, or, usually, a mixture of the two. They do not think they are becoming involved, for they do not know that, apart from the supernatural, it is only society which prevents us from falling naturally into the most fearful vice and crime. They do not know that they are going to become different, for they do not know the extent of the region within themselves which can be changed by environment. They always become involved without knowing.

Rome is the Great Beast of atheism and materialism, adoring nothing but itself. Israel is the Great Beast of religion. Neither the one nor the other is likeable. The Great Beast is always repulsive.

Would a society in which only gravity reigned be able to exist, or is a little of the supernatural element a vital necessity?

In Rome, perhaps, there was only gravity.

With the Hebrews too, perhaps. Their God was heavy.

Perhaps there was only one ancient people absolutely without mysticism: Rome. By what mystery? It was an artificial city, made up of fugitives, just as Israel was.

The Great Beast of Plato. The whole of Marxism, in so far as it is true, is contained in the page of Plato on the Great Beast; and its refutation is there too.

The power of the social element. Agreement between several men brings with it a feeling of reality. It brings with it also a sense of duty. Divergence, where this agreement is concerned, appears as a sin. Hence *all* returns to the fold are possible. The state of conformity is an imitation of grace.

By a strange mystery – which is connected with the power of the social element – a profession can confer on quite ordinary men in their exercise of it, virtues which, if they were extended to all circumstances of life, would make of them heroes or saints.

But the power of the social element makes these virtues *natural*. Accordingly they need a compensation.

Pharisees: 'Verily I say unto you, they have received their reward.' Inversely, Christ could have said of the publicans and prostitutes: 'Verily I say unto you, they have received their punishment' – that is to say social reprobation. In so far as they have received this, the Father who is in secret does not punish them. Whereas the sins which are not accompanied by social reprobation receive their full measure of punishment from the Father who is in secret. Thus social reprobation is a favour on the part of destiny. It turns into a supplementary evil, however, for those who, under the pressure of this reprobation, manufacture for themselves eccentric social surroundings within which they have full licence. Criminal and homosexual circles, etc.

The service of the false God (of the social Beast under whatever form it may be) purifies evil by eliminating its horror. Nothing seems evil to those who serve it except failure in its service. The service of the true God, on the other hand, allows the horror of evil to remain and even makes it more intense. Whilst this evil horrifies us, we yet love it as emanating from the will of God.

Those who think today that one of the adversaries is on the side of the good, think also that that side will be victorious.[1]

To watch a good, loved as such, condemned as it were by the oncoming tide of events is an intolerable suffering.

The idea that that which does not exist any more may be a good is painful and we thrust it aside. That is submission to the Great Beast.

The force of soul of the Communists comes from the fact that they are going, not only towards what they believe to be the good, but towards what they believe will surely and soon be brought about. Thus without being saints – they are a long way from that – they can endure dangers and sufferings which only a saint would bear for justice alone.

In some respects the state of mind of the Communists is very analogous to that of the early Christians.

That eschatological propaganda explains very well the persecutions of the first period.

'He to whom little is forgiven, the same loveth little.' This concerns someone with whom social virtue occupies a very large place. Grace finds little room to spare in him. Obedience to the Great Beast which conforms to the good – that is social virtue.

A Pharisee is someone who is virtuous out of obedience to the Great Beast.

---

[1] These lines were written in 1942.

Charity can and should love in every country all that is a condition of the spiritual development of individuals, that is to say, on the one hand, social order, even if it is bad, as being less bad than disorder, on the other hand the language, ceremonies, customs – all that contains beauty – all the poetry which the life of a country embraces.

But a nation as such cannot be the object of supernatural love. It has no soul. It is a Great Beast.

And yet a city. . . .

But that is not social; it is a human environment of which one is no more conscious than of the air one breathes. A contact with nature, the past, tradition.

Rootedness lies in something other than the social.

Patriotism. We must not have any love other than charity. A nation cannot be an object of charity. But a country can be one – as an environment bearing traditions which are eternal. Every country can be that.

From *Gravity and Grace*, translated by Emma Craufurd, Routledge and Kegan Paul, London, 1952; originally published as *La Pesanteur et la Grâce*, Plon, Paris, 1947.

ANALYSIS OF OPPRESSION

———————— ◎ ————————

This work, an extract from a much longer piece entitled 'Reflections concerning the Causes of Liberty and Social Oppression' is one of her major contributions to political theory. Sketches for the essay were in progress ever since Simone Weil's return from Germany in 1932. Many of the ideas contained in it formed part of a course on Marxism she gave at the miners' study group sessions in Saint-Etienne. She presented a brief history of science and a history of the struggles against oppression, which she described as being finally united in Marxism.

It has been suggested that work on this paper was the spur which decided her to enter the factory and which began to separate her from the political theorists within the revolutionary-syndicalist movement. She herself attached some importance to it and after the outbreak of war, when many of her papers were left behind in her parents' apartment in the rue Auguste Comte, she wrote to an old friend, Guindy, who had become a customs inspector and could travel easily between Paris and Vichy, asking him if he would go there and find it for her:

there is in Paris in my briefcase a prose piece, very long, typewritten, whose title I forget, but it has a quotation from

*Spinoza as an epigraph. It is essentially an analysis of political
and social oppression, its permanent causes, its mechanism and
its present forms. It dates from 1934. It too is very pertinent today.
It surely is good enough not be lost I think. But I don't know
whether it would be prudent to take it home with you. Read it and
evaluate it for yourself . . . I really regret now that I didn't publish
it . . .*

The quotation from Spinoza reads: 'With regard to human
affairs, not to laugh, not to cry, not to become indignant, but
to understand'.

    The conclusion to this critique echoes the themes that were
to occupy her for the rest of her life, both in the factory and
outside it. It seems to be a question, she says, of

*separating, in present-day civilization, what belongs of right to
man, considered as an individual, and what is of a nature to
place weapons in the hands of the collectivity for use against him
[. . .] Technique [. . .] ought to be studied [. . .] from an entirely
new point of view, which would no longer be that of output, but
that of the relation between the worker and his work[. . . .] [My
deletions S.M.]*

The problem is, in short, to know what it is that links
oppression in general and each form of oppression in particular to the system of production; in other words, to
succeed in grasping the mechanism of oppression, in understanding by what means it arises, subsists, transforms itself,
by what means, perhaps, it might theoretically disappear.
This is, to all intents and purposes, a novel question. For
centuries past, noble minds have regarded the power of
oppressors as constituting a usurpation pure and simple,
which one had to try to oppose either by simply expressing
a radical disapproval of it, or else by armed force placed at
the service of justice. In either case, failure has always been
complete; and never was it more strikingly so than when it
took on momentarily the appearance of victory, as happened
with the French Revolution, when, after having effectively
succeeded in bringing about the disappearance of a certain

form of oppression, people stood by, helpless, watching a new oppression immediately being set up in its place.

In his ponderings over this resounding failure, which had come to crown all previous ones, Marx finally came to understand that you cannot abolish oppression so long as the causes which make it inevitable remain, and that these causes reside in the objective – that is to say material – conditions of the social system. He consequently elaborated a completely new conception of oppression, no longer considered as the usurpation of a privilege, but as the organ of a social function. This function is that very one which consists in developing the productive forces, in so far as this development calls for severe efforts and serious hardships; and Marx and Engels perceived a reciprocal relationship between this development and social oppression.

In the first place, according to them, oppression becomes established only when improvements in production have brought about a division of labour sufficiently advanced for exchange, military command and government to constitute distinct functions; on the other hand, oppression, once established, stimulates the further development of the productive forces, and changes in form as and when this development so demands, until the day when, having become a hindrance to it instead of a help, it disappears purely and simply.

However brilliant the concrete analyses may be by which Marxists have illustrated this thesis, and although it constitutes an improvement on the naïve expressions of indignation which it replaced, one cannot say that it throws light on the mechanism of oppression. It only partially describes its origins; for why should the division of labour necessarily turn into oppression? It by no means entitles us to a reasonable expectation of its ending; for if Marx believed himself to have shown how the capitalist system finally hinders production, he did not even attempt to prove that, in our day, any other oppressive system would hinder it in like manner. Furthermore, one fails to understand why oppression should not manage to continue, even after it has become a factor of economic regression. Above all, Marx omits to explain why oppression is invincible as long as it is useful, why the oppressed in revolt have never succeeded in founding a non-oppressive society, whether on the basis of the productive forces of their time, or even at the cost of an economic regression which could hardly increase their misery; and, lastly, he leaves completely in the dark the general principles of the mechanism by which a given form of oppression is replaced by another.

What is more, not only have Marxists not solved a single one of these problems, but they have not even thought it their duty to formulate them. It has seemed to them that they had sufficiently accounted for social oppression by assuming that it corresponds to a function in the struggle against nature. Even then, they have only really brought out this correspondence in the case of the capitalist system; but, in any case, to suppose that such a correspondence constitutes an explanation of the phenomenon is to apply unconsciously to social organisms Lamarck's famous principle, as unintelligible as it is convenient, 'the function creates the organ'. Biology only started to be a science on the day when Darwin replaced this principle by the notion of conditions of existence. The improvement lies in the fact that the function is no longer considered as the cause, but as the result of the organ – the only intelligible order; the part played by cause is henceforth attributed only to a blind mechanism, that of heredity combined with accidental variations. Actually, by itself, all this blind mechanism can do is to produce haphazardly anything whatsoever; the adaptation of the organ to the function here enters into play in such a manner as to limit chance by eliminating the non-viable structures, no longer as a mysterious tendency, but as a condition of existence; and this condition is defined by the relationship of the organism under consideration to its partly inert, partly living environment, and more especially to similar rival organisms. Adaptation is henceforth conceived in regard to living beings as an exterior and no longer an interior necessity.

It is clear that this luminous method is not only valid in

biology, but wherever one is confronted by organized structures which have not been organized by anybody. In order to be able to appeal to science in social matters, we ought to have effected with respect to Marxism an improvement similar to that which Darwin effected with respect to Lamarck. The causes of social evolution must no longer be sought elsewhere than in the daily efforts of men considered as individuals. These efforts are certainly not directed haphazardly; they depend, in each individual case, on temperament, education, routine, customs, prejudices, natural or acquired needs, environment, and above all, broadly speaking, human nature, a term which, although difficult to define, is probably not devoid of meaning. But given the almost infinite diversity of individuals, and especially the fact that human nature includes among other things the ability to innovate, to create, to rise above oneself, this warp and woof of incoherent efforts would produce anything whatever in the way of social organization, were it not that chance found itself restricted in this field by the conditions of existence to which every society has to conform on pain of being either subdued or destroyed. The men who submit to these conditions of existence are more often than not unaware of them, for they act not by imposing a definite direction on the efforts of each one, but by rendering ineffective all efforts made in directions disallowed by them.

These conditions of existence are determined in the first place, as in the case of living beings, on the one hand by the natural environment and on the other hand by the existence, activity and especially competition of other organisms of the same species, that is to say here of other social groups. But still a third factor enters into play, namely, the organization of the natural environment, capital equipment, armaments, methods of work and of warfare; and this factor occupies a special position owing to the fact that, though it acts upon the form of social organization, it in turn undergoes the latter's reaction upon it. Furthermore, this factor is the only one over which the members of a society can perhaps exercise some control.

This outline is too abstract to serve as a guide; but if on the basis of this summary view we could arrive at some concrete analyses, it would at last become possible to formulate the social problem. The enlightened goodwill of men acting in an individual capacity is the only possible principle of social progress; if social necessities, once clearly perceived, were found to lie outside the range of this goodwill in the same way as those which govern the stars, each man would have nothing more to do but to watch history unfolding as one watches the seasons go by, while doing his best to spare himself and his loved ones the misfortune of being either an instrument or a victim of social oppression. If this is not so, it would be necessary first of all to define by way of an ideal limit the objective conditions that would permit of a social organization absolutely free from oppression; then seek out by what means and to what extent the conditions actually given can be transformed so as to bring them nearer to this ideal; find out what is the least oppressive form of social organization for a body of specific objective conditions; and lastly, define in this field the power of action and responsibilities of individuals as such. Only on this condition could political action become something analogous to a form of work, instead of being, as has been the case hitherto, either a game or a branch of magic.

Unfortunately, in order to reach this stage, what is required is not only searching, rigorous thinking, subjected, so as to avoid all possibility of error, to the most exacting checking, but also historical, technical and scientific investigations of an unparalleled range and precision, and conducted from an entirely new point of view. However, events do not wait; time will not stop in order to afford us leisure; the present forces itself urgently on our attention and threatens us with calamities which would bring in their train, amongst many other harrowing misfortunes, the material impossibility of studying or writing otherwise than in the service of the oppressors. What are we to do? There would be no point in letting oneself be swept along in the *mêlée* by an ill-considered enthusiasm. No one has the faintest idea of either the objectives or the means of what is still from force of habit called revolutionary action. As for reformism, the principle of the lesser evil on which it is based is certainly eminently reasonable, however discredited it may be through the fault of those who have hitherto made use of it; though remember, if it has so far served only as a pretext for capitulation, this is due not to the cowardice of a few leaders, but to an ignorance unfortunately common to all; for as long as the worst and the best have not been defined in terms of a clearly and concretely conceived ideal, and then the precise margin of possibilities determined, we do not know which is the lesser evil, and consequently we are compelled to accept under this name anything effectively imposed by those who dispose of force, since any existing evil whatever is always less than the possible evils which uncalculating action invariably runs the risk of bringing about. Broadly speaking, blind men such as we are in these days have only the choice between surrender and adventure. And yet we cannot avoid the duty of determining here and now the attitude to adopt with regard to the present situation. This is why, until we have – if, indeed, such a thing is possible – taken to pieces the social mechanism, it is permissible perhaps to try to outline its principles; provided it be clearly understood that such a rough sketch rules out any kind of categorical assertion, and aims solely at submitting a few ideas, by way of hypotheses, to the critical examination of honest people. Besides, we are far from being without a guide on the subject. If Marx's system, in its broad outlines, is of little assistance, it is a different matter when it comes to the analyses he was led to make by the concrete study of capitalism, and in which, while believing that he was limiting himself to describing a system, he probably more than once seized upon the hidden nature of oppression itself.

Among all the forms of social organization which history has to show, there are very few which appear to be really free from oppression; and these few are not very well known. All of them correspond to an extremely low level of production,

so low that the division of labour is pretty well unknown, except between the sexes, and each family produces
little more than its own requirements. It is sufficiently obvious, moreover, that such material conditions necessarily
rule out oppression, since each man, compelled to sustain
himself personally, is continually at grips with outside
nature; war itself, at this stage, is war of pillage and extermination, not of conquest, because the means of consoli-
dating a conquest and especially of turning it to account are
lacking. What is surprising is not that oppression should
make its appearance only after higher forms of economy
have been reached, but that it should always accompany
them. This means, therefore, that as between a completely
primitive economy and more highly developed forms of
economy there is a difference not only of degree, but also of
kind. And, in fact, although from the point of view of
consumption there is but a change-over to slightly better
conditions, production, which is the decisive factor, is itself
transformed in its very essence. This transformation consists at first sight in a progressive emancipation with respect
to nature. In completely primitive forms of production –
hunting, fishing, gathering – human effort appears as a
simple reaction to the inexorable pressure continually exercised on man by nature, and that in two ways. To start
with, it takes place, to all intents and purposes, under
immediate compulsion, under the ever-present spur of
natural needs; and, by an indirect consequence, the action
seems to receive its form from nature herself, owing to the
important part played therein by an intuition comparable to
animal instinct and a patient observation of the most frequent natural phenomena, also owing to the indefinite
repetition of methods that have often succeeded without
men's knowing why, and which are doubtless regarded as
being welcomed by nature with special favour. At this
stage, each man is necessarily free with respect to other
men, because he is in direct contact with the conditions of
his own existence, and because nothing human interposes
itself between them and him; but, on the other hand, and

to the same extent, he is narrowly subjected to nature's dominion, and he shows this clearly enough by deifying her. At higher stages of production, nature's compulsion continues certainly to be exercised, and still pitilessly, but in an apparently less immediate fashion; it seems to become more and more liberalized and to leave an increasing margin to man's freedom of choice, to his faculty of initiative and decision. Action is no longer tied moment by moment to nature's exigencies; men learn how to store up reserves on a long-term basis for meeting needs not yet actually felt; efforts which can be only of indirect usefulness become more and more numerous; at the same time a systematic co-ordination in time and in space becomes possible and necessary, and its importance increases continually. In short, man seems to pass by stages, with respect to nature, from servitude to dominion. At the same time nature gradually loses her divine character, and divinity more and more takes on human shape. Unfortunately, this emancipation is only a flattering semblance. In reality, at these higher stages, human action continues, as a whole, to be nothing but pure obedience to the brutal spur of an immediate necessity; only, instead of being harried by nature, man is henceforth harried by man. However, it is still the same pressure exerted by nature that continues to make itself felt, although indirectly; for oppression is exercised by force, and in the long run all force originates in nature.

The notion of force is far from simple, and yet it is the first that has to be elucidated in order to formulate the problems of society. Force and oppression — that makes two; but what needs to be understood above all is that it is not the manner in which use is made of some particular force, but its very nature, which determines whether it is oppressive or not. Marx clearly perceived this in connection with the State; he understood that this machine for grinding men down, cannot stop grinding as long as it goes on functioning, no matter in whose hands it may be. But this insight has a far more general application. Oppression proceeds exclusively from objective conditions. The first of these is the existence of privileges; and it is not men's laws or decrees which determine privileges, nor yet titles to property; it is the very nature of things. Certain circumstances, which correspond to stages, no doubt inevitable, in human development, give rise to forces which come between the ordinary man and his own conditions of existence, between the effort and the fruit of the effort, and which are, inherently, the monopoly of a few, owing to the fact that they cannot be shared among all; thenceforward these privileged beings, although they depend, in order to live, on the work of others, hold in their hands the fate of the very people on whom they depend, and equality is destroyed. This is what happens to begin with when the religious rites by which man thinks to win nature over to his side, having become too numerous and complicated to be known by all, finally become the secret and consequently the monopoly of a few priests; the priest then disposes, albeit only through a fiction, of all of nature's powers, and it is in their name that he exercises authority. Nothing essential is changed when this monopoly is no longer made up of rites but of scientific processes, and when those in possession of it are called scientists and technicians instead of priests.

Arms, too, give rise to a privilege from the day when, on the one hand, they are sufficiently powerful to render any defence by unarmed against armed men impossible, and, on the other, the handling of them has become sufficiently advanced, and consequently difficult, to require a long apprenticeship and continuous practice. For henceforth the workers are powerless to defend themselves, whereas the warriors, albeit incapable of production, can always take forcible possession of the fruits of other people's labour; the workers are thus at the mercy of the warriors, and not the other way about. The same thing applies to gold, and more generally to money, as soon as the division of labour is so far developed that no worker can live off his own products without having exchanged at any rate some of them for those of others; the organization of exchange then becomes necessarily the monopoly of a few specialists who, having money under their control, can both obtain for themselves, in order to live, the products of others' labour, and at the same time deprive the producers of the indispensably necessary.

In short, wherever, in the struggle against men or against nature, efforts need to be multiplied and co-ordinated to be effective, co-ordination becomes the monopoly of a few leaders as soon as it reaches a certain degree of complexity, and execution's primary law is then obedience; this is true both for the management of public affairs and for that of private undertakings. There may be other sources of privilege, but these are the chief ones; furthermore, except in the case of money, which appears at a given moment of history, all these factors enter into play under all systems of oppression; what changes is the way in which they are distributed and combined, the degree of concentration of power, and also the more or less closed and consequently more or less mysterious character of each monopoly. Nevertheless, privileges, of themselves, are not sufficient to cause oppression. Inequality could be easily mitigated by the resistance of the weak and the feeling for justice of the strong; it would not lead to a still harsher form of necessity than that of natural needs themselves, were it not for the intervention of a further factor, namely, the struggle for power.

As Marx clearly understood in the case of capitalism, and as a few moralists have perceived in a more general way, power contains a sort of fatality which weighs as pitilessly on those who command as on those who obey; nay more, it is in so far as it enslaves the former that, through their agency, it presses down upon the latter. The struggle against nature entails certain inescapable necessities which nothing can turn aside, but these necessities contain within themselves their own limits; nature resists, but she does not defend herself, and where she alone is involved, each situation presents certain well-defined obstacles which arouse the best in human effort. It is altogether different as soon as relations between man and man take the place of direct contact between man and nature. The preservation of power is a vital necessity for the powerful, since it is their power which provides their sustenance; but they have to preserve it both against their rivals and against their inferiors, and these latter cannot do otherwise than try to rid themselves of dangerous masters, for, through a vicious circle, the master produces fear in the slave by the very fact that he is afraid of him, and vice versa; and the same is true as between rival powers.

What is more, the two struggles that every man of power has to wage – first against those over whom he rules, secondly against his rivals – are inextricably bound up together and each is all the time rekindling the other. A power, whatever it may be, must always tend towards strengthening itself at home by means of successes gained abroad, for such successes provide it with more powerful means of coercion; besides, the struggle against its rivals rallies behind it its own slaves, who are under the illusion they have a personal interest in the result of the battle. But, in order to obtain from the slaves the obedience and sacrifices indispensable to victory, that power has to make itself more oppressive; to be in a position to exercise this oppression, it is still more imperatively compelled to turn outwards; and so on. We can follow out the same chain of events by starting from another link; show how a given social group, in order to be in a position to defend itself against the outside powers threatening to lay hands on it, must itself submit to an oppressive form of authority; how the power thus set up, in order to maintain its position, must stir up conflicts with rival powers; and so on, once again. Thus it is that the most fatal of vicious circles drags the whole society in the wake of its masters in a mad merry-go-round.

There are only two ways of breaking the circle, either by abolishing inequality, or else by setting up a stable power, a power such that there exists a balance between those who command and those who obey. It is this second solution that has been sought by all whom we call upholders of

order, or at any rate all those among them who have been
moved neither by servility nor by ambition; it was doubtless so with the Latin writers who praised 'the immense
majesty of the Roman peace', with Dante, with the reactionary school at the beginning of the nineteenth century,
with Balzac, and is so today with sincere and thoughtful
men of the Right. But this stability of power – objective of
those who call themselves realists – shows itself to be a
chimera, if one examines it closely, on the same grounds as
the anarchists' utopia.

Between man and matter, each action, whether successful
or not, establishes a balance that can only be upset from outside; for matter is inert. A displaced stone accepts its new
position; the wind consents to guide to her destination the
same ship which it would have sent off her course if sails and
rudder had not been properly adjusted. But men are essentially active beings and have a faculty of self-determination
which they can never renounce, even should they so desire,
except on the day when, through death, they drop back into
the state of inert matter; so that every victory won over men
contains within itself the germ of a possible defeat, unless it
goes as far as extermination. But extermination abolishes
power by abolishing its object. Thus there is, in the very
essence of power, a fundamental contradiction that prevents it from ever existing in the true sense of the word;
those who are called the masters, ceaselessly compelled to
reinforce their power for fear of seeing it snatched away
from them, are for ever seeking a dominion essentially
impossible to attain; beautiful illustrations of this search are
offered by the infernal torments in Greek mythology. It
would be otherwise if one man could possess in himself a
force superior to that of many other men put together; but
such is never the case; the instruments of power – arms,
gold, machines, magical or technical secrets – always exist
independently of him who disposes of them, and can be
taken up by others. Consequently all power is unstable.

Generally speaking, among human beings, since the
relationships between rulers and ruled are never fully

acceptable, they always constitute an irremediable disequilibrium which is continually aggravating itself; the same is true even in the sphere of private life, where love, for example, destroys all balance in the soul as soon as it seeks to dominate or to be dominated by its object. But here at any rate there is nothing external to prevent reason from returning and putting everything to rights by establishing liberty and equality; whereas social relationships, in so far as the very methods of labour and of warfare rule out equality, seem to cause madness to weigh down on mankind in the manner of an external fatality. For, owing to the fact that there is never power, but only a race for power, and that there is no term, no limit, no proportion set to this race, neither is there any limit or proportion set to the efforts that it exacts; those who give themselves up to it, compelled to do always better than their rivals, who in their turn strive to do better than they, must sacrifice not only the existence of the slaves, but their own also and that of their nearest and dearest; so it is that Agamemnon sacrificing his daughter lives again in the capitalists who, to maintain their privileges, acquiesce lightheartedly in wars that may rob them of their sons.

Thus the race for power enslaves everybody, strong and weak alike. Marx saw this clearly with reference to the capitalist system. Rosa Luxemburg used to inveigh against the aspect of 'aimless merry-go-round' presented by the Marxist picture of capitalist accumulation, that picture in which consumption appears as a 'necessary evil' to be reduced to the minimum, a mere means for keeping alive those who devote themselves, whether as leaders or as workers, to the supreme object, which is none other than the manufacture of capital equipment, that is to say of the means of production. And yet it is the profound absurdity of this picture which gives it its profound truth; a truth which extends singularly beyond the framework of the capitalist system. The only characteristic peculiar to this system is that the instruments of industrial production are at the same time the chief weapons in the race for power;

but always the methods pursued in the race for power, whatever they may be, bring men under their subjection through the same frenzy and impose themselves on them as absolute ends. It is the reflection of this frenzy that lends an epic grandeur to works such as the *Comédie Humaine*, Shakespeare's *Histories*, the *chansons de geste*, or the *Iliad*. The real subject of the *Iliad* is the sway exercised by war over the warriors, and, through them, over humanity in general; none of them knows why each sacrifices himself and all his family to a bloody and aimless war, and that is why, all through the poem, it is the gods who are credited with the mysterious influence which nullifies peace negotiations, continually revives hostilities, and brings together again the contending forces urged by a flash of good sense to abandon the struggle.

Thus in this ancient and wonderful poem there already appears the essential evil besetting humanity, the substitution of means for ends. At times war occupies the forefront, at other times the search for wealth, at other times production; but the evil remains the same. The common run of moralists complain that man is moved by his private interest: would to heaven it were so! Private interest is a self-centred principle of action, but at the same time restricted, reasonable and incapable of giving rise to unlimited evils. Whereas, on the other hand, the law of all activities governing social life, except in the case of primitive communities, is that here each one sacrifices human life – in himself and in others – to things which are only means to a better way of living. This sacrifice takes on various forms, but it all comes back to the question of power. Power, by definition, is only a means; or to put it better, to possess a power is simply to possess means of action which exceed the very limited force that a single individual has at his disposal. But power-seeking, owing to its essential incapacity to seize hold of its object, rules out all consideration of an end, and finally comes, through an inevitable reversal, to take the place of all ends. It is this reversal of the relationship between means and end, it is this fundamental folly that accounts for all that is senseless and bloody right through history. Human history is simply the history of the servitude which makes men – oppressors and oppressed alike – the plaything of the instruments of domination they themselves have manufactured, and thus reduces living humanity to being the chattel of inanimate chattels.

Thus it is things, not men, that prescribe the limits and laws governing this giddy race for power. Men's desires are powerless to control it. The masters may well dream of moderation, but they are prohibited from practising this virtue, on pain of defeat, except to a very slight extent; so that, apart from a few almost miraculous exceptions, such as Marcus Aurelius, they quickly become incapable even of conceiving it. As for the oppressed, their permanent revolt, which is always simmering, though it only breaks out now and then, can operate in such a way as to aggravate the evil as well as to restrict it; and on the whole it rather constitutes an aggravating factor in that it forces the masters to make their power weigh ever more heavily for fear of losing it.

From time to time the oppressed manage to drive out one team of oppressors and to replace it by another, and sometimes even to change the form of oppression; but as for abolishing oppression itself, that would first mean abolishing the sources of it, abolishing all the monopolies, the magical and technical secrets that give a hold over nature, armaments, money, co-ordination of labour. Even if the oppressed were sufficiently conscious to make up their minds to do so, they could not succeed. It would be condemning themselves to immediate enslavement by the social groupings that had not carried out the same change; and even were this danger to be miraculously averted, it would be condemning themselves to death, for, once men have forgotten the methods of primitive production and have transformed the natural environment into which these fitted, they cannot recover immediate contact with nature.

It follows that, in spite of so many vague desires to put an end to madness and oppression, the concentration of power and the aggravation of its tyrannical character would know no bounds were these not by good fortune found in the nature of things. It behoves us to determine roughly what these bounds can be; and for this purpose we must keep in mind the fact that, if oppression is a necessity of social life, this necessity has nothing providential about it. It is not because it becomes detrimental to production that oppression can come to an end; the 'revolt of the productive forces', so naïvely invoked by Trotsky as a factor in history, is a pure fiction. We should be mistaken likewise in assuming that oppression ceases to be ineluctable as soon as the productive forces have been sufficiently developed to ensure welfare and leisure for all. Aristotle admitted that there would no longer be anything to stand in the way of the abolition of slavery if it were possible to have the indispensable jobs done by 'mechanical slaves', and when Marx attempted to forecast the future of the human species, all he did was to take up this idea and develop it. It would be true if men were guided by considerations of welfare; but from the days of the *Iliad* to our own times, the senseless demands made by the struggle for power have taken away even the leisure for thinking about welfare. The raising of the output of human effort will remain powerless to lighten the load of this effort as long as the social structure implies the reversal of the relationship between means and ends, in other words, as long as the methods of labour and of warfare give to a few men a discretionary power over the masses; for the fatigues and privations that have become unnecessary in the struggle against nature will be absorbed by the war carried on between men for the defence or acquisition of privileges. Once society is divided up into men who command and men who execute, the whole of social life is governed by the struggle for power, and the struggle for subsistence only enters in as one factor, indispensable to be sure, of the former.

The Marxist view, according to which social existence is determined by the relations between man and nature established by production, certainly remains the only sound basis for any historical investigation; only these relations must be considered first of all in terms of the problem of power, the means of subsistence forming simply one of the data of this problem. This order seems absurd, but it merely reflects the essential absurdity lying at the very heart of social life. A scientific study of history would thus be a study of the actions and reactions which are perpetually arising between the organization of power and the methods of production; for although power depends on the material conditions of life, it never ceases to transform these conditions themselves. Such a study goes very far beyond our possibilities at the moment; but before grappling with the infinite complexity of the facts, it is useful to make an abstract diagram of this interplay of actions and reactions, rather in the same way as astronomers have had to invent an imaginary celestial sphere so as to find their way about among the movements and positions of the stars.

We must try first of all to draw up a list of the inevitable necessities which limit all species of power. In the first place, any sort of power relies upon instruments which have in each situation a given scope. Thus you do not command in the same way, by means of soldiers armed with bows and arrows, spears and swords as you do by means of aeroplanes and incendiary bombs; the power of gold depends on the role played by exchanges in economic life; that of technical secrets is measured by the difference between what you can accomplish with their aid and what you can accomplish without them; and so on. As a matter of fact, one must always include in this balance-sheet the subterfuges by which the powerful obtain through persuasion what they are totally unable to obtain by force, either by placing the oppressed in a situation such that they have or think they have an immediate interest in doing what is asked of them, or by inspiring them with a fanaticism calculated to make them accept any and every sacrifice. Secondly, since the power that a human being really exercises extends only to what is effectively under his control, power is always running up against the actual limits of the controlling faculty, and these are extremely narrow. For no single mind can encompass a whole mass of ideas at once; no man can be in several places at once; and for master and slave alike there are never more than twenty-four hours in a day. Collaboration apparently constitutes a remedy for this drawback; but as it is never absolutely free from rivalry, it gives rise to infinite complications. The faculties of examining, comparing, weighing, deciding, combining are essentially individual, and consequently the same thing applies also to power, whose exercise is inseparable from these faculties; collective power is a fiction, at any rate in the final analysis. As for the number of interests that can come under the control of one single man, that depends to a very large extent on individual factors such as breadth and quickness of intelligence, capacity for work, firmness of character; but it also depends on the objective conditions of the control exercised, more or less rapid methods of transport and communication, simplicity or otherwise of the machinery of power. Lastly, the exercise of any form of power is subject to the existence of a surplus in the production of commodities, and a sufficiently large surplus so that all those engaged, whether as masters or as slaves, in the struggle for power, may be able to live. Obviously, the extent of such surplus depends on the methods of production, and consequently also on the social organization. Here, therefore, are three factors that enable one to conceive political and social power as constituting at each moment something analogous to a measurable force. However, in order to complete the picture, one must bear in mind that the men who find themselves in relationship, whether as masters or as slaves, with the phenomenon of power are unconscious of this analogy. The powerful, be they priests, military leaders, kings or capitalists, always believe that they command by divine right; and those who are under them feel themselves crushed by a power which seems to them either divine or diabolical, but in any case supernatural. Every oppressive society is cemented by this religion of power, which falsifies all social relations by enabling the powerful to command over and above what they are able to impose; it is only otherwise in times of popular agitation, times when, on the contrary, all – rebellious slaves and threatened masters alike – forget how heavy and how solid the chains of oppression are.

Thus a scientific study of history ought to begin by analysing the reactions brought to bear at each moment by power on the conditions which assign to it objectively its limits; and a hypothetical sketch of the play of these reactions is indispensable in order to conduct such an analysis, far too difficult, incidentally, considering our present possibilities. Some of these reactions are conscious and willed. Every power consciously strives, in proportion to the means at its disposal – a proportion determined by the social organization – to improve production and official control within its own sphere; history offers many an example of this, from the Pharaohs down to the present day, and it is on this that the notion of enlightened despotism is founded. On the other hand, every power strives also, and again consciously, to destroy among its competitors the means whereby to produce and govern, and is the object on their part of a similar attempt. Thus the struggle for power is at the same time constructive and destructive, and brings about economic progress or decadence, depending on whichever aspect wins the day; and it is clear that in a given civilization destruction will take place to an extent all the greater the more difficult it is for a power to expand without coming up against rival powers approximately as strong as itself. But the indirect consequences of the exercise of power are far more important than the conscious efforts of the wielders of power.

Every power, from the mere fact that it is exercised, extends to the farthest possible limit the social relations on which it is based; thus military power multiplies wars, commercial capital multiplies exchanges. Now it sometimes happens, through a sort of providential accident, that this extension gives rise, by some mechanism or other, to new resources that make a new extension possible, and so on, more or less in the same way as food strengthens living beings in full process of growth and enables them thus to win still more food so as to acquire still greater strength. All regimes provide examples of such providential accidents; for without them no form of power could endure, and consequently those powers that benefit from them are the only ones to subsist. Thus war enabled the Romans to carry off slaves, that is to say workers in the prime of life, whom others had had to provide for during childhood; the profit derived from slave labour made it possible to reinforce the army, and the stronger army undertook more important wars which brought in new and bigger consignments of slaves as booty. Similarly, the roads which the Romans built for military purposes later facilitated the government and exploitation of the conquered provinces, and thus contributed towards storing up resources for future wars.

If we turn now to modern times, we see, for example, that the extension of exchanges has brought about a greater division of labour, which in its turn has made a wider circulation of commodities indispensable; furthermore, the increased productivity which has resulted from this has furnished new resources that have been able to transform themselves into commercial and industrial capital. As far as big industry is concerned, it is clear that each important advance in mechanization has created at the same time resources, instruments and a stimulus towards a further advance. Similarly, it was the technique of big industry which came to provide the means of control and information indispensable to the centralized economy that is the inevitable outcome of big industry, such as the telegraph, the telephone, the daily press. The same may be said with regard to the means of transport. One could find all through history an immense number of similar examples, bearing on the widest and the narrowest aspects of social life. One may define the growth of a system by the fact that all it needs to do is to function in order to create new resources enabling it to function on a larger scale.

This phenomenon of automatic development is so striking

that one would be tempted to imagine that a happily constituted system, if one may so express it, would go on enduring and progressing endlessly. That is exactly what the nineteenth century, socialists included, imagined with regard to the system of big industry. But if it is easy to imagine in a vague way an oppressive system that would never fall into decadence, it is no longer the same if one wants to conceive clearly and concretely the indefinite extension of a specific power. If it could extend endlessly its means of control, it would tend indefinitely towards a limit which would be something like ubiquity; if it could extend its resources endlessly, everything would be as though surrounding nature were evolving gradually towards that unqualified abundance from which Adam and Eve benefited in the earthly paradise; and, finally, if it could extend indefinitely the range of its own instruments – whether it be a question of arms, gold, technical secrets, machines or anything else – it would tend towards abolishing that correlation which, by indissolubly linking together the notions of master and of slave, establishes between master and slave a relationship of mutual dependence.

One cannot prove that all this is impossible; but one must assume that it is impossible, or else decide to think of human history as a fairy-tale. In general, one can only regard the world in which we live as subject to laws if one admits that every phenomenon in it is limited; and it is the same for the phenomenon of power, as Plato had understood. If we want to consider power as a conceivable phenomenon, we must think that it can extend the foundations on which it rests up to a certain point only, after which it comes up, as it were, against an impassable wall. But even so it is not in a position to stop; the spur of competition forces it to go ever farther and farther, that is to say to go beyond the limits within which it can be effectively exercised. It extends beyond what it is able to control; it commands over and above what it can impose; it spends in excess of its own resources. Such is the internal contradiction which every oppressive system carries within itself like a seed of death; it is made up of the opposition between the necessarily limited character of the material bases of power and the necessarily unlimited character of the race for power considered as relationship between men.

For as soon as a power goes beyond the limits assigned to it by the nature of things, it narrows down the bases on which it rests, renders these limits themselves narrower and narrower. By spreading beyond what it is able to control, it breeds a parasitism, a waste, a confusion which, once they have appeared, increase automatically. By attempting to command where actually it is not in a position to compel obedience, it provokes reactions which it can neither foresee nor deal with. Finally, by wishing to spread the exploitation of the oppressed beyond what the objective resources make possible, it exhausts these resources themselves; this is doubtless what is meant by the ancient and popular tale of the goose with the golden eggs. Whatever may be the sources from whence the exploiters draw the material goods which they appropriate, a day arrives when such and such a method of development, which was at first, as it went on spreading, more and more productive, finally becomes, on the other hand, increasingly costly. That is how the Roman army, which had first of all brought wealth to Rome, ended by ruining it; that is how the knights of the Middle Ages, whose battles had first of all brought a relative security to the peasants, who found themselves to a certain extent protected against acts of brigandage, ended in the course of their interminable wars by laying waste the countryside which fed them; and it certainly seems as though capitalism is passing through a phase of this kind. Once more, it cannot be proved that it must always be so; but it has to be assumed, unless the possibility of inexhaustible resources is also assumed. Thus it is the nature itself of things which constitutes that justice-dealing divinity the Greeks worshipped under the name of Nemesis, and which punishes excess.

When a specific form of domination finds itself thus arrested in its development and faced with decadence, it does not follow that it begins to disappear progressively; sometimes it is then, on the contrary, that it becomes most harshly oppressive, that it crushes human beings under its weight, that it grinds down body, heart and spirit without mercy. However, since everyone begins little by little to feel the lack of the resources required by some to maintain their supremacy, by others to live, a time comes when, on every hand, there is a feverish search for expedients. There is no reason why such a search should not remain fruitless; and in that case the regime can only end by collapsing for want of the means of subsistence and being replaced, not by another and better organized regime, but by a disorder, a poverty, a primitive condition of existence which continue until some new factor or other gives rise to new relationships of force. If it happens otherwise, if the search for new material resources is successful, new patterns of social life arise and a change of regime begins to form slowly and, as it were, subterraneously. Subterraneously, because these new forms can only develop in so far as they are compatible with the established order and do not represent, in appearance at any rate, any danger for the powers that be; otherwise nothing could prevent these powers from destroying them, as long as they remain the stronger. For the new social patterns to triumph over the old, this continued development must already have brought them to play effectively a more important role in the functioning of the social organism; in other words, they must have given rise to more powerful forces than those at the disposal of the official authorities. Thus there is never really any break in continuity, not even when the change of regime seems to be the result of a bloody struggle; for all that victory then does is to sanction forces that, even before the struggle, were the decisive factor in the life of the community, social patterns that had long since begun gradually to replace those on which the declining regime rested. So it was that, under the Roman Empire, the barbarians had begun to occupy the most important posts, the army was disintegrating little by little into armed bands led by adventurers, and the system of military colonies gradually replaced slavery by serfdom – all this long before the great invasions. Similarly, the French bourgeoisie did not by any means wait until 1789 to get the better of the nobility. The Russian Revolution, thanks to a singular conjunction of circumstances, certainly seemed to give rise to something entirely new; but the truth is that the privileges it abolished had not for a long time rested on any social foundation other than tradition; that the institutions arising out of the insurrection did not perhaps effectively function for as long as a single morning; and that the real forces, namely big industry, the police, the army, the bureaucracy, far from being smashed by the Revolution, attained, thanks to it, a power unknown in other countries.

Generally speaking, the sudden reversal of the relationship between forces which is what we usually understand by the term 'revolution' is not only a phenomenon unknown in history, but furthermore, if we examine it closely, something literally inconceivable, for it would be a victory of weakness over force, the equivalent of a balance whose lighter scale were to go down. What history offers us is slow transformations of regimes, in which the bloody events to which we give the name 'revolutions' play a very secondary role, and from which they may even be absent; such is the case when the social class which ruled in the name of the old relationships of force manages to keep a part of the power under cover of the new relationships, and the history of England supplies an example. But whatever may be the patterns taken by social transformations, all one finds, if one tries to lay bare the mechanism, is a dreary play of blind forces that unite together or clash, that progress or decline, that replace each other, without ever ceasing to grind beneath them the unfortunate race of human beings. At first sight there seems to be no weak spot in this sinister mesh of circumstances through which an attempt at deliverance might find its way. But it is not from such a vague, abstract and miserably hasty sketch as this that one can claim to draw any conclusion.

We must pose once again the fundamental problem, namely, what constitutes the bond which seems hitherto to have united social oppression and progress in the relations between man and nature? If one considers human development as a whole up to our own time, if, above all, one contrasts primitive tribes, organized practically without inequality, with our present-day civilization, it seems as if man cannot manage to lighten the yoke imposed by natural necessities without an equal increase in the weight of that imposed by social oppression, as though by the play of a mysterious equilibrium. And even, what is stranger still, it would seem that if, in fact, the human collectivity has to a large extent freed itself from the crushing burden which the gigantic forces of nature place on frail humanity, it has, on the other hand, taken in some sort nature's place to the point of crushing the individual in a similar manner.

What makes primitive man a slave? The fact that he hardly orders his own activity at all; he is the plaything of need, which dictates each of his movements or very nearly, and harries him with its relentless spur; and his actions are regulated not by his own intelligence, but by the customs and caprices – both equally incomprehensible – of a nature that he can but worship with blind submission. If we consider simply the collectivity, men seem nowadays to have raised themselves to a condition that is diametrically the opposite of that servile state. Hardly a single one of their tasks constitutes a mere response to the imperative impulsion of need; work is accomplished in such a way as to take charge of nature and to organize her so that needs can be satisfied. Humanity no longer believes itself to be in the presence of capricious divinities whose good graces must be won over; it knows that it has merely to handle inert matter, and acquits itself of this task by methodically following out clearly conceived laws. At last we seem to have reached that epoch predicted by Descartes when men would use 'the force and actions of fire, water, air, the stars and all the other bodies' in the same way as they do the artisans' tools, and would thus make themselves masters of nature. But, by a strange inversion, this collective dominion transforms itself into servitude as soon as one descends to the scale of the individual, and into a servitude fairly closely resembling that associated with primitive conditions of existence.

The efforts of the modern worker are imposed on him by a constraint as brutal, as pitiless and which holds him in as tight a grip as hunger does the primitive hunter. From the time of that primitive hunter up to that of the worker in our large factories, passing by way of the Egyptian workers driven by the lash, the slaves of antiquity, the serfs of the Middle Ages constantly threatened by the seigneurial sword, men have never ceased to be goaded to work by some outside force and on pain of almost immediate death. And as for the sequence of movements in work, that, too, is often imposed from outside on our workers, exactly as in the case of primitive men, and is as mysterious for the ones as it was for the others; what is more, in this respect, the constraint is in certain cases incomparably more brutal today than it has ever been. However tied and bound a primitive man was to routine and blind gropings, he could at least try to think things out, to combine and innovate at his own risk, a liberty which is absolutely denied to a worker engaged in a production line. Lastly, if humanity appears to have reached the stage of controlling those forces of nature which, however, in Spinoza's words, 'infinitely surpass those of mankind' – and that in almost as sovereign a fashion as a rider controls his horse – that victory does not belong to men taken individually; only the largest collectivities are in a position to handle 'the force and actions of fire, water, air . . . and all the other bodies that surround us'; as for the members of these collectivities, both oppressors and oppressed are alike subjected to the implacable demand of the struggle for power.

Thus, in spite of progress, man has not emerged from the servile condition in which he found himself when he was handed over weak and naked to all the blind forces that make up the universe; it is merely that the power which keeps him on his knees has been as it were transferred from inert matter to the human society of which he is a member. That is why it is this society which is imposed on his worship through all the various forms that religious feeling takes in turn. Hence the social question poses itself in a fairly clear manner; the mechanism of this transfer must be examined; we must try to find out why man has had to pay this price for his power over nature; form an idea of what would constitute the least unhappy position for him to be in, that is to say the one in which he would be the least enslaved to the twin domination of nature and society; and lastly, discern what roads can lead towards such a position, and what instruments present-day civilization could place in men's hands if they aspired to transform their lives in this way.

We accept material progress too easily as a gift of the gods, as something which goes without saying; we must look fairly and squarely at the conditions at the cost of which it takes place. Primitive life is something easy to understand; man is spurred on by hunger, or at any rate by the anguished thought that he will soon go hungry, and he sets off in search of food; he shivers in the cold, or at any rate at the thought that he will soon feel cold, and he goes in search of heat-creating or heat-preserving materials; and so on. As for the way in which to set about the matter, this is given him in the first place by the habit acquired in child-hood of imitating his seniors, and also as a result of the habits which he has given himself in the course of innumer-able tentative efforts, by repeating those methods which have succeeded; when caught off his guard, he continues to proceed by trial and error, spurred on as he is to act by a sharp urge which never leaves him a moment's peace. In all this process, man has only to yield to his own nature, not master it.

On the other hand, as soon as we pass to a more advanced stage of civilization, everything becomes miraculous. Men are then found laying by things that are good to consume, desirable things, which they nevertheless go without. They are found giving up to a large extent the search for food, warmth, etc., and spending the best part of their energy on apparently unprofitable labours. As a matter of fact, most of these labours, far from being unprofitable, are infinitely more profitable than the efforts of primitive man, for they result in an organization of outside nature in a manner favourable to human existence; but this efficacy is indirect and often separated from the actual effort by so many intermediaries that the mind has difficulty in covering them; it is a long-term efficacy, often so long-term that it is only future generations which will benefit from it; while, on the other hand, the utter fatigue, physical pains and dangers connected with these labours are felt immediately, and all the time. Now, everybody knows from his own experience how unusual it is for an abstract idea having a long-term utility to triumph over present pains, needs and desires. It must, however, do so in the matter of social existence, on pain of a regression to a primitive form of life.

But what is more miraculous still is the co-ordination of labour. Any reasonably high level of production presupposes a more or less extensive co-operation; and co-operation shows itself in the fact that the efforts of each one have meaning and efficacy only through their relationship to and exact correspondence with the efforts of all the rest, in such a way that all the efforts together form one single collective piece of work. In other words, the movements of several men must be combined according to the manner in which the movements of a single man are combined. But how can this be done? A combination can only take place if it is intellectually conceived; while a relationship is never formed except within one mind. The number 2 thought of by one man cannot be added to the number 2 thought of by another man so as to make up the number 4; similarly, the idea that one of the co-operators has of the partial work he is carrying out cannot be combined with the idea that each of the others has of his respective task so as to form a coherent piece of work. Several human minds cannot become united in one collective mind, and the expressions 'collective soul', 'collective thought', so commonly employed nowadays, are altogether devoid of meaning. Consequently, for the efforts of several to be combined, they all need to be directed by one and the same mind, as the famous line in *Faust* expresses it: 'One mind is enough for a thousand hands.'

In the egalitarian organization of primitive tribes, it is not possible to solve a single one of these problems, neither that of privation, nor that of incentive to effort, nor that of co-ordination of labour; on the other hand, social oppression provides an immediate solution, by creating, to put it broadly, two categories of men – those who command and those who obey. The leader co-ordinates without difficulty the efforts of those who are under his orders; he has no temptation to overcome in order to reduce them to what is strictly necessary; and as for the stimulus to effort, an oppressive organization is admirably equipped for driving men beyond the limit of their strength, some being whipped by ambition, others, in Homer's words, 'under the goad of a harsh necessity'.

The results are often extraordinary when the division between social categories is deep enough for those who decide what work shall be done never to be exposed to feeling or even knowing about the exhausting fatigue, the pains and the dangers of it, while those who do it and suffer have no choice, being continually under the sway of a more or less disguised menace of death. Thus it is that man escapes to a certain extent from the caprices of blind nature only by handing himself over to the no less blind caprices of the struggle for power. This is never truer than when man reaches – as in our case – a technical development suffi-ciently advanced to give him the mastery over the forces of nature; for, in order that this may be so, co-operation has to take place on such a vast scale that the leaders find they have to deal with a mass of affairs which lie utterly beyond their capacity to control. As a result, humanity finds itself as much the plaything of the forces of nature, in the new form that technical progress has given them, as it ever was in primitive times; we have had, are having, and will continue to have bitter experience of this. As for attempts to preserve technique while shaking off oppression, they at once provoke such laziness and such confusion that those who have engaged in them are more often than not obliged to place themselves again almost immediately under the yoke; the experiment was tried out on a small scale in the producers' co-operatives, on a vast scale at the time of the Russian Revolution. It would seem that man is born a slave, and that servitude is his natural condition.

From 'Reflections concerning the Causes of Liberty and Social Oppression' in *Oppression and Liberty*, translated by Arthur Wills and John Petrie, Routledge and Kegan Paul, London 1958.

THE MYSTICISM OF WORK

———————— ◎ ————————

The secret of the human condition is that there is no equilibrium between man and the surrounding forces of nature, which infinitely exceed him when in inaction; there is only equilibrium in action by which man recreates his own life through work.

Man's greatness is always to recreate his life, to recreate what is given to him, to fashion that very thing which he undergoes. Through work he produces his own natural existence. Through science he recreates the universe by means of symbols. Through art he recreates the alliance between his body and his soul (cf. the speech of Eupalinos). It is to be noticed that each of these three things is something poor, empty and vain taken by itself and not in relation to the two others. Union of the three: a working people's culture (that will not be just yet) . . .

Plato himself is only a forerunner. The Greeks knew about art and sport, but not about work. The master is the slave of the slave in the sense that the slave *makes* the master.

Two tasks:
  To individualize machinery.

To individualize science (popularization, a people's university on the Socratic model for the study of the elements of the various trades).

Manual work. Why has there never been a mystic, workman or peasant, to write on the use to be made of disgust for work? Our souls fly from this disgust which is so often there, ever threatening, and try to hide it from themselves by reacting vegetatively. There is mortal danger in admitting it to ourselves. This is the source of the falsehood peculiar to the working classes. (There is a falsehood peculiar to each level.)

This disgust is the burdensomeness of time. To acknowledge it to ourselves without giving way under it makes us mount upwards.

Disgust in all its forms is one of the most precious trials sent to man as a ladder by which to rise. I have a very large share of this favour.

We have to turn all our disgust into a disgust for ourselves.

Monotony is the most beautiful or the most atrocious thing. The most beautiful if it is a reflection of eternity – the most atrocious if it is the sign of an unvarying perpetuity. It is time surpassed or time sterilized.

The circle is the symbol of monotony which is beautiful, the swinging of a pendulum of monotony which is atrocious.

The spirituality of work. Work makes us experience in the most exhausting manner the phenomenon of finality rebounding like a ball; to work in order to eat, to eat in order to work. If we regard one of the two as an end, or the one and the other taken separately, we are lost. Only the cycle contains the truth.

A squirrel turning in its cage and the rotation of the celestial sphere – extreme misery and extreme grandeur.

It is when man sees himself as a squirrel turning round

and round in a circular cage that, if he does not lie to himself, he is close to salvation.

The great hardship in manual work is that we are compelled to expend our efforts for such long hours simply in order to exist.

The slave is he to whom no good is proposed as the object of his labour except mere existence.

Accordingly he must either be detached or fall to the vegetative level.

No terrestial finality separates the workers from God. They alone are so situated. All other conditions imply special aims which form a screen between man and pure good. But for them no such screen exists. They have nothing superfluous of which they have to strip themselves.

To strive from necessity and not for some good – driven not drawn – in order to maintain our existence just as it is – that is always slavery.

In this sense the slavery of manual workers is irreducible.

Effort without finality.

It is terrible – or the most beautiful thing of all – if it is finality without an end. The beautiful alone enables us to be satisfied by that which is.

Workers need poetry more than bread. They need that their life should be a poem. They need some light from eternity.

Religion alone can be the source of such poetry.

It is not religion but revolution which is the opium of the people.

Deprivation of this poetry explains all forms of demoralization.

Slavery is work without any light from eternity, without poetry, without religion.

May the eternal light give, not a reason for living and

working, but a sense of completeness which makes the search for any such reason unnecessary.

Failing that, the only incentives are fear and gain – fear, which implies the oppression of the people; gain, which implies the corruption of the people.

Manual labour. Time entering into the body. Through work man turns himself into matter, as Christ does through the Eucharist. Work is like a death.

We have to pass through death. We have to be killed – to endure the weight of the world. When the universe is weighing upon the back of a human creature, what is there to be surprised at if it hurts him?

Work is like a death if it is without an incentive. We have to act, renouncing the fruits of action.

To work – if we are worn out it means that we are becoming submissive to time as matter is. Thought is forced to pass from one instant to the next without laying hold of the past or the future. That is what it means to obey.

Joys parallel to fatigue: tangible joys, eating, resting, the pleasures of Sunday . . . but not money.

No poetry concerning the people is authentic if fatigue does not figure in it, and the hunger and thirst which come from fatigue.

From *Gravity and Grace*, translated by Emma Craufurd, Routledge and Kegan Paul, London, 1952. Originally published as *La Pesanteur et la Grâce*, Plon, Paris, 1947.

THE *ILIAD*
or
THE POEM OF FORCE

———————— Ⓒ ————————

This was written during the first year of the war and begun at the same time as an essay on the origins of Hitlerism. A fundamental mistake, as she saw it, was to consider a particular people, epoch or individual as essentially barbarous or evil. She said it was dangerously easy to dismiss Hitler as an unusual phenomenon existing outside 'normal' society and with which civilized people have to cope only once in a while. No particular class is predestined as the one and only bearer of civilization. Not class but force was the key to history. 'I believe,' she said, 'that the concept of force must be made central in any attempt to think clearly about human relations just as the concept of relation is central to mathematics.'

It first appeared in the only important literary magazine published in the free zone at the time, the Cahiers du Sud, *and it was through her association with the* Cahiers *that she was to meet groups interested in Catharism: 'the last living expression in Europe of pre-Roman antiquity.'*

The essay, which she was obliged to sign with an anagram of her name, Emile Novis, marks a turning point in her thinking. It was from then on, while living in Marseille, that she came to think and write increasingly on religion and religious subjects.

Through her contacts with these groups Simone Weil was put in touch with a Resistance network. In the hope that they would be able to get her to England, she attended some of their meetings. Evidently there had been a traitor amongst them since early one morning the police came to interview her and to search the apartment. Several times she was summoned to the police station and several times threatened with imprisonment. She was not in the least bit afraid. Writing to André, now already in America, she describes her conversations with 'Oscar', their code name for the police. ' ... He was bizarre. Now he was polite, now agreeable and now angry in quick succession, but above all terribly lazy and not very conscientious. He spoke of inviting me to his house for a rather prolonged stay, but after that it never came up again and I really believe he forgot all about it ... '

The true hero, the true subject, the centre of the *Iliad* is force. Force employed by man, force that enslaves man, force before which man's flesh shrinks away. In this work, at all times, the human spirit is shown as modified by its relations with force, as swept away, blinded, by the very force it imagined it could handle, as deformed by the weight of the force it submits to. For those dreamers who considered that force, thanks to progress, would soon be a thing of the past, the *Iliad* could appear as an historical document; for others, whose powers of recognition are more acute and who perceive force, today as yesterday, at the very centre of human history, the *Iliad* is the purest and the loveliest of mirrors.

To define force – it is that x that turns anybody who is subjected to it into a *thing*. Exercised to the limit, it turns man into a thing in the most literal sense: it makes a corpse out of him. Somebody was here, and the next minute there is nobody here at all; this is a spectacle the *Iliad* never wearies of showing us:

> . . . the horses
> Rattled the empty chariots through the files of battle,
> Longing for their noble drivers. But they on the ground
> Lay, dearer to the vultures than to their wives.

The hero becomes a *thing* dragged behind a chariot in the dust:

> All around, his black hair
> Was spread; in the dust his whole head lay,
> That once-charming head; now Zeus had let his
>   enemies
> Defile it on his native soil.

The bitterness of such a spectacle is offered us absolutely undiluted. No comforting fiction intervenes; no consoling prospect of immortality; and on the hero's head no washed-out halo of patriotism descends.

> His soul, fleeing his limbs, passed to Hades,
> Mourning its fate, forsaking its youth and its vigour.

Still more poignant – so painful is the contrast – is the sudden evocation, as quickly rubbed out, of another world: the faraway, precarious, touching world of peace, of the family, the world in which each man counts more than anything else to those about him.

> She ordered her bright-haired maids in the palace
> To place on the fire a large tripod, preparing
> A hot bath for Hector, returning from battle.
> Foolish woman! Already he lay, far from hot baths,
> Slain by grey-eyed Athena, who guided Achilles' arm.

Far from hot baths he was indeed, poor man. And not he alone. Nearly all the *Iliad* takes place far from hot baths. Nearly all of human life, then and now, takes place far from hot baths.

Here we see force in its grossest and most summary form – the force that kills. How much more varied in its processes, how much more surprising in its effects is the other

force, the force that does *not* kill, i.e., that does not kill just
yet. It will surely kill, it will possibly kill, or perhaps it
merely hangs, poised and ready, over the head of the creature it *can* kill, at any moment, which is to say at every
moment. In whatever aspect, its effect is the same: it turns
a man into a stone. From its first property (the ability to
turn a human being into a thing by the simple method of
killing him) flows another, quite prodigious too in its own
way, the ability to turn a human being into a thing while he
is still alive. He is alive; he has a soul; and yet – he is a
thing. An extraordinary entity this – a thing that has a soul.
And as for the soul, what an extraordinary house it finds
itself in! Who can say what it costs it, moment by moment,
to accommodate itself to this residence, how much writhing
and bending, folding and pleating are required of it? It was
not made to live inside a thing; if it does so, under pressure
of necessity, there is not a single element of its nature to
which violence is not done.

A man stands disarmed and naked with a weapon pointing at him; this person becomes a corpse before anybody or
anything touches him. Just a minute ago, he was thinking,
acting, hoping:

> Motionless, he pondered. And the other drew near,
> Terrified, anxious to touch his knees, hoping in his
>   heart
> To escape evil death and black destiny . . .
> With one hand he clasped, suppliant, his knees,
> While the other clung to the sharp spear, not letting
>   go . . .

Soon, however, he grasps the fact that the weapon which is
pointing at him will not be diverted; and now, still breathing, he is simply matter; still thinking, he can think no
longer:

> Thus spoke the brilliant son of Priam
> In begging words. But he heard a harsh reply:
> He spoke. And the other's knees and heart failed him.

> Dropping his spear, he knelt down, holding out his
>   arms.
> Achilles, drawing his sharp sword, struck
> Through the neck and breastbone. The two-edged
>   sword
> Sunk home its full length. The other, face down
> Lay still, and the black blood ran out, wetting the
>   ground.

If a stranger, completely disabled, disarmed, strengthless, throws himself on the mercy of a warrior, he is not by this very act, condemned to death; but a moment of impatience on the warrior's part will suffice to relieve him of his life. In any case, his flesh has lost that very important property which in the laboratory distinguishes living flesh from dead, the galvanic response. If you give a frog's leg an electric shock, it twitches. If you confront a human being with the touch or sight of something horrible or terrifying, this bundle of muscles, nerves, and flesh likewise twitches. Alone of all living things, the suppliant we have just described neither quivers nor trembles. He has lost the right to do so. As his lips advance to touch the object that is for him of all things most charged with horror, they do not draw back on his teeth – they cannot:

> No one saw great Priam enter. He stopped,
> Clasped the knees of Achilles, kissed his hands,
> Those terrible man-killing hands that had slaughtered
>   so many of his sons.

The sight of a human being pushed to such an extreme of suffering chills us like the sight of a dead body:

> As when harsh misfortune strikes a man if in his own
>   country,
> He has killed a man, and arrives at last at someone else's
>   door,
> The door of a rich man; a shudder seizes those who see
>   him.
> So Achilles shuddered to see divine Priam;

The others shuddered too, looking one at the other.

But this feeling lasts only a moment. Soon the very presence of the suffering creature is forgotten:

> He spoke. The other, remembering his own father,
>   longed to weep;
> Taking the old man's arm, he pushed him away.
> Both were remembering. Thinking of Hector, killer of
>   men,
> Priam wept, abased at the feet of Achilles.
> But Achilles wept, now for his father,
> Now for Patroclus. And their sobs resounded through
>   the house.

It was not insensibility that made Achilles with a single movement of his hand push away the old man who had been clinging to his knees; Priam's words, recalling his own old father, had moved him to tears. It was merely a question of his being as free in his attitudes and movements as if, clasping his knees, there were not a suppliant but an inert object. Anybody who is in our vicinity exercises a certain power over us by his very presence, and a power that belongs to him alone, that is, the power of halting, repressing, modifying each movement that our body sketches out. If we step aside for a passer-by on the road, it is not the same thing as stepping aside to avoid a billboard; alone in our rooms, we get up, walk about, sit down again quite differently from the way we do when we have a visitor. But this indefinable influence that the presence of another human being has on us is not exercised by men whom a moment of impatience can deprive of life, who can die before even thought has a chance to pass sentence on them. In their presence, people move about as if they were not there; they, on their side, running the risk of being reduced to nothing in a single instant, imitate nothingness in their own persons. Pushed, they fall. Fallen, they lie where they are, unless chance gives somebody the idea of raising them up again. But supposing that at long last they have been picked up, honoured with cordial remarks, they still do not venture to take this resurrection seriously; they dare not express a wish lest an irritated voice return them forever to silence:

> He spoke; the old man trembled and obeyed.

At least a suppliant, once his prayer is answered, becomes a human being again, like everybody else. But there are other, more unfortunate creatures who have become things for the rest of their lives. Their days hold no pastimes, no free spaces, no room in them for any impulse of their own. It is not that their life is harder than other men's nor that they occupy a lower place in the social hierarchy; no, they are another human species, a compromise between a man and a corpse. The idea of a person's being a thing is a logical contradiction. Yet what is impossible in logic becomes true in life, and the contradiction lodged within the soul tears it to shreds. This thing is constantly aspiring to be a man or a woman, and never achieving it – here, surely, is death but death strung out over a whole lifetime; here, surely, is life, but life that death congeals before abolishing.

This strange fate awaits the virgin, the priest's daughter:

> I will not give her up. Sooner shall old age come upon
>   her
> In our house in Argos, far from her native land,
> Tending the loom and sharing my bed.

It awaits the young wife, the young mother, the prince's bride:

> And perhaps one day, in Argos, you will weave cloth for
>   another,
> And the Messeian or Hyperian water you will fetch,
> Much against your will, yielding to a harsh necessity.

It awaits the baby, heir to the royal sceptre:

> Soon they will be carried off in the hollow ships,
> I with them. And you, my child, will either go with me,

> To a land where you will work at wretched tasks,
> Labouring for a pitiless master . . .

In the mother's eyes, such a fate is, for her child, as terrible as death; the husband would rather die than see his wife reduced to it; all the plagues of heaven are invoked by the father against the army that subjects his daughter to it. Yet the victims themselves are beyond all this. Curses, feelings of rebellion, comparisons, reflections on the future and the past, are obliterated from the mind of the captive; and memory itself barely lingers on. Fidelity to his city and his dead is not the slave's privilege.

And what does it take to make the slave weep? The misfortune of his master, his oppressor, despoiler, pillager, of the man who laid waste his town and killed his dear ones under his very eyes. This man suffers or dies; *then* the slave's tears come. And really why not? This is for him the only occasion on which tears are permitted, are, indeed, required. A slave will always cry whenever he can do so with impunity – his situation keeps tears on tap for him.

> She spoke, weeping, and the women groaned,
> Using the pretext of Patroclus to bewail their own
> torments.

Since the slave has no licence to express anything except what is pleasing to his master, it follows that the only emotion that can touch or enliven him a little, that can reach him in the desolation of his life, is the emotion of love for his master. There is no place else to send the gift of love; all other outlets are barred, just as, with the horse in harness, bit, shafts, reins bar every way but one. And if, by some miracle, in the slave's breast a hope is born, the hope of becoming, some day, through somebody's influence, *someone* once again, how far won't these captives go to show love and thankfulness, even though these emotions are addressed to the very men who should, considering the very recent past, still reek with horror for them:

My husband, to whom my father and respected mother
    gave me,
I saw before the city transfixed by the sharp bronze.
My three brothers, children, with me, of a single mother,
So dear to me! They all met their fatal day.
But you did not allow me to weep, when swift Achilles
Slaughtered my husband and laid waste the city of
    Mynes.
You promised me that I would be taken by divine
    Achilles,
For his legitimate wife, that he would carry me away in
    his ships,
To Pythia, where our marriage would be celebrated
    among the Myrmidons,
So without respite I mourn for you, you who have always
    been gentle.

To lose more than the slave does is impossible, for he
loses his whole inner life. A fragment of it he may get back
if he sees the possibility of changing his fate, but this is his
only hope. Such is the empire of force, as extensive as the
empire of nature. Nature, too, when vital needs are at stake,
can erase the whole inner life, even the grief of a mother:

But the thought of eating came to her, when she was tired
    of tears.

Force, in the hands of another, exercises over the soul the
same tyranny that extreme hunger does; for it possesses,
and *in perpetuo*, the power of life and death. Its rule,
moreover, is as cold and hard as the rule of inert matter.
The man who knows himself weaker than another is more
alone in the heart of a city than a man lost in the desert.

Two casks are placed before Zeus's doorsill,
Containing the gifts he gives, the bad in one, the good in
    the other . . .
The man to whom he gives baneful gifts, he exposes to
    outrage;

> A frightful need drives him across the divine earth;
> He is a wanderer, and gets no respect from gods or men.

Force is as pitiless to the man who possesses it, or thinks he does, as it is to its victims; the second it crushes, the first it intoxicates. The truth is, nobody really possesses it. The human race is not divided up, in the *Iliad*, into conquered persons, slaves, suppliants, on the one hand, and conquerors and chiefs on the other. In this poem there is not a single man who does not at one time or another have to bow his neck to force. The common soldier in the *Iliad* is free and has the right to bear arms; nevertheless he is subject to the indignity of orders and abuse;

> But whenever he came upon a commoner shouting out,
> He struck him with his sceptre and spoke sharply:
> 'Good for nothing! Be still and listen to your betters,
> You are weak and cowardly and unwarlike,
> You count for nothing, neither in battle nor in council.'

Thersites pays dear for the perfectly reasonable comments he makes, comments not at all different, moreover, from those made by Achilles:

> He hit him with his sceptre on back and shoulders,
> So that he doubled over, and a great tear welled up,
> And a bloody welt appeared on his back
> Under the golden sceptre. Frightened, he sat down,
> Wiping away his tears, bewildered and in pain.
> Troubled though they were, the others laughed long at
>   him.

Achilles himself, that proud hero, the undefeated, is shown us at the outset of the poem, weeping with humiliation and helpless grief – the woman he wanted for his bride has been taken from under his nose, and he has not dared to oppose it:

> . . . But Achilles
> Weeping, sat apart from his companions,

> By the white-capped waves, staring over the
> boundless ocean.

What has happened is that Agamemnon has deliberately
humiliated Achilles, to show that he himself is the master:

> ... So you will learn
> That I am greater than you, and anyone else will
>   hesitate
> To treat me as an equal and set himself against me.

But a few days pass, and now the supreme commander is
weeping in his turn. He must humble himself, he must
plead, and have, moreover, the added misery of doing it all
in vain.

In the same way, there is not a single one of the combatants who is spared the shameful experience of fear. The
heroes quake like everybody else. It only needs a challenge
from Hector to throw the whole Greek force into consterna-
tion – except for Achilles and his men, and they did not
happen to be present:

> He spoke and all grew still and held their peace,
> Ashamed to refuse, afraid to accept.

But once Ajax comes forward and offers himself, fear
quickly changes sides:

> A shudder of terror ran through the Trojans, making
>   their limbs weak;
> And Hector himself felt his heart leap in his breast.
> But he no longer had the right to tremble, or to run
>   away ...

Two days later, it is Ajax's turn to be terrified:

> Zeus the father on high, makes fear rise in Ajax.
> He stops, overcome, puts behind him his buckler made
>   of seven hides,
> Trembles, looks at the crowd around, like a wild
>   beast ...

Even to Achilles the moment comes; he too must shake and stammer with fear, though it is a river that has this effect on him, not a man. But, with the exception of Achilles, every man in the *Iliad* tastes a moment of defeat in battle. Victory is less a matter of valour than of blind destiny, which is symbolized in the poem by Zeus's golden scales:

> Then Zeus the father took his golden scales,
> In them he put the two fates of death that cuts down all
>   men,
> One for the Trojans, tamers of horses, one for the
>   bronze-sheathed Greeks.
> He seized the scales by the middle; it was the fatal day of
>   Greece that sank.

By its very blindness, destiny establishes a kind of justice. Blind also is she who decrees to warriors punishment in kind. He that takes the sword, will perish by the sword. The *Iliad* formulated the principle long before the Gospels did, and in almost the same terms:

> Ares is just, and kills those who kill.

Perhaps all men, by the very act of being born, are destined to suffer violence; yet this is a truth to which circumstance shuts men's eyes. The strong are, as a matter of fact, never absolutely strong, nor are the weak absolutely weak, but neither is aware of this. They have in common a refusal to believe that they both belong to the same species: the weak see no relation between themselves and the strong, and vice versa. The man who is the possessor of force seems to walk through a non-resistant element; in the human substance that surrounds him nothing has the power to interpose, between the impulse and the act, the tiny interval that is reflection. Where there is no room for reflection, there is none either for justice or prudence. Hence we see men in arms behaving harshly and madly. We see their sword bury itself in the breast of a disarmed enemy who is in the very act of pleading at their knees. We see them triumph over a dying man by describing to him the outrages his corpse will endure. We see Achilles cut the throats of twelve Trojan boys on the funeral pyre of Patroclus as naturally as we cut flowers for a grave. These men, wielding power, have no suspicion of the fact that the consequences of their deeds will at length come home to them – they too will bow the neck in their turn. If you can make an old man fall silent, tremble, obey, with a single word of your own, why should it occur to you that the curses of this old man, who is after all a priest, will have their own importance in the gods' eyes? Why should you refrain from taking Achilles' girl away from him if you know that neither he nor she can do anything but obey you? Achilles rejoices over the sight of the Greeks fleeing in misery and confusion. What could possibly suggest to him that this rout, which will last exactly as long as he wants it to and end when his mood indicates it, that this very rout will be the cause of his friend's death, and, for that matter, of his own? Thus it happens that those who have force on loan from fate count on it too much and are destroyed.

But at the time their own destruction seems impossible to them. For they do not see that the force in their possession is only a limited quantity; nor do they see their relations with other human beings as a kind of balance between unequal amounts of force. Since other people do not impose on their movements that halt, that interval of hesitation, wherein lies all our consideration for our brothers in humanity, they conclude that destiny has given complete licence to them, and none at all to their inferiors. And at this point they exceed the measure of the force that is actually at their disposal. Inevitably they exceed it, since they are not aware that it is limited. And now we see them committed irretrievably to chance; suddenly things cease to obey them. Sometimes chance is kind to them, sometimes cruel. But in any case there they are, exposed, open to misfortune; gone is the armour of power that formerly protected their naked souls; nothing, no shield, stands between them and tears.

This retribution, which has a geometrical rigour, which operates automatically to penalize the abuse of force, was the main subject of Greek thought. It is the soul of the epic. Under the name of Nemesis, it functions as the mainspring of Aeschylus's tragedies. To the Pythagoreans, to Socrates and Plato, it was the jumping-off point of speculation upon the nature of man and the universe. Wherever Hellenism has penetrated, we find the idea of it familiar. In Oriental countries which are steeped in Buddhism, it is perhaps this Greek idea that has lived on under the name of Kharma. The Occident, however, has lost it, and no longer even has a word to express it in any of its languages: conceptions of limit, measure, equilibrium, which ought to determine the conduct of life are, in the West, restricted to a servile function in the vocabulary of technics. We are only geometricians of matter; the Greeks were, first of all, geometricians in their apprenticeship to virtue.

The progress of the war in the *Iliad* is simply a continual game of seesaw. The victor of the moment feels himself invincible, even though, only a few hours before, he may have experienced defeat; he forgets to treat victory as a transitory thing. At the end of the first day of combat described in the *Iliad*, the victorious Greeks were in a position to obtain the object of all their efforts, i.e. Helen and her riches – assuming of course as Homer did, that the Greeks had reason to believe that Helen was in Troy. Actually, the Egyptian priests, who ought to have known, affirmed later on to Herodotus that she was in Egypt. In any case, that evening the Greeks are no longer interested in her or her possessions:

> 'For the present, let us not accept the riches of Paris;
> Nor Helen; everybody sees, even the most ignorant,
> That Troy stands on the verge of ruin.'
> He spoke, and all the Achaians acclaimed him.

What they want is, in fact, everything. For booty, all the riches of Troy; for their bonfires, all the palaces, temples, houses; for slaves, all the women and children; for corpses, all the men. They forget one detail, that *everything* is not within their power, for they are not in Troy. Perhaps they will be there tomorrow; perhaps not. Hector, the same day, makes the same mistake:

> For I know well in my entrails and in my heart,
> A day will come when Holy Troy will perish,
> And Priam, and the nation of Priam of the good
> lance.
> But I think less of the grief that is in store for the
> Trojans.
> And of Hecuba herself, and of Priam the king,
> And of my brothers, so numerous and so brave,
> Who will fall in the dust under the blows of the
> enemy,
> Than of you that day when a Greek in his bronze
> breastplate
> Will drag you away weeping and deprive you of your
> liberty.
> But as for me, may I be dead, and may the earth have
> covered me
> Before I hear you cry out or see you dragged away!

At this moment what would he not give to turn aside those horrors which he believes to be inevitable? But at this moment nothing he *could* give would be of any use. The next day but one, however, the Greeks have run away miserably, and Agamemnon himself is in favour of putting to the sea again. And now Hector, by making a very few concessions, could readily secure the enemy's departure; yet now he is even unwilling to let them go empty-handed:

> Set fires everywhere and let the brightness mount
> the skies
> Lest in the night the long-haired Greeks,
> Escaping, sail over the broad back of ocean. . . .
> Let each of them take home a wound to heal
> . . . thus others will fear

> To bring dolorous war to the Trojans, tamers of
> horses.

His wish is granted; the Greeks stay; and the next day they
reduce Hector and his men to a pitiable condition:

> As for them – they fled across the plain like cattle
> Whom a lion hunts before him in the dark
> midnight. . . .
> Thus the mighty Agamemnon, son of Atreus,
> pursued them,
> Steadily killing the hindmost; and still they fled.

In the course of the afternoon, Hector regains the ascen-
dancy, withdraws again, then puts the Greeks to flight,
then is repulsed by Patroclus, who has come in with his
fresh troops. Patroclus, pressing his advantage, ends by
finding himself exposed, wounded and without armour, to
the sword of Hector. And finally that evening the victorious
Hector hears the prudent counsel of Polydamas and repudi-
ates it sharply:

> Now that wily Kronos's son has given me
> Glory at the ships; now that I have driven the Greeks
> to the sea,
> Do not offer, fool, such counsels to the people.
> No Trojan will listen to you; nor would I permit
> it. . . .
> So Hector spoke, and the Trojans acclaimed him. . . .

The next day Hector is lost. Achilles has harried him across
the field and is about to kill him. He has always been the
stronger of the two in combat; how much the more so now,
after several weeks of rest, ardent for vengeance and victory, against an exhausted enemy? And Hector stands
alone, before the walls of Troy, absolutely alone, alone to
wait for death and to steady his soul to face it:

> Alas, were I to slip through the gate, behind the
> rampart,
> Polydamas at once would heap dishonour on me. . . .

And now that through my recklessness I have
     destroyed my people,
I fear the Trojans and the long-robed Trojan women,
I fear to hear from someone far less brave than I:
'Hector, trusting in his own strength too far, has ruined
     his people.' . . .
Suppose I were to down my bossed shield,
My massive helmet, and, leaning my spear against the
     wall,
Should go to meet renowned Achilles? . . .
But why spin out these fancies? Why such dreams?
I would not reach him, nor would he pity me,
Or respect me. He would kill me like a woman
If I came naked thus. . . .

Not a jot of the grief and ignominy that fall to the unfortunate is Hector spared. Alone, stripped of the prestige of force, he discovers that the courage that kept him from taking to the shelter of the walls is not enough to save him from flight:

Seeing him, Hector began to tremble. He had not the
     heart
To stay . . .
. . . It is not for a ewe nor the skin of an ox,
That they are striving, not these ordinary rewards of the
     race;
It is for a life that they run, the life of Hector, tamer of
     horses.

Wounded to death, he enhances his conqueror's triumph by vain supplications:

I implore you, by your soul, by your knees, by your
     parents. . . .

But the auditors of the *Iliad* knew that the death of Hector would be but a brief joy to Achilles, and the death of Achilles but a brief joy to the Trojans, and the destruction of Troy but a brief joy to the Achaians.

Thus violence obliterates anybody who feels its touch. It comes to seem just as external to its employer as to its victim. And from this springs the idea of a destiny before which executioner and victim stand equally innocent, before which conquered and conqueror are brothers in the same distress. The conquered brings misfortune to the conqueror, and vice versa:

> A single son, short-lived, was born to him.
> Neglected by me, he grows old – for far from home
> I camp before Troy, injuring you and your sons.

A moderate use of force, which alone would enable man to escape being enmeshed in its machinery, would require superhuman virtue, which is as rare as dignity in weakness. Moreover, moderation itself is not without its perils, since prestige, from which force derives at least three-quarters of its strength, rests principally upon that marvellous indifference that the strong feel toward the weak, an indifference so contagious that it infects the very people who are the objects of it. Yet ordinarily excess is not arrived at through prudence or politic considerations. On the contrary, man dashes to it as to an irresistible temptation. The voice of reason is occasionally heard in the mouths of the characters in the *Iliad*. Thersites' speeches are reasonable to the highest degree; so are the speeches of the angry Achilles:

> Nothing is worth my life, not all the goods
> They say the well-built city of Ilium contains. . . .
> A man can capture steers and fatted sheep
> But, once gone, the soul cannot be captured back.

But words of reason drop into the void. If they come from an inferior, he is punished and shuts up; if from a chief, his actions betray them. And failing everything else, there is always a god handy to advise him to be unreasonable. In the end, the very idea of wanting to escape the role fate has allotted one – the business of killing and dying – disappears from the mind:

> We to whom Zeus
> Has assigned suffering, from youth to old age,
> Suffering in grievous wars, till we perish to the
> last man.

Already these warriors, like Craonne's so much later, felt,
themselves to be 'condemned men'.

It was the simplest trap that pitched them into this situation. At the outset, at the embarkation, their hearts are
light, as hearts always are if you have a large force on your
side and nothing but space to oppose you. Their weapons
are in their hands; the enemy is absent. Unless your spirit
has been conquered in advance by the reputation of the
enemy, you always feel yourself to be much stronger than
anybody who is not there. An absent man does not impose
the yoke of necessity. To the spirits of those embarking no
necessity yet presents itself; consequently they go off as
though to a game, as though on holiday from the confine-
ment of daily life.

> Where have they gone, those braggadocio boasts
> We proudly flung upon the air at Lemnos,
> Stuffing ourselves with flesh of horned steers,
> Drinking from cups brimming over with wine?
> As for Trojans – a hundred or two each man of us
> Could handle in battle. And now one is too much
>   for us.

But the first contact of war does not immediately destroy
the illusion that war is a game. War's necessity is terrible,
altogether different in kind from the necessity of peace. So
terrible is it that the human spirit will not submit to it so
long as it can possibly escape; and whenever it can escape it
takes refuge in long days empty of necessity, days of play, of
revery, days arbitrary and unreal. Danger then becomes an
abstraction; the lives you destroy are like toys broken by a
child, and quite as incapable of feeling; heroism is but a
theatrical gesture and smirched with boastfulness. This

becomes doubly true if a momentary access of vitality comes to reinforce the divine hand that wards off defeat and death. Then war is easy and basely, coarsely loved.

But with the majority of the combatants this state of mind does not persist. Soon there comes a day when fear, or defeat, or the death of beloved comrades touches the warrior's spirit, and it crumples in the hand of necessity. At that moment war is no more a game or a dream; now at last the warrior cannot doubt the reality of its existence. And this reality, which he perceives, is hard, much too hard to be borne, for it enfolds death. Once you acknowledge death to be a practical possibility, the thought of it becomes unendurable, except in flashes. True enough, all men are fated to die; true enough also, a soldier may grow old in battles; yet for those whose spirits have bent under the yoke of war, the relation between death and the future is different than for other men. For other men death appears as a limit set in advance on the future; for the soldier death *is* the future, the future his profession assigns him. Yet the idea of man's having death for a future is abhorrent to nature. Once the experience of war makes visible the possibility of death that lies locked up in each moment, our thoughts cannot travel from one day to the next without meeting death's face. The mind is then strung up to a pitch it can stand for only a short time; but each new dawn reintroduces the same necessity; and days piled on days make years. On each one of these days the soul suffers violence. Regularly, every morning, the soul castrates itself of aspiration, for thought cannot journey through time without meeting death on the way. Thus war effaces all conceptions of purpose or goal, including even its own 'war aims'. It effaces the very notion of war's being brought to an end. To be outside a situation so violent as this is to find it inconceivable; to be inside it is to be unable to conceive its end. Consequently, nobody does anything to bring this end about. In the presence of an armed enemy, what hand can relinquish its weapon? The mind ought to find a way out, but the mind has lost all capacity to so much as look outward.

The mind is completely absorbed in doing itself violence. Always in human life, whether war or slavery is in question, intolerable sufferings continue, as it were, by the force of their own specific gravity, and so look to the outsider as though they were easy to bear; actually, they continue because they have deprived the sufferer of the resources which might serve to extricate him.

Nevertheless, the soul that is enslaved to war cries out for deliverance, but deliverance itself appears to it in an extreme and tragic aspect, the aspect of destruction. Any other solution, more moderate, more reasonable in character, would expose the mind to suffering so naked, so violent that it could not be borne, even as memory. Terror, grief, exhaustion, slaughter, the annihilation of comrades – is it credible that these things should not continually tear at the soul, if the intoxication of force had not intervened to drown them? The idea that an unlimited effort should bring in only a limited profit or no profit at all is terribly painful.

> What? Will we let Priam and the Trojans boast
> Of Argive Helen, she for whom so many Greeks
> Died before Troy, far from their native land?
> What? Do you want us to leave the city, wide-streeted
> Troy,
> Standing, when we have suffered so much for it?

But actually what is Helen to Ulysses? What indeed is Troy, full of riches that will not compensate him for Ithaca's ruin? For the Greeks, Troy and Helen are in reality mere sources of blood and tears; to master them is to master frightful memories. If the existence of an enemy has made a soul destroy in itself the thing nature put there, then the only remedy the soul can imagine is the destruction of the enemy. At the same time the death of dearly loved comrades arouses a spirit of sombre emulation, a rivalry in death:

> May I die, then, at once! Since fate has not let me
> Protect my dead friend, who far from home
> Perished, longing for me to defend him from death.

So now I go to seek the murderer of my friend,
Hector. And death shall I find at the moment
Zeus wills it –
Zeus and the other immortals.

It is the same despair that drives him on toward death, on
the one hand, and slaughter on the other:

I know it well, my fate is to perish here,
Far from father and dearly loved mother; but meanwhile
I shall not stop till the Trojans have had their fill of war.

The man possessed by this twofold need for death belongs,
so long as he has not become something still different, to a
different race from the race of the living.

What echo can the timid hopes of life strike in such a
heart? How can it hear the defeated begging for another
sight of the light of day? The threatened life has already
been relieved of nearly all its consequences by a single,
simple distinction: it is now unarmed; its adversary
possesses a weapon. Furthermore, how can a man who has
rooted out of himself the notion that the light of day is sweet
to the eyes respect such a notion when it makes its
appearance in some futile and humble lament?

I clasp tight your knees, Achilles. Have a thought, have
        pity for me.
I stand here, O son of Zeus, a suppliant, to be respected.
In your house it was I first tasted Demeter's bread,
That day in my well-pruned vineyard you caught me
And sold me, sending me far from father and friends,
To holy Lemnos; a hundred oxen was my price.
And now I will pay you three hundred for ransom.
This dawn is for me my twelfth day in Troy,
After so many sorrows. See me here, in your hands,
Through some evil fate. Zeus surely must hate me
Who again puts me into your hands. Alas, my poor
        mother, Laothoe,
Daughter of the old man, Altes – a short-lived son you
        have borne.

What a reception this feeble hope gets!

> Come, friend, you too must die. Why make a fuss
>   about it?
> Patroclus, he too has died – a far better man than you are.
> Don't you see how handsome I am, how mighty?
> A noble father begat me, and I have a goddess for mother.
> Yet even I, like you, must some day encounter my fate,
> Whether the hour strikes at noon, or evening, or sunrise,
> The hour that comes when some arms-bearing warrior
>   will kill me.

To respect life in somebody else when you have had to castrate yourself of all yearning for it demands a truly heartbreaking exertion of the powers of generosity. It is impossible to imagine any of Homer's warriors being capable of such an exertion, unless it is that warrior who dwells, in a peculiar way, at the very centre of the poem – I mean Patroclus, who 'knew how to be sweet to everybody', and who throughout the *Iliad* commits no cruel or brutal act. But then how many men do we know, in several thousand years of human history, who would have displayed such god-like generosity? Two or three? – even this is doubtful. Lacking this generosity, the conquering soldier is like a scourge of nature. Possessed by war, he, like the slave, becomes a thing, though his manner of doing so is different – over him too, words are as powerless as over matter itself. And both, at the touch of force, experience its inevitable effects: they become deaf and dumb.

Such is the nature of force. Its power of converting a man into a thing is a double one, and in its application double-edged. To the same degree, though in different fashions, those who use it and those who endure it are turned to stone. This property of force achieves its maximum effectiveness during the clash of arms, in battle, when the tide of the day has turned, and everything is rushing toward a decision. It is not the planning man, the man of strategy, the man acting on the resolution taken, who wins or loses a battle; battles are fought and decided by men deprived of these faculties, men who have undergone a transformation, who have dropped either to the level of inert matter, which is pure passivity, or to the level of blind force, which is pure momentum. Herein lies the last secret of war, a secret revealed by the *Iliad* in its similes, which liken the warriors either to fire, flood, wind, wild beasts, or God knows what blind cause of disaster, or else to frightened animals, trees, water, sand, to anything in nature that is set into motion by the violence of external forces. Greeks and Trojans, from one day to the next, sometimes even from one hour to the next, experience, turn and turn about, one or the other of these transmutations:

> As when a lion, murderous, springs among the cattle
> Which by thousands are grazing over some vast marshy
>   field. . . .
> And their flanks heave with terror; even so the
>   Achaians
> Scattered in panic before Hector and Zeus, the great
>   father.
>
> As when a ravening fire breaks out deep in a bushy
>   wood
> And the wheeling wind scatters sparks far and wide,
> And trees, root and branch, topple over in flames;
> So Atreus' son, Agamemnon, roared through the ranks
> Of the Trojans in flight. . . .

The art of war is simply the art of producing such transformations, and its equipment, its processes, even the casualties it inflicts on the enemy, are only means directed towards this end – its true object is the warrior's soul. Yet these transformations are always a mystery; the gods are their authors, the gods who kindle men's imagination. But however caused, this petrifactive quality of force, twofold always, is essential to its nature; and a soul which has entered the province of force will not escape this except by a miracle. Such miracles are rare and of brief duration.

The wantonness of the conqueror that knows no respect for any creature or thing that is at its mercy or is imagined to be so, the despair of the soldier that drives him on to destruction, the obliteration of the slave or the conquered man, the wholesale slaughter – all these elements combine in the *Iliad* to make a picture of uniform horror, of which force is the sole hero. A monotonous desolation would result were it not for those few luminous moments, scattered here and there throughout the poem, those brief, celestial moments in which man possesses his soul. The soul that awakes then, to live for an instant only and be lost almost at once in force's vast kingdom, awakes pure and whole; it contains no ambiguities, nothing complicated or turbid; it has no room for anything but courage and love. Sometimes it is in the course of inner deliberation that a man finds his soul: he meets it, like Hector before Troy, as he tries to face destiny on his own terms, without the help of gods or men. At other times, it is in a moment of love that men discover their souls – and there is hardly any form of pure love known to humanity of which the *Iliad* does not treat. The tradition of hospitality persists, even through several generations, to dispel the blindness of combat.

> Thus I am for you a beloved guest in the breast of
>   Argos . . .
> Let us turn our lances away from each other, even in
>   battle.

The love of the son for the parents, of father for son, of mother for son, is continually described, in a manner as touching as it is curt:

> Thetis answered, shedding tears,
> 'You were born to me for a short life,
>   my child, as you say . . .'

Even brotherly love:

> My three brothers whom the same mother bore
>   for me,
> So dear. . . .

Conjugal love, condemned to sorrow, is of an astonishing purity. Imagining the humiliations of slavery which await a beloved wife, the husband passes over the one indignity which even in anticipation would stain their tenderness. What could be simpler than the words spoken by his wife to the man about to die?

> ... Better for me
> Losing you, to go under the earth. No other comfort
> Will remain, when you have encountered your
>   death-heavy fate,
> Only grief, only sorrow. ...

Not less touching are the words addressed to a dead husband:

> Dear husband, you died young, and left me your
>   widow
> Alone in the palace. Our child is still tiny,
> The child you and I, crossed by fate, had together.
> I think he will never grow up ...
> For not in your bed did you die, holding my hand
> And speaking to me prudent words which forever
> Night and day, as I weep, might live in my memory.

The most beautiful friendship of all, the friendship between comrades-at-arms, is the final theme of The Epic:

> ... But Achilles
> Wept, dreaming of the beloved comrade;
>   sleep, all-prevailing,
> Would not take him; he turned over again and
>   again.

But the purest triumph of love, the crowning grace of war, is the friendship that floods the hearts of mortal enemies. Before it a murdered son or a murdered friend no longer cries out for vengeance. Before it – even more miraculous – the distance between benefactor and suppliant, between victor and vanquished, shrinks to nothing:

But when thirst and hunger had been appeased,
Then Dardanian Priam fell to admiring Achilles.
How tall he was, and handsome; he had the face of a god;
And in his turn Dardanian Priam was admired by
   Achilles,
Who watched his handsome face and listened to his words.
And when they were satisfied with contemplation of each
   other . . .

These moments of grace are rare in the *Iliad*, but they are
enough to make us feel with sharp regret what it is that
violence has killed and will kill again.

However, such a heaping-up of violent deeds would have a
frigid effect, were it not for the note of incurable bitterness
that continually makes itself heard, though often only a
single word marks its presence, often a mere stroke of the
verse, or a run-on line. It is in this that the *Iliad* is absolutely unique, in this bitterness that proceeds from tenderness and that spreads over the whole human race, impartial
as sunlight. Never does the tone lose its colouring of bitterness; yet never does the bitterness drop into lamentation.
Justice and love, which have hardly any place in this study
of extremes and of unjust acts of violence, nevertheless
bathe the work in their light without ever becoming noticeable themselves, except as a kind of accent. Nothing precious is scorned, whether or not death is its destiny; everyone's unhappiness is laid bare without dissimulation or
disdain; no man is set above or below the condition common to all men; whatever is destroyed is regretted. Victors
and vanquished are brought equally near us; under the
same head, both are seen as counterparts of the poet, and
the listener as well. If there is any difference, it is that the
enemy's misfortunes are possibly more sharply felt.

So he fell there, put to sleep in the sleep of bronze,
Unhappy man, far from his wife, defending his own
   people. . . .

And what accents echo the fate of the lad Achilles sold at Lemnos!

> Eleven days he rejoiced his heart among those he loved,
> Returning from Lemnos; the twelfth day, once
>> more,
> God delivered him into the hands of Achilles,
> To him who had to send him, unwilling, to Hades.

And the fate of Euphorbus, who saw only a single day of war.

> Blood soaked his hair, that hair like to the Graces' . . .

When Hector is lamented:

> . . . guardian of chaste wives and little children. . . .

In these few words, chastity appears, dirtied by force, and childhood, delivered to the sword. The fountain at the gates of Troy becomes an object of poignant nostalgia when Hector runs by, seeking to elude his doom:

> Close by there stood the great stone tanks,
> Handsomely built, where silk-gleaming garments
> Were washed clean by Troy's lovely daughters and
>> housewives
> In the old days of peace, long ago, when the Greeks
>> had not come.
> Past these did they run their race, pursued and
>> pursuer.

The whole of the *Iliad* lies under the shadow of the greatest calamity the human race can experience – the destruction of a city. This calamity could not tear more at the heart had the poet been born in Troy. But the tone is not different when the Achaeans are dying, far from home.

In so far as this other life, the life of the living, seems calm and full, the brief evocations of the world of peace are felt as pain:

> With the break of dawn and the rising of the day,
> On both sides arrows flew, men fell.

But at the very hour that the woodcutter goes home to fix
 his meal
In the mountain valleys when his arms have had enough
Of hacking great trees, and disgust rises in his heart,
And the desire for sweet food seizes his entrails,
At that hour, by their valour, the Danaans broke the
 front.

Whatever is not war, whatever war destroys or threatens,
the *Iliad* wraps in poetry; the realities of war, never. No
reticence veils the step from life to death:

Then his teeth flew out; from two sides,
Blood came to his eyes; the blood that from lips
 and nostrils
He was spilling, open-mouthed; death enveloped him
 in its black cloud.

The cold brutality of the deeds of war is left undisguised;
neither victors nor vanquished are admired, scorned, or
hated. Almost always, fate and the gods decide the changing lot of battle. Within the limits fixed by fate, the gods
determine with sovereign authority victory and defeat. It is
always they who provoke those fits of madness, those
treacheries, which are forever blocking peace; war is their
true business; their only motives, caprice and malice. As for
the warriors, victors or vanquished, those comparisons
which liken them to beasts or things can inspire neither
admiration nor contempt, but only regret that men are
capable of being so transformed.

There may be, unknown to us, other expressions of the
extraordinary sense of equity which breathes through the
Iliad; certainly it has not been imitated. One is barely
aware that the poet is a Greek and not a Trojan. The tone of
the poem furnishes a direct clue to the origin of its oldest
portions; history perhaps will never be able to tell us more.
If one believes with Thucydides that eighty years after the
fall of Troy, the Achaeans in their turn were conquered,

one may ask whether these songs, with their rare references to iron, are not the songs of a conquered people, of whom a few went into exile. Obliged to live and die 'very far from the homeland', like the Greeks who fell before Troy, having lost their cities like the Trojans, they saw their own image both in the conquerors, who had been their fathers, and in the conquered, whose misery was like their own. They could still see the Trojan war over that brief span of years in its true light, unglossed by pride or shame. They could look at it as conquered and as conquerors simultaneously, and so perceive what neither conqueror nor conquered ever saw, for both were blinded. Of course, this is mere fancy; one can see such distant times only in fancy's light.

In any case, this poem is a miracle. Its bitterness is the only justifiable bitterness, for it springs from the subjection of the human spirit to force, that is, in the last analysis, to matter. This subjection is the common lot, although each spirit will bear it differently, in proportion to its own virtue. No one in the *Iliad* is spared by it, as no one on earth is. No one who succumbs to it is by virtue of this fact regarded with contempt. Whoever, within his own soul and in human relations, escapes the dominion of force is loved but loved sorrowfully because of the threat of destruction that constantly hangs over him.

Such is the spirit of the only true epic the Occident possesses. The *Odyssey* seems merely a good imitation, now of the *Iliad*, now of Oriental poems; the *Aeneid* is an imitation which, however brilliant, is disfigured by frigidity, bombast, and bad taste. The *chansons de geste*, lacking the sense of equity, could not attain greatness: in the *Chanson de Roland*, the death of an enemy does not come home to either author or reader in the same way as does the death of Roland.

Attic tragedy, or at any rate the tragedy of Aeschylus and Sophocles, is the true continuation of the epic. The conception of justice enlightens it, without ever directly intervening in it; here force appears in its coldness and hardness, always attended by effects from whose fatality neither those who use it or those who suffer it can escape; here the shame of the coerced spirit is neither disguised, nor enveloped in facile pity, nor held up to scorn; here more than one spirit bruised and degraded by misfortune is offered for our admiration. The Gospels are the last marvellous expression of the Greek genius, as the *Iliad* is the first: here the Greek spirit reveals itself not only in the injunction given mankind to seek above all other goods, 'the kingdom and justice of our Heavenly Father', but also in the fact that human suffering is laid bare, and we see it in a being who is at once divine and human. The accounts of the Passion show that a divine spirit, incarnate, is changed by misfortune, trembles before suffering and death, feels itself, in the depths of its agony, to be cut off from man and God. The sense of human misery gives the Gospels that accent of simplicity that is the mark of the Greek genius, and that endows Greek tragedy and the *Iliad* with all their value. Certain phrases have a ring strangely reminiscent of the epic, and it is the Trojan lad dispatched to Hades, though he does not wish to go, who comes to mind when Christ says to Peter: 'Another shall gird thee and carry thee whither thou wouldst not.' This accent cannot be separated from the idea that inspired the Gospels, for the sense of human misery is a pre-condition of justice and love. He who does not realize to what extent shifting fortune and necessity hold in subjection every human spirit, cannot regard as fellow-creatures nor love as he loves himself those whom chance separated from him by an abyss. The variety of constraints pressing upon man give rise to the illusion of several distinct species that cannot communicate. Only he who has measured the dominion of force, and knows how not to respect it, is capable of love and justice.

The relations between destiny and the human soul, the extent to which each soul creates its own destiny, the question of what elements in the soul are transformed by merciless necessity as it tailors the soul to fit the requirements of shifting fate, and of what elements can on the other hand be preserved, through the exercise of virtue and through grace – this whole question is fraught with temptations to false-hood, temptations that are positively enhanced by pride, by shame, by hatred, contempt, indifference, by the will to oblivion or to ignorance. Moreover, nothing is so rare as to see misfortune fairly portrayed; the tendency is either to treat the unfortunate person as though catastrophe were his natural vocation, or to ignore the effects of misfortune on the soul, to assume, that is, that the soul can suffer and remain unmarked by it, can fail, in fact, to be recast in misfortune's image. The Greeks, generally speaking, were endowed with spiritual force that allowed them to avoid self-deception. The rewards of this were great; they dis-covered how to achieve in all their acts the greatest lucidity, purity, and simplicity. But the spirit that was transmitted from the *Iliad* to the Gospels by way of the tragic poets never jumped the borders of Greek civilization; once Greece was destroyed, nothing remained of this spirit but pale reflections.

Both the Romans and the Hebrews believed themselves to be exempt from the misery that is the common human lot. The Romans saw their country as the nation chosen by destiny to be mistress of the world; with the Hebrews, it was their God who exalted them and they retained their superior position just as long as they obeyed Him. Strang-ers, enemies, conquered peoples, subjects, slaves, were ob-jects of contempt to the Romans; and the Romans had no epics, no tragedies. In Rome gladiatorial fights took the place of tragedy. With the Hebrews, misfortune was a sure indication of sin and hence a legitimate object of contempt; to them a vanquished enemy was abhorrent to God himself and condemned to expiate all sorts of crimes – this is a view that makes cruelty permissible and indeed indispensable. And no text of the Old Testament strikes a note comparable to the note heard in the Greek epic, unless it be certain parts of the book of Job. Throughout twenty centuries of Christianity, the Romans and the Hebrews have been admired, read, imitated, both in deed and word; their masterpieces have yielded an appropriate quotation every time anybody had a crime he wanted to justify.

Furthermore, the spirit of the Gospels was not handed down in a pure state from one Christian generation to the next. To undergo suffering and death joyfully was from the very beginning considered a sign of grace in the Christian martyrs – as though grace could do more for a human being than it could for Christ. Those who believe that God himself, once he became man, could not face the harshness of destiny without a long tremor of anguish, should have understood that the only people who can give the impression of having risen to a higher plane, who seem superior to ordinary human misery, are the people who resort to the aids of illusion, exaltation, fanaticism, to conceal the harshness of destiny from their own eyes. The man who does not wear the armour of the lie cannot experience force without being touched by it to the very soul. Grace can prevent this touch from corrupting him, but it cannot spare him the wound. Having forgotten it too well, Christian tradition can only rarely recover that simplicity that renders so poignant every sentence in the story of the Passion. On the other hand, the practice of forcible proselytization threw a veil over the effects of force on the souls of those who used it.

In spite of the brief intoxication induced at the time of the Renaissance by the discovery of Greek literature, there has been, during the course of twenty centuries, no revival of the Greek genius. Something of it was seen in Villon, in Shakespeare, Cervantes, Molière, and – just once – in Racine. The bones of human suffering are exposed in *L'Ecole des femmes* and in *Phèdre*, love being the context – a strange century indeed, which took the opposite view from that of the epic period, and would only acknowledge human suffering in the context of love, while it insisted on swathing with glory the effects of force in war and in politics. To the list of writers given above, a few other names might be added. But nothing the peoples of Europe have produced is worth the first known poem that appeared among them. Perhaps they will yet rediscover the epic genius, when they learn that there is no refuge from fate, learn not to admire force, not to hate the enemy, nor to scorn the unfortunate. How soon this will happen is another question.

Translated by Mary McCarthy, *Politics*, New York, November 1945. Originally published as *'L'Iliade* ou le poème de la force' [signed Emile Novis], *Cahiers du Sud*, XIX, 230, December 1940–January 1941.

VOID AND COMPENSATION

———————— ◉ ————————

Human mechanics. Whoever suffers tries to communicate his suffering (either by ill-treating someone or calling forth their pity) in order to reduce it, and he does really reduce it in this way. In the case of a man in the uttermost depths, whom no one pities, who is without power to ill-treat anyone (if he has no child or being who loves him), the suffering remains within and poisons him.

This is imperative, like gravity. How can one gain deliverance? How gain deliverance from a force which is like gravity?

The tendency to spread evil beyond oneself: I still have it! Beings and things are not sacred enough to me. May I never sully anything, even though I be utterly transformed into mud. To sully nothing, even in thought. Even in my worst moments I would not destroy a Greek statue or a fresco by Giotto. Why anything else then? Why, for example, a moment in the life of a human being who could have been happy for that moment.

It is impossible to forgive whoever has done us harm if that harm has lowered us. We have to think that it has not lowered us, but has revealed our true level.

The wish to see others suffer exactly what we are suffering. It is because of this that, except in periods of social instability, the spite of those in misfortune is directed against their fellows.

That is a factor making for social stability.

The tendency to spread the suffering beyond ourselves. If through excessive weakness we can neither call forth pity nor do harm to others, we attack *what the universe itself represents for us*.

Then every good or beautiful thing is like an insult.

To harm a person is to receive something from him. What? What have we gained (and what will have to be repaid) when we have done harm? We have gained in importance. We have expanded. We have filled an emptiness in ourselves by creating one in somebody else.

To be able to hurt others with impunity – for instance to pass our anger on to an inferior who is obliged to be silent – is to spare ourselves from an expenditure of energy, an expenditure which the other person will have to make. It is the same in the case of the unlawful satisfaction of any desire. The energy we economize in this way is immediately debased.

To forgive. We cannot do this. When we are harmed by someone, reactions are set up within us. The desire for vengeance is a desire for essential equilibrium. We must seek equilibrium on another plane. We have to go as far as this limit by ourselves. There we reach the void. (Heaven helps those who help themselves. . . .)

Headaches. At a certain moment, the pain is lessened by projecting it into the universe, but the universe is impaired; the pain is more intense when it comes home again, but something in me does not suffer and remains in contact with a universe which is not impaired. Act in the same way with the passions. Make them come down like a deposit, collect them into a point and become detached from them. Especially, treat all sufferings in this way. Prevent them from having access to *things*.

The search for equilibrium is bad because it is imaginary. Revenge. Even if in fact we kill or torture our enemy it is, in a sense, imaginary.

A man who lived for his city, his family, his friends, to acquire wealth, improve his social position, etc. – a war: he is led away as a slave and henceforth for evermore he must wear himself out to the utmost limit of his strength merely in order to exist.

That is frightful, impossible, and for this reason he will cling to any aim which presents itself no matter how wretched, be it only to have the slave punished who works at his side. He has no more choice about aims. Any aim at all is like a branch to a drowning man.

Those whose city had been destroyed and who were led away into slavery had no longer either past or future: what had they with which to fill their minds? Lies and the meanest and most pitiful of covetous desires. They were perhaps more ready to risk crucifixion for the sake of stealing a chicken than they had formerly been to risk death in battle for the defence of their town. This is surely so, or those frightful tortures would not have been necessary.

Otherwise they had to be able to endure a void in their minds.

In order to have the strength to contemplate affliction when we are afflicted we need supernatural bread.

A situation which is too hard degrades us through the following process: as a general rule the energy supplied by higher emotions is limited. If the situation requires us to go beyond this limit we have to fall back on lower feelings (fear, covetousness, desire to beat the record, love of outward honours) which are richer in energy.

This limitation is the key to many a retrogression.

Tragedy of those who, having been guided by the love of the Good into a road where suffering has to be endured, after a certain time reach their limit and become debased.

A rock in our path. To hurl ourselves upon this rock as though after a certain intensity of desire had been reached it could not exist any more. Or else to retreat as though we ourselves did not exist. Desire contains something of the absolute and if it fails (once its energy has been used up) the absolute is transferred to the obstacle. This produces the state of mind of the defeated, the oppressed.

To grasp (in each thing) that there is a limit and that without supernatural help that limit cannot be passed – or only by very little and at the price of a terrible fall afterwards.

Energy, freed by the disappearance of the objects which provide motives, always tends to go downwards.
   Base feelings (envy, resentment) are degraded energy.

Every kind of reward constitutes a degradation of energy.

Self-satisfaction over a good action (or a work of art) is a degradation of higher energy. That is why the left hand should not know. . . .

A purely imaginary reward (a smile from Louis XIV) is the exact equivalent of what we have expended, for it has exactly the same value as what we have expended – unlike real rewards which, as such, are either of higher or lower value. Hence *imaginary advantages* alone supply the energy for unlimited effort. But it is necessary that Louis XIV should really smile; if he does not, it is an unutterable deprivation. A king can only pay out imaginary rewards most of the time or he would be insolvent.

It is the same with religion at a certain level. Instead of receiving the smile of Louis XIV, we invent a God who smiles on us.

Or again we praise ourselves. There must be an equivalent reward. This is as inevitable as gravity.

A beloved being who disappoints me. I have written to him. It is impossible that he should not reply by saying what I have said to myself in his name.

Men owe us what we imagine they will give us. We must forgive them this debt.

To accept the fact that they are other than the creatures of our imagination is to imitate the renunciation of God.

I also am other than what I imagine myself to be. To know this is forgiveness.

From *Gravity and Grace*, translated by Emma Craufurd, Routledge and Kegan Paul, London, 1952. Originally published as *La Pesanteur et la Grâce*, Plon, Paris, 1947.

DRAFT FOR A
STATEMENT OF HUMAN OBLIGATIONS

———————— ⊙ ————————

In this essay written in 1943, Simone Weil translates the word 'God' into terms meaningful to the religious, the agnostic and the atheist. She sets out what she believes should be the rules governing political life. Vast though the problems were in drawing up such a document, she saw the need for some kind of guidelines as essential. This was particularly so since de Gaulle and the State Reform Commission, whose work had already begun, were using the old Declarations of 1789 and 1793 as the starting points of their proposed constitutional reforms. Her infinitely more radical view was that the very idea of rights was too weak and diffuse to be of any use and should be replaced by something else.

It is possible that some of the ideas introduced in this work were not rejected out of hand. Indeed, in the Declaration published in the press of the Free French movement on 4 August 1943, a list of rights is accompanied by a corresponding list of duties or obligations.

PROFESSION OF FAITH

There is a reality outside the world, that is to say, outside space and time, outside man's mental universe, outside any sphere whatsoever that is accessible to human faculties.

Corresponding to this reality, at the centre of the human heart, is the longing for an absolute good, a longing which is always there and is never appeased by any object in this world.

Another terrestrial manifestation of this reality lies in the absurd and insoluble contradictions which are always the terminus of human thought when it moves exclusively in this world.

Just as the reality of this world is the sole foundation of facts, so that other reality is the sole foundation of good.

That reality is the unique source of all the good that can exist in this world: that is to say, all beauty, all truth, all justice, all legitimacy, all order, and all human behaviour that is mindful of obligations.

Those minds whose attention and love are turned towards that reality are the sole intermediary through which good can descend from there and come among men.

Although it is beyond the reach of any human faculties, man has the power of turning his attention and love towards it.

Nothing can ever justify the assumption that any man, whoever he may be, has been deprived of this power.

It is a power which is only real in this world in so far as it is exercised. The sole condition for exercising it is consent.

This act of consent may be expressed, or it may not be, even tacitly; it may not be clearly conscious, although it has really taken place in the soul. Very often it is verbally expressed although it has not in fact taken place. But whether expressed or not, the one condition suffices: that it shall in fact have taken place.

To anyone who does actually consent to directing his attention and love beyond the world, towards the reality that exists outside the reach of all human faculties, it is given to succeed in doing so. In that case, sooner or later, there descends upon him a part of the good, which shines through him upon all that surrounds him.

The combination of these two facts – the longing in the depth of the heart for absolute good, and the power, though only latent, of directing attention and love to a reality beyond the world and of receiving good from it – constitutes a link which attaches every man without exception to that other reality.

Whoever recognizes that reality recognizes also that link. Because of it, he holds every human being without any exception as something sacred to which he is bound to show respect.

This is the only possible motive for universal respect towards all human beings. Whatever formulation of belief or disbelief a man may choose to make, if his heart inclines him to feel this respect, then he in fact also recognizes a reality other than this world's reality. Whoever in fact does not feel this respect is alien to that other reality also.

The reality of the world we live in is composed of variety. Unequal objects unequally solicit our attention. Certain people personally attract our attention, either through the hazard of circumstances or some chance affinity. For the lack of such circumstance or affinity other people remain unidentified. They escape our attention or, at the most, it only sees them as items of a collectivity.

If our attention is entirely confined to this world it is entirely subject to the effect of these inequalities, which it is all the less able to resist because it is unaware of it.

It is impossible to feel equal respect for things that are in fact unequal unless the respect is given to something that is identical in all of them. Men are unequal in all their relations with the things of this world, without exception. The only thing that is identical in all men is the presence of a link with the reality outside the world.

All human beings are absolutely identical in so far as they can be thought of as consisting of a centre, which is an unquenchable desire for good, surrounded by an accretion of psychical and bodily matter.

Only by really directing the attention beyond the world can there be real contact with this central and essential fact of human nature. Only an attention thus directed possesses the faculty, always identical in all cases, of irradiating with light any human being whatsoever.

If anyone possesses this faculty, then his attention is in reality directed beyond the world, whether he is aware of it or not.

The link which attaches the human being to the reality outside the world is, like the reality itself, beyond the reach of human faculties. The respect that it inspires as soon as it is recognized cannot be expressed to it.

This respect cannot, in this world, find any form of direct expression. But unless it is expressed it has no existence. There is a possibility of indirect expression for it.

The respect inspired by the link between man and the reality outside the world can be expressed to that part of man which exists in the reality of this world.

The reality of this world is necessity. The part of man which is in this world is the part which is in bondage to necessity and subject to the misery of need.

The one possibility of indirect expression of respect for the human being is offered by men's needs, the needs of the soul and of the body, in this world.

It is based upon the connection in human nature between the desire for good, which is the essence of man, and his sensibility. There is never any justification for doubting the existence in any man of this connection.

Because of it, when a man's life is destroyed or damaged by some wound or privation of soul or body, which is due to other men's actions or negligence, it is not only his sensibility that suffers but also his aspiration towards the good. Therefore there has been sacrilege towards that which is sacred in him.

On the other hand, there are cases where it is only a man's sensibility that is affected; for example, where his wound or privation is solely the result of the blind working of natural forces, or where he recognizes that the people who seem to be making him suffer are far from bearing him any ill will, but are acting solely in obedience to a necessity which he also acknowledges.

The possibility of indirect expression of respect for the human being is the basis of obligation. Obligation is concerned with the needs in this world of the souls and bodies of human beings, whoever they may be. For each need there is a corresponding obligation; for each obligation a corresponding need. There is no other kind of obligation, so far as human affairs are concerned.

If there seem to be others, they are either false or else it is only by error that they have not been classed among the obligations mentioned.

Anyone whose attention and love are really directed towards the reality outside the world recognizes at the same time that he is bound, both in public and private life, by the single and permanent obligation to remedy, according to his responsibilities and to the extent of his power, all the privations of soul and body which are liable to destroy or damage the earthly life of any human being whatsoever.

This obligation cannot legitimately be held to be limited by the insufficiency of power or the nature of the responsibilities until everything possible has been done to explain the necessity of the limitation to those who will suffer by it; the explanation must be completely truthful and must be such as to make it possible for them to acknowledge the necessity.

No combination of circumstances ever cancels this obligation. If there are circumstances which seem to cancel it as regards a certain man or category of men, they impose it in fact all the more imperatively.

The thought of this obligation is present to all men, but in very different forms and in very varying degrees of clarity. Some men are more and some are less inclined to accept – or to refuse – it as their rule of conduct.

Its acceptance is usually mixed with self-deception, and even when it is quite sincere it is not consistently acted upon. To refuse it is to become criminal.

The proportions of good and evil in any society depend partly upon the proportion of consent to that of refusal and partly upon the distribution of power between those who consent and those who refuse.

If any power of any kind is in the hands of a man who has

not given total, sincere, and enlightened consent to this obligation such power is misplaced.

If a man has wilfully refused to consent, then it is in itself a criminal activity for him to exercise any function, major or minor, public or private, which gives him control over people's lives. All those who, with knowledge of his mind, have acquiesced in his exercise of the function are accessories to the crime.

Any State whose whole official doctrine constitutes an incitement to this crime is itself wholly criminal. It can retain no trace of legitimacy.

Any State whose official doctrine is not primarily directed against this crime in all its forms is lacking in full legitimacy.

Any legal system which contains no provisions against this crime is without the essence of legality. Any legal system which provides against some forms of this crime but not others is without the full character of legality.

Any government whose members commit this crime, or authorize it in their subordinates, has betrayed its function.

Any collectivity, institution, or form of collective life whatsoever whose normal functioning implies or induces the practice of this crime is convicted *ipso facto* of illegitimacy and should be reformed or abolished.

Any man who has any degree of influence, however small, upon public opinion becomes an accessory to this crime if he refrains from denouncing it whenever it comes to his knowledge, or if he purposely avoids knowledge of it in order not to have to denounce it.

A country is not innocent of this crime if public opinion, being free to express itself, does not denounce any current examples of it, or if, freedom of expression being forbidden, the crime is not denounced clandestinely.

It is the aim of public life to arrange that all forms of power are entrusted, so far as possible, to men who effectively consent to be bound by the obligation towards all human beings which lies upon everyone, and who understand the obligation.

Law is the totality of the permanent provisions for making this aim effective.

To understand the obligation involves two things: understanding the principle and understanding its application.

Since it is with human needs in this world that the application is concerned, it is for the intelligence to conceive the idea of need and to discern, discriminate, and enumerate, with all the accuracy of which it is capable, the earthly needs of the soul and of the body.

This is a study which is permanently open to revision.

STATEMENT OF OBLIGATIONS

A concrete conception of obligation towards human beings and a subdivision of it into a number of obligations is obtained by conceiving the earthly needs of the body and of the human soul. Each need entails a corresponding obligation.

The needs of a human being are sacred. Their satisfaction cannot be subordinated either to reasons of state, or to any consideration of money, nationality, race, or colour, or to the moral or other value attributed to the human being in question, or to any consideration whatsoever.

There is no legitimate limit to the satisfaction of the needs of a human being except as imposed by necessity and by the needs of other human beings. The limit is only legitimate if the needs of all human beings receive an equal degree of attention.

The fundamental obligation towards human beings is subdivided into a number of concrete obligations by the enumeration of the essential needs of the human being. Each need is related to an obligation, and each obligation to a need.

The needs in question are earthly needs, for those are the only ones that man can satisfy. They are needs of the soul as well as of the body; for the soul has needs whose non-satisfaction leaves it in a state analogous to that of a starved or mutilated body.

The principal needs of the human body are food, warmth, sleep, health, rest, exercise, fresh air.

The needs of the soul can for the most part be listed in pairs of opposites which balance and complete one another.

The human soul has need of equality and of hierarchy.

Equality is the public recognition, effectively expressed in institutions and manners, of the principle that an equal degree of attention is due to the needs of all human beings. Hierarchy is the scale of responsibilities. Since attention is inclined to direct itself upwards and remain fixed, special provisions are necessary to ensure the effective compatibility of equality and hierarchy.

The human soul has need of consented obedience and of liberty.

Consented obedience is what one concedes to an authority because one judges it to be legitimate. It is not possible in relation to a political power established by conquest or *coup d'état* nor to an economic power based upon money.

Liberty is the power of choice within the latitude left between the direct constraint of natural forces and the authority accepted as legitimate. The latitude should be sufficiently wide for liberty to be more than a fiction, but it should include only what is innocent and should never be wide enough to permit certain kinds of crime.

The human soul has need of truth and of freedom of expression.

The need for truth requires that intellectual culture should be universally accessible, and that it should be able to be acquired in an environment neither physically remote nor psychologically alien. It requires that in the domain of thought there should never be any physical or moral pressure exerted for any purpose other than an exclusive concern for truth; which implies an absolute ban on all propaganda without exception. It calls for protection against error and lies; which means that every avoidable material falsehood publicly asserted becomes a punishable offence. It calls for public health measures against poisons in the domain of thought.

But, in order to be exercised, the intelligence requires to

be free to express itself without control by any authority. There must therefore be a domain of pure intellectual research, separate but accessible to all, where no authority intervenes.

The human soul has need of some solitude and privacy and also of some social life.

The human soul has need of both personal property and collective property.

Personal property never consists in the possession of a sum of money, but in the ownership of concrete objects like a house, a field, furniture, tools, which seem to the soul to be an extension of itself and of the body. Justice requires that personal property, in this sense, should be, like liberty, inalienable.

Collective property is not defined by a legal title but by the feeling among members of a human milieu that certain objects are like an extension or development of the milieu. This feeling is only possible in certain objective conditions.

The existence of a social class defined by the lack of personal and collective property is as shameful as slavery.

The human soul has need of punishment and of honour.

Whenever a human being, through the commission of a crime, has become exiled from good, he needs to be reintegrated with it through suffering. The suffering should be inflicted with the aim of bringing the soul to recognize freely some day that its infliction was just. This reintegration with the good is what punishment is. Every man who is innocent, or who has finally expiated guilt, needs to be recognized as honourable to the same extent as anyone else.

The human soul has need of disciplined participation in a common task of public value, and it has need of personal initiative within this participation.

The human soul has need of security and also of risk. The fear of violence or of hunger or of any other extreme evil is a sickness of the soul. The boredom produced by a complete absence of risk is also a sickness of the soul.

The human soul needs above all to be rooted in several natural environments and to make contact with the universe through them.

Examples of natural human environments are: a man's

country, and places where his language is spoken, and places with a culture or a historical past which he shares, and his professional milieu, and his neighbourhood.

Everything which has the effect of uprooting a man or of preventing him from becoming rooted is criminal.

Any place where the needs of human beings are satisfied can be recognized by the fact that there is a flowering of fraternity, joy, beauty, and happiness. Wherever people are lonely and turned in on themselves, wherever there is sadness or ugliness, there are privations that need remedying.

PRACTICAL APPLICATION

For this statement to become the practical inspiration of the country's life, the first condition is that it should be adopted by the people with that intention.

The second condition is that anyone who wields or desires to wield any power of any kind – political, administrative, legal, economic, technical, spiritual, or other – should have to pledge himself to adopt it as his practical rule of conduct.

In such cases the equal and universal character of the obligation is to some extent modified by the particular responsibilities attaching to a particular office. It would therefore be necessary to amplify the pledge with the words: '... paying especial attention to the needs of the human beings who are in my charge.'

The violation of such a pledge, either in word or deed, should always in principle be punishable. But, in most cases, the institutions and public morals which would make such punishment possible would take several generations to create.

Assent to this Statement implies a continual effort to bring such institutions and such morals into existence as rapidly as possible.

From *Selected Essays 1934–43 by Simone Weil*, chosen and translated by Richard Rees, Oxford University Press, London, 1962.

ATTENTION AND WILL

———————— ⓒ ————————

We do not have to understand new things, but by dint of patience, effort and method to come to understand with our whole self the truths which are evident.

Stages of belief. The most commonplace truth when it floods the *whole soul*, is like a revelation.

We have to try to cure our faults by attention and not by will.

The will only controls a few movements of a few muscles, and these movements are associated with the idea of the change of position of nearby objects. I can will to put my hand flat on the table. If inner purity, inspiration or truth of thought were necessarily associated with attitudes of this kind, they might be the object of will. As this is not the case, we can only beg for them. To beg for them is to believe that we have a Father in heaven. Or should we cease to desire them? What could be worse? Inner supplication is the only reasonable way, for it avoids stiffening muscles which have nothing to do with the matter. What could be more stupid than to tighten up our muscles and set our jaws about virtue, or poetry, or the solution of a problem. Attention is something quite different.

Pride is a tightening up of this kind. There is a lack of grace (we can give the word its double meaning here) in the proud man. It is the result of a mistake.

Attention, taken to its highest degree, is the same thing as prayer. It presupposes faith and love.

Absolutely unmixed attention is prayer.

If we turn our minds towards the good, it is impossible that little by little the whole soul will not be attracted thereto in spite of itself.

Extreme attention is what constitutes the creative faculty in man and the only extreme attention is religious. The amount of creative genius in any period is strictly in proportion to the amount of extreme attention and thus of authentic religion at that period.

The wrong way of seeking. The attention fixed on a problem. Another phenomenon due to horror of the void. We do not want to have lost our labour. The heat of the chase. We must not want to find: as in the case of an excessive devotion, we become dependent on the object of our efforts. We need an outward reward which chance sometimes provides and which we are ready to accept at the price of a deformation of the truth.

It is only effort without desire (not attached to an object) which infallibly contains a reward.

To draw back before the object we are pursuing. Only an indirect method is effective. We do nothing if we have not first drawn back.

By pulling at the bunch, we make all the grapes fall to the ground.

There are some kinds of effort which defeat their own object (example: the soured disposition of certain pious females, false asceticism, certain sorts of self-devotion, etc.). Others are always useful, even if they do not meet with success.

How are we to distinguish between them?

Perhaps in this way: some efforts are always accompanied by the (false) negation of our inner wretchedness; with others the attention is continually concentrated on the distance there is between what we are and what we love.

Love is the teacher of gods and men, for no one learns without desiring to learn. Truth is sought not because it is truth but because it is good.

Attention is bound up with desire. Not with the will but with desire – or more exactly, consent.

We liberate energy in ourselves, but it constantly reattaches itself. How are we to liberate it entirely? We have to desire that it should be done in us – to desire it truly – simply to desire it, not to try to accomplish it. For every attempt in that direction is vain and has to be dearly paid for. In such a work all that I call 'I' has to be passive. Attention alone – that attention which is so full that the 'I' disappears – is required of me. I have to deprive all that I call 'I' of the light of my attention and turn it on to that which cannot be conceived.

The capacity to drive a thought away once and for all is the gateway to eternity. The infinite in an instant.

As regards temptations, we must follow the example of the truly chaste woman who, when the seducer speaks to her, makes no answer and pretends not to hear him.

We should be indifferent to good and evil but, when we are indifferent, that is to say when we project the light of our attention equally on both, the good gains the day. This phenomenon comes about automatically. There lies the essential grace. And it is the definition, the criterion of good.

A divine inspiration operates infallibly, irresistibly, if we do not turn away our attention, if we do not refuse it. There is not a choice to be made in its favour, it is enough not to refuse to recognize that it exists.

The attention turned with love towards God (or in a lesser degree, towards anything which is truly beautiful) makes certain things impossible for us. Such is the non-acting action of prayer in the soul. There are ways of behaviour which would veil such attention should they be indulged in and which, reciprocally, this attention puts out of the question.

As soon as we have a point of eternity in the soul, we have nothing more to do but to take care of it, for it will grow of itself like a seed. It is necessary to surround it with an armed guard, waiting in stillness, and to nourish it with the contemplation of numbers, of fixed and exact relationships.
    We nourish the changeless which is in the soul by the contemplation of that which is unchanging in the body.

Writing is like giving birth: we cannot help making the supreme effort. But we also act in like fashion. I need have no fear of not making the supreme effort – provided only that I am honest with myself and that I pay attention.

The poet produces the beautiful by fixing his attention on something real. It is the same with the act of love. To know that this man who is hungry and thirsty really exists as much as I do – that is enough, the rest follows of itself.
    The authentic and pure values – truth, beauty and goodness – in the activity of a human being are the result of one and the same act, a certain application of the full attention to the object.
    Teaching should have no aim but to prepare, by training the attention, for the possibility of such an act.
    All the other advantages of instruction are without interest.

Studies and faith. Prayer being only attention in its pure form and studies being a form of gymnastics of the attention, each school exercise should be a refraction of spiritual life.

There must be method in it. A certain way of doing a Latin prose, a certain way of tackling a problem in geometry (and not just any way) make up a system of gymnastics of the attention calculated to give it a greater aptitude for prayer.

Method for understanding images, symbols, etc. Not to try to interpret them, but to look at them till the light suddenly dawns.
    Generally speaking, a method for the exercise of the intelligence, which consists of looking.
    Application of this rule for the discrimination between the real and the illusory. In our sense perceptions, if we are not sure of what we see we change our position while looking, and what is real becomes evident. In the inner life, time takes the place of space. With time we are altered, and, if as we change we keep our gaze directed towards the same thing, in the end illusions are scattered and the real becomes visible. This is on condition that the attention be a looking and not an attachment.

When a struggle goes on between the will attached to some obligation and a bad desire, there is a wearing away of the energy attached to good. We have to endure the biting of the desire passively, as we do a suffering which brings home to us our wretchedness, and we have to keep our attention turned towards the good. Then the quality of our energy is raised to a higher degree.
    We must steal away the energy from our desires by taking away from them their temporal orientation.

Our desires are infinite in their pretensions but limited by the energy from which they proceed. That is why with the help of grace we can become their master and finally destroy them by attrition. As soon as this has been clearly understood, we have virtually conquered them, if we keep our attention in contact with this truth.

Video meliora . . . In such states, it seems as though we were thinking of the good, and in a sense we are doing so, but we are not thinking of its possibility.

It is incontestable that the void which we grasp with the pincers of contradiction is from on high, for we grasp it the better the more we sharpen our natural faculties of intelligence, will and love. The void which is from below is that into which we fall when we allow our natural faculties to become atrophied.

Experience of the transcendent: this seems contradictory, and yet the transcendent can be known only through contact since our faculties are unable to prevent it.

Solitude. Where does its value lie? For in solitude we are in the presence of mere matter (even the sky, the stars, the moon, trees in blossom), things of less value (perhaps) than a human spirit. Its value lies in the greater possibility of attention. If we could be attentive to the same degree in the presence of a human being. . . .

We can only know one thing about God – that he is what we are not. Our wretchedness alone is an image of this. The more we contemplate it, the more we contemplate him.

Sin is nothing else but the failure to recognize human wretchedness. It is unconscious wretchedness and for that very reason guilty wretchedness. The story of Christ is the experimental proof that human wretchedness is irreducible, that it is as great in the absolutely sinless man as in the sinner. But in him who is without sin it is enlightened. . . .

The recognition of human wretchedness is difficult for whoever is rich and powerful because he is almost invincibly led to believe that he is something. It is equally difficult for the man in miserable circumstances because he is almost invincibly led to believe that the rich and powerful man is something.

It is not the fault which constitutes mortal sin, but the degree of light in the soul when the fault, whatever it may be, is accomplished.

Purity is the power to contemplate defilement.

Extreme purity can contemplate both the pure and the impure: impurity can do neither: the pure frightens it, the impure absorbs it. It has to have a mixture.

From *Gravity and Grace*, translated by Emma Craufurd, Routledge and Kegan Paul, London, 1952. Originally published as *La Pesanteur et la Grâce*, Plon, Paris, 1947.

THE POWER OF WORDS

———————— ◉ ————————

Simone Weil wrote this essay when she was twenty-five, during the year of her return from the Spanish Civil War. In that year, it was rumoured that Germany was sending troops into Morocco and a great stir of jingoistic fury was created as a result in the French press. She wrote a scathing attack on French foreign policy pointing out the patent absurdity and falseness of the idea of 'protection' not only in that part of North Africa but in other parts of the globe as well.

She was suffering very badly from her old headaches at the time and was eventually admitted to hospital on her way to Italy, which she was now longing to see. She had promised herself a treat there and memories of the trip were to give her immense pleasure and consolation till the end of her life. She wrote angrily of surrealism that it was the literary and artistic equivalent to the sacking of a city. In this brilliant essay she produced a powerful indictment of 'war based on no definable object'. The power of words such as 'national interest' is the power of 'myths and monsters' it is quite possible to destroy, provided the idea of limit is introduced and provided the idea of the victory of an absolute good over an equally illusory absolute evil is seen to be invalid. Earlier she had written:

I predict ... that we shall enter a period in which one will see throughout the country the most incredible absurdities – and they will appear natural. There will be less and less civilian life. Military preoccupations will more and more dominate all the everyday aspects of existence ...

Later, she wrote:

The effort of expression has a bearing not only on the form but on the thought and on the whole inner being. So long as bare simplicity of expression is not attained, the thought has not touched or even come near to, true greatness ... The real way of writing is to write as we translate. When we translate a text written in some foreign language, we do not seek to add anything to it; on the contrary, we are scrupulously careful not to add anything to it. That is how we have to translate a text which is not written down.

The relative security we enjoy in this age, thanks to a technology which gives us a measure of control over nature, is more than cancelled out by the dangers of destruction and massacre in conflicts between groups of men.[1] If the danger is grave it is no doubt partly because of the power of the destructive weapons supplied by our techniques; but these weapons do not fire themselves, and it is dishonest to blame inert matter for a situation in which the entire responsibility is our own. Common to all our most threatening troubles is one characteristic which might appear reassuring to a superficial eye, but which is in reality the great danger: *they are conflicts with no definable objective*. The whole of history bears witness that it is precisely such conflicts that are the most bitter. It may be that a clear recognition of this paradox is one of the keys to history; that it is the key to our own period there is no doubt.

In any struggle for a well-defined stake each combatant

[1]   This essay first appeared in *Nouveaux Cahiers*, 1 and 15 April 1937, under the title: *Ne recommençons pas la guerre de Troie*. Simone Weil at one time held pacifist opinions, which may have influenced certain passages in this essay. They do not appear in her writing after 1939 [R. Rees].

can weigh the value of the stake against the probable cost of the struggle and decide how great an effort it justifies; indeed, it is generally not difficult to arrive at a compromise which is more advantageous to both contending parties than even a successful battle. But when there is no objective there is no longer any common measure or proportion; no balance or comparison of alternatives is possible, and compromise is inconceivable. In such circumstances the importance of the battle can only be measured by the sacrifices it demands, and from this it follows that the sacrifices already incurred are a perpetual argument for new ones. Thus there would never be any reason to stop killing and dying, except that there is fortunately a limit to human endurance. This paradox is so extreme as to defy analysis. And yet the most perfect example of it is known to every so-called educated man, but, by a sort of taboo, we read it without understanding.

The Greeks and Trojans massacred one another for ten years on account of Helen. Not one of them except the dilettante warrior Paris cared two straws about her; all of them agreed in wishing she had never been born. The person of Helen was so obviously out of scale with this gigantic struggle that in the eyes of all she was no more than the symbol of what was really at stake; but the real issue was never defined by anyone, nor could it be, because it did not exist. For the same reason it could not be calculated. Its importance was simply imagined as corresponding to the deaths incurred and the further massacres expected; and this implied an importance beyond all reckoning. Hector foresaw that his city would be destroyed, his father and brothers massacred, his wife degraded to a slavery worse than death; Achilles knew that he was condemning his father to the miseries and humiliations of a defenceless old age; all were aware that their long absence at the war would bring ruin on their homes; yet no one felt that the cost was too great, because they were all in pursuit of a literal non-entity whose only value was in the price paid for it. When the Greeks began to think of returning to their homes it

seemed to Minerva and Ulysses that a reminder of the sufferings of their dead comrades was a sufficient argument to
put them to shame. They used, in fact, exactly the same
arguments as three thousand years later were employed by
Poincaré to castigate the proposal for a negotiated peace.
Nowadays the popular mind has an explanation for this
sombre zeal in piling up useless ruin; it imagines the
machinations of economic interests. But there is no need to
look so far. In the time of Homer's Greeks there were no
organized bronze manufacturers or international cartels.
The truth is that the role which we attribute to mysterious
economic oligarchies was attributed by Homer's contemporaries to the gods of the Greek mythology. But there is no
need of gods or conspiracies to make men rush headlong
into the most absurd disasters. Human nature suffices.

For the clear-sighted, there is no more distressing symptom
of this truth than the unreal character of most of the conflicts that are taking place today. They have even less reality
than the war between the Greeks and Trojans. At the heart
of the Trojan War there was at least a woman and, what is
more, a woman of perfect beauty. For our contemporaries
the role of Helen is played by words with capital letters. If
we grasp one of these words, all swollen with blood and
tears, and squeeze it, we find it is empty. Words with
content and meaning are not murderous. If one of them
occasionally becomes associated with bloodshed, it is rather
by chance than by inevitability, and the resulting action is
generally controlled and efficacious. But when empty words
are given capital letters, then, on the slightest pretext, men
will begin shedding blood for them and piling up ruin in
their name, without effectively grasping anything to which
they refer, since what they refer to can never have any
reality, for the simple reason that they mean nothing. In
these conditions, the only definition of success is to crush a
rival group of men who have a hostile word on their banners;
for it is a characteristic of these empty words that each of
them has its complementary antagonist. It is true, of course,
that not all of these words are intrinsically meaningless;

some of them do have meaning if one takes the trouble to define them properly. But when a word is properly defined it loses its capital letter and can no longer serve either as a banner or as a hostile slogan; it becomes simply a sign, helping us to grasp some concrete reality or concrete objective, or method of activity. To clarify thought, to discredit the intrinsically meaningless words, and to define the use of others by precise analysis – to do this, strange though it may appear, might be a way of saving human lives.

★

Our age seems almost entirely unfitted for such a task. The glossy surface of our civilization hides a real intellectual decadence. There is no area in our minds reserved for superstition, such as the Greeks had in their mythology; and superstition, under cover of an abstract vocabulary, has revenged itself by invading the entire realm of thought. Our science is like a store filled with the most subtle intellectual devices for solving the most complex problems, and yet we are almost incapable of applying the elementary principles of rational thought. In every sphere, we seem to have lost the very elements of intelligence: the ideas of limit, measure, degree, proportion, relation, comparison, contingency, interdependence, interrelation of means and ends. To keep to the social level, our political universe is peopled exclusively by myths and monsters; all it contains is absolutes and abstract entities. This is illustrated by all the words of our political and social vocabulary: nation, security, capitalism, communism, fascism, order, authority, property, democracy. We never use them in phrases such as: There is democracy *to the extent that* ... or: There is capitalism *in so far as* ... The use of expressions like 'to the extent that' is beyond our intellectual capacity. Each of these words seems to represent for us an absolute reality, unaffected by conditions, or an absolute objective, independent of methods of action, or an absolute evil; and at the same time we make all these words mean, successively or simultaneously, anything whatsoever. Our lives are lived, in actual fact, among changing, varying realities, subject to the casual play of external necessities, and modifying themselves according to specific conditions within specific limits; and yet we act and strive and sacrifice ourselves and others by reference to fixed and isolated abstractions which cannot possibly be related either to one another or to any concrete facts. In this so-called age of technicians, the only battles we know how to fight are battles against windmills.

So it is easy to find examples of lethal absurdity wherever one looks. The prime specimen is the antagonism between nations. People often try to explain this as a simple cover for capitalist rivalries; but in so doing they ignore a glaringly obvious fact, namely, that the world-wide and complex system of capitalist rivalries and wars and alliances in no way corresponds to the world's division into nations. Two French groups, in the form of limited companies, for example, may find themselves opposed to one another while each of them is in alliance with a German group. The German steel industry may be regarded with hostility by producers of steel goods in France; but it makes little difference to the mining companies whether the iron of Lorraine is worked in France or Germany; and the wine-growers, manufacturers of Parisian articles, and others have an interest in the prosperity of German industry. In the light of these elementary truths the current explanation of international rivalry breaks down. Whoever insists that nationalism is always a cover for capitalist greed should specify whose greed. The mining companies'? The electricity companies'? The steel magnates'? The textile industry's? The banks'? It cannot be all of them, because their interests do not coincide; and if one is referring only to a minority of them, then one must show how it is that this minority has got control of the State. It is true that the policy of a State at any given moment always coincides with the interests of some sector of capitalism, and this offers an explanation whose very superficiality makes it applicable everywhere. But in view of the international circulation of capital it is not clear why a capitalist should look to his own State for protection rather than to some foreign State, or why he should not find it as easy to use pressure and influence with foreign statesmen as with those of his own country. The world's economic structure coincides with its political structure only in so far as States exert their authority in economic affairs; and, moreover, the way they use this authority is not explicable solely in terms of economic interest. If we examine the term 'national interest' we find it does not even mean the interest of capitalist business. 'A man thinks he is dying for his country,' said Anatole France, 'but he is dying for a few industrialists.' But even that is saying too much. What one dies for is not even so substantial and tangible as an industrialist.

The national interest cannot be defined as a common interest of the great industrial, commercial, and financial companies of a country, because there is no such common interest; nor can it be defined as the life, liberty, and well-being of the citizens, because they are continually being adjured to sacrifice their well-being, their liberty, and their lives to the national interest. In the end, a study of modern history leads to the conclusion that the national interest of every State consists in its capacity to make war. In 1911 France nearly went to war for Morocco; but why was Morocco so important? Because the populations of North Africa would make a reserve of cannon fodder; and because, for the purpose of war, a country needs to make its economy as self-supporting as possible in raw materials and markets. What a country calls its vital economic interests are not the things which enable its citizens to live, but the things which enable it to make war; petrol is much more likely than wheat to be a cause of international conflict. Thus when war is waged it is for the purpose of safeguarding or increasing one's capacity to make war. International politics are wholly involved in this vicious circle. What is called national prestige consists in behaving always in such a way as to demoralize other nations by giving them the impression that, if it comes to war, one would certainly defeat them. What is called national security is an imaginary state of affairs in which one would retain the capacity to make war while depriving all other countries of it. It amounts to this, that a self-respecting nation is ready for anything, including war, except for a renunciation of its option to make war. But why is it so essential to be able to make war? No one knows, any more than the Trojans knew why it was necessary for them to keep Helen. That is why the good intentions of peace-loving statesmen are so ineffectual. If the countries were divided by a real opposition of interests, it would be possible to arrive at satisfactory compromises. But when economic and political interests have no meaning apart from war, how can they be peacefully reconciled? It is the very concept of the nation that needs to be suppressed – or rather, the manner in which the word is used. For the word national and the expressions of which it forms part are empty of all meaning; their only content is millions of corpses, and orphans, and disabled men, and tears and despair.

Another good example of murderous absurdity is the opposition between fascism and communism. The fact that this opposition constitutes today a double threat of civil war and world war is perhaps the gravest of all our symptoms of intellectual atrophy, because one has only to examine the present-day meaning of the two words to discover two almost identical political and social conceptions. In each of them the State seizes control of almost every department of individual and social life; in each there is the same frenzied militarization, and the same artificial unanimity, obtained by coercion, in favour of a single party which identifies itself with the State and derives its character from this false identification, and finally there is the same serfdom imposed upon the working masses in place of the ordinary wage system. No two nations are more similar in structure than Germany and Russia, each threatening an international crusade against the other and each pretending to see the other as the Beast of the Apocalypse. Therefore one can safely assert that the opposition between fascism and communism is strictly meaningless. Victory for fascism can only mean extermination of the communists and victory for communism extermination of the fascists. In these circumstances it follows, of course, that anti-fascism and anti-communism are also meaningless. The anti-fascist position is this: Anything rather than fascism; anything, including fascism, so long as it is labelled communism. And the anti-communist position: Anything rather than communism; anything, including communism, so long as it is labelled fascism. For such a noble cause everyone in either camp is resolved to die, and above all to kill. In Berlin, in the summer of 1932, it was common to see a little group of people gather around two workmen or two petty bourgeois, one a communist and the other a Nazi, who were arguing. After a time it always became clear to both disputants that they were defending exactly the same programme; and this made their heads swim, but it only exacerbated in each of them his hatred for an opponent separated from him by such a gulf as to remain an enemy even when expressing the same ideas. That was four and a half years ago; the Nazis are still torturing German communists in the concentration camps today, and it is possible that France is threatened with a war of extermination between anti-fascists and anti-communists. If such a war took place it would make the Trojan war look perfectly reasonable by comparison; for even if the Greek poet was wrong who said that there was only Helen's phantom at Troy, a phantom Helen is a substantial reality compared to the distinction between fascism and communism.

The distinction between dictatorship and democracy, however, which is related to that between order and freedom, is indeed an example of a real opposition. Nevertheless, it loses its meaning if we see each of the two terms as a thing-in-itself, as is usually done nowadays, instead of seeing it as a point of reference for judging the character of a social structure. It is clear that neither absolute dictatorship nor absolute democracy exists anywhere, and that every

social organism everywhere is always a compound of democracy and dictatorship in different proportions; it is clear,
too, that the extent to which there is democracy is defined
by the relations between different parts of the social mechanism and upon the conditions which control its functioning; it is therefore upon these relations and these conditions
that we should try to act. Instead of which we generally
imagine that dictatorship or democracy are intrinsically inherent in certain groups of men, whether nations or parties,
so that we become obsessed with the desire to crush one or
other of these groups, according to whether we are tem-
peramentally more attached to order or to liberty. Many
Frenchmen, for example, believe in all good faith that a
military victory for France over Germany would be a victory for democracy. As they see it, freedom inheres in the
French nation and tyranny in the German, in much the
same way that for Molière's contemporaries there was a
dormitive virtue inherent in opium. If a day comes when
the requirements of so-called 'national defence' transform
France into a fortified camp in which the whole nation is
totally subjected to the military authority, and if this transformed France goes to war with Germany, then these
Frenchmen will allow themselves to be killed, having first
killed as many Germans as possible, in the touching belief
that their blood is being shed for democracy. It does not
occur to them that dictatorship arose in Germany as the
result of certain conditions and that an alteration of those
conditions, in such a way as to make possible some relax-
ation of the State authority in Germany, might be more
effective than killing the young men of Berlin and Hamburg.

Another example: suppose one dared to suggest to any
party man the idea of an armistice in Spain. If he is a man of
the right he will indignantly reply that the fight must continue until the forces of order are triumphant and anarchy is
crushed; if he is a man of the left he will reply with equal
indignation that the fight must continue until the people's
freedom and well-being are assured and the oppressors and
exploiters crushed. The man of the right forgets that no

political regime, of whatever kind, involves disorders re-
motely comparable to those of a civil war, with its deliberate
destruction, its non-stop massacre in the firing-line, its
slowing down of production, and the hundreds of crimes it
permits every day, on both sides, by the fact that any
hooligan can get hold of a gun. The man of the left, for his
part, forgets that even on his own side liberty is suppressed
far more drastically by the necessities of civil war than it
would be by the coming to power of a party of the extreme
right; in other words, he forgets that there is a state of siege,
that militarization is in force both at the front and behind it,
that there is a police terror, and that the individual has no
security and no protection against arbitrary injustice; he
forgets, too, that the cost of the war, and the ruin it causes,
and the slowing down of production condemn the people to
a long period of far more cruel privation than their exploiters would. And both of them forget that during the
long months of civil war an almost identical regime has
grown up on both sides. Each of them has unconsciously
lost sight of his ideal and replaced it by an entity without
substance. For each, the victory of what he still calls his
idea can no longer mean anything except the extermination
of the enemy; and each of them will scorn any suggestion of
peace, replying to it with the same knock-out argument as
Minerva in Homer and Poincaré in 1917: 'The dead do not
wish it.'[1]

★

Of all the conflicts which set groups of men against one
another the most legitimate and serious – one could perhaps
say, the only serious one – is what is called today the *class
struggle* (an expression which needs clarifying). But this is
only true in so far as it is not confused by imaginary entities
which obstruct controlled action, lead efforts astray, and
entail the risk of ineradicable hatred, idiotic destructiveness,

---

[1] Simone Weil was one of the first foreign volunteers in the Spanish Civil War.
She went to the Aragon front with the anarchist militia in August 1936 [R. Rees].

and senseless butchery. What is well founded, vital, and essential is the eternal struggle of those who obey against those who command when the mechanism of social power involves a disregard for the human dignity of the former. It is an eternal struggle because those who command are always inclined, whether they know it or not, to trample on the human dignity of those below them. The function of command cannot, except in special cases, be exercised in a way that respects the personal humanity of those who carry out orders. When exercised as though men were objects, and unresisting ones at that, it inevitably acts upon them as exceptionally pliable objects; for a man exposed to the threat of death, which is really the final sanction of all authority, can become more pliable than inert matter. So long as there is a stable social hierarchy, of whatever form, those at the bottom must struggle so as not to lose all the rights of a human being. But the resistance of those at the top, although it usually appears unjust, is also inspired by concrete motives. First, personal motives; for except in rather rare cases of generosity the privileged hate to lose any of their material and moral privileges. But there are also higher motives. To those in whom the functions of command are vested it seems to be their duty to defend order, without which no social life can survive; and the only order they conceive is the existing one. Nor are they entirely wrong, for until a different order has been, in fact, established no one can say with certainty that it is possible. It is just for this reason that social progress depends upon a pressure from below sufficient to change effectively the relations of power and thus to compel the actual establishment of new social relationships. The tension between pressure from below and resistance from above creates and maintains an unstable equilibrium, which defines at each moment the structure of a society. This tension is a struggle but not a war; and although it may in certain circumstances turn into a war, it does not inevitably do so. The story of the interminable and useless massacres around Troy is not our only legacy from antiquity; there is also the vigorous and concerted action of the Roman plebeians, who, without shedding a drop of blood, escaped from a condition verging upon slavery and obtained the institution of tribunes to guarantee their new rights. In exactly the same way the French workers, by occupying the factories, without violence, enforced the recognition of certain elementary rights and obtained elected delegates to guarantee them.

★

But early Rome had one important advantage over modern France. In social matters she knew nothing of abstract entities, or words in capitals, or words ending in -ism; nor any of those things which, with us, are liable to stultify the most serious efforts or to degrade the social struggle into a war as ruinous, as bloody, and as irrational in every way as a war between nations. On inspection, almost all the words and phrases of our political vocabulary turn out to be hollow. What, for example, can be the meaning of that slogan which was so popular at the recent elections – 'the fight against the trusts'? A trust is an economic monopoly in the hands of financial powers, which is used by them not in the public interest but in such a way as to increase their own influence. What is it that is wrong about this? The fact that a monopoly is serving as the instrument of a will-to-power uninterested in the public good. But it is not this fact that is attacked; what is attacked is the fact, which is in itself morally indifferent, that the will-to-power belongs to an economic oligarchy. The aim is to replace economic oligarchies by the State, which has a will-to-power of its own and is quite as little concerned with the public good; and a will-to-power, moreover, which is not economic but military and therefore much more dangerous to any good folk who have a taste for staying alive. And on the bourgeois side what on earth is the sense of objecting to State control in economic affairs if one accepts private monopolies which have all the economic and technical disadvantages of State monopolies and possibly some others as well? One could make a long list of pairs of complementary slogans of this kind, all of them equally unreal. The two considered above are relatively harmless, but this is not true of all of them.

★

For example, whatever can be in the heads of those for whom the word 'capitalism' signifies the absolute of evil? The society in which we live includes forms of coercion and oppression by which those who suffer from them are all too often overwhelmed; it includes the most grievous inequalities and unnecessary miseries. On the other hand, the economic character of this society consists in certain methods of production, consumption, and exchange, which are continually varying, however, and which depend upon certain fundamental relationships: between the production and the circulation of goods, between the circulation of goods and money, between money and production, between money and consumption. This whole interplay of varied and changing economic phenomena is arbitrarily converted into an abstraction, which defies all definition, and is then made responsible, under the name of capitalism, for every hardship endured by oneself or others. After that, it is only natural that any man of character should devote his life to the destruction of capitalism, or rather (it comes to the same thing) to revolution – for this negative meaning is the only one possessed today by the word revolution.

Since the 'destruction of capitalism' has no meaning – capitalism being an abstraction – and since it does not refer to any precise modifications that might be applied to the regime (such modifications are contemptuously dismissed as 'reforms'), the slogan can only imply the destruction of capitalists and, more generally, of everyone who does not call himself an opponent of capitalism. Apparently it is easier to kill, and even to die, than to ask ourselves a few quite simple questions like the following: Can the laws and conventions which control our present economic life be said to constitute a system? To what extent is this or that feature of our economic life necessarily connected with the others? To what extent would the modification of this or that economic law produce repercussions among the others? How far can the ills arising from the social relations which exist today be attributed to this or that convention and how far are they attributable to the totality of conventions of our economic life? How far are they attributable to other factors, either permanent factors which would persist after the transformation of the economic system or, on the contrary, factors which could be eliminated without putting an end to what is called the regime? What kind of hardships, either transitory or permanent, would necessarily be involved by the chosen method for transforming the regime? What new hardships might be introduced by the proposed new organization of society? If we gave serious thought to these problems we might reach the point where we could give some meaning to the assertion that capitalism is an evil; but we should mean only a relative evil, and the proposal to transform the regime would be only for the purpose of substituting a lesser evil. And the proposed transformation would be a clearly defined and limited one.

The same criticism is applicable in its entirety to those in the opposite camp, except that the concern for maintaining order replaces the concern about the sufferings of the depressed social classes and the instinct of conservation replaces the desire for change. The bourgeois always tend to regard anyone who wishes to put an end to capitalism, and sometimes even anyone who wants to reform it, as an agent of disorder; and they do so because they are ignorant as to what extent and in what circumstances the various economic relations, which are subsumed today under the general name of capitalism, are factors in preserving order. Many of them are in favour of changing nothing, because they do not know what modifications of the system may or may not be dangerous; they fail to realize that, since conditions are always changing, the refusal to modify the system is itself a modification which may be productive of disorders. Most of them appeal to economic laws as religiously as if they were the unwritten laws invoked by Antigone, and this although they can see them changing day by day in front of their eyes. The preservation of the capitalist regime is a meaningless expression, in their mouths, because they do not know what ought to be preserved, nor how much of it; all they can mean, in practice, is the suppression of everyone who wants to put an end to the regime. The struggle between the opponents and the defenders of capitalism is a struggle between innovators who do not know what innovation to make and conservatives who do not know what to conserve; it is a battle of blind men struggling in a void, and for that very reason it is liable to become a war of extermination. The same situation exists on a smaller scale in the struggle within any industrial firm. In general, the worker instinctively blames his employer for all the hardships of work in a factory; he does not ask himself whether under any other property system the management would not inflict some of the same hardships on him, or indeed exactly the same ones, or even perhaps some worse ones; nor does he ask himself how many of these hardships might be abolished, by abolishing their causes, without any alteration of the existing property system. He identifies the struggle 'against the boss' with the undying protest of the human being oppressed by too many hardships. The head of the firm, for his part, is rightly concerned to maintain his authority. But his authority is strictly limited to overall direction, to the due co-ordination of the branches of production, and to ensuring, with some compulsion if necessary, that the work is properly executed. Any industrial regime, of whatever kind, in which these functions of co-ordination and control can be effectively exercised is allowing sufficient authority to the heads of the firms. But the feeling of authority, in these men's minds, is especially connected with a certain atmosphere of deference and subservience which has no necessary connection with a high standard of work; and, above all, when they become aware of latent or overt opposition among their personnel they always attribute it to certain individuals, whereas in reality a spirit of revolt, whether loud or silent, aggressive or despairing, is always present wherever life is physically or morally oppressive. In the worker's mind the struggle 'against the boss' is confused with the assertion of human dignity, and in the manager's mind the struggle against the 'ringleaders' is confused with his duty to the job and his professional conscience. Both of them are tilting at windmills, so their efforts cannot be confined to reasonable objectives. When strikes are undertaken for clearly defined claims a settlement is attainable without too great difficulty, as we have sometimes seen; but we have also seen strikes which resembled wars, in the sense that neither side had any objective, strikes in which there were no real or tangible issues – apart from arrested production, deteriorating machines, destitution, want, weeping women, and hungry children; and such bitterness on both sides that any agreement seemed impossible. In events like these there are the seeds of civil war.

If we analysed in this way all the words and formulas which have served throughout history to call forth the spirit of self-sacrifice and cruelty combined, we should doubtless discover them all to be just as empty. And yet, all these bloodthirsty abstractions must have some sort of connection with real life; and indeed they have. It may be that there was only Helen's phantom at Troy, but the Greek and Trojan armies were not phantoms; and in the same way although there is no meaning in the word nation and the slogans in which it occurs, the different States with their offices, prisons, arsenals, barracks, and customs are real enough. The theoretical distinction between the two forms of totalitarian regime, fascism and communism, is imaginary, but in Germany in 1932 there existed very concretely two political organizations each of which wanted to achieve complete power and consequently to exterminate the other. A democratic party may gradually change into a party of dictatorship but it still remains distinct from the dictatorial party it is striving to suppress. France, for the purpose of defence against Germany, may submit in her turn to a totalitarian regime, but the French State and the German State will not cease to be two separate States. Both the destruction and the preservation of capitalism are meaningless slogans, but these slogans are supported by real organizations. Corresponding to each empty abstraction there is an actual human group, and any abstraction of which this is not true remains harmless. Conversely, any group wich has not secreted an abstract entity will probably not be dangerous. This particular kind of secretion is superbly illustrated by the 'Dr Knock' of Jules Romains with his maxim: 'Above the interest of the patient and the interest of the doctor stands the interest of Medicine.' It is pure comedy, because the medical profession has not so far secreted such an entity; it is always by organizations concerned with guarding or acquiring power that these entities are secreted. All the absurdities which make history look like a prolonged delirium have their root in one essential absurdity, which is the nature of power. The necessity for power is obvious, because life cannot be lived without order; but the allocation of power is arbitrary because all men are alike, or very nearly. Yet power must not seem to be arbitrarily allocated, because it will not then be recognized as power. Therefore prestige, which is illusion, is of the very essence of power. All power is based, in fact, upon the interrelation of human activities; but in order to be stable it must appear as something absolute and sacrosanct, both to those who wield and those who submit to it and also to other external powers. The conditions which ensure order are essentially contradictory, and men seem to be compelled to choose between the anarchy which goes with inadequate power and the wars of every kind which go with the preoccupation of prestige.

All the absurdities we have enumerated cease to appear absurd when translated into the language of power. Is it not natural that every State should define the national interest as the capacity to make war, when it is surrounded by States capable of subduing it by arms if it is weak? One must either join the race to prepare for war or else be resigned to enduring whatever some other armed State may choose to inflict; no third choice seems possible. Nothing but complete and universal disarmament could resolve this dilemma, and that is hardly conceivable. And, further, a State cannot appear weak in its external relations without the risk of weakening its authority with its own subjects. If Priam and Hector had delivered Helen to the Greeks this might merely have increased the Greeks' inclination to sack a town that seemed so ill prepared to defend itself; and they would also have risked a general uprising in Troy – not because the Trojans would have been upset by the surrender of Helen, but because it would have suggested to them that their chiefs could not be so very powerful. In Spain, if one of the two sides gave the impression of wanting peace this would first have the effect of encouraging its enemies and stimulating their aggressiveness, and then it would involve the risk of uprisings among its own supporters. Again, for a man who is outside both the anti-communist and the anti-fascist blocs the clash between two almost identical ideologies may appear ridiculous; but since these two blocs exist the members of one of them are bound to see absolute evil in the other, because it will exterminate them if they are the weaker. The leaders on each side must seem prepared to annihilate the enemy, in order to maintain their authority with their own troops; and once these blocs have achieved a certain degree of power, neutrality becomes an almost untenable position. In the same way, when those at the bottom of any social hierarchy begin to fear that unless they dispossess those above them they will be completely crushed, then, so soon as either side becomes strong enough to have nothing to fear, it will yield to the intoxication of power mixed with spite. Power, in general, is always essentially vulnerable; and therefore it is bound to defend itself, for otherwise society would lack the necessary minimum of stability. But it is nearly always believed, with or without reason, by all parties, that the only defence is attack. And it is natural that the most implacable conflicts should arise out of imaginary disputes, because these take place solely on the level of power and prestige. It would probably be easier for France to cede raw materials to Germany than a few acres of ground with the title of 'colony', and easier for Germany to do without raw materials than without the title of 'colonial power'. The essential contradiction in human society is that every social status quo rests upon an equilibrium of forces or pressures, similar to the equilibrium of fluids; but between one prestige and another there can be no equilibrium. Prestige has no bounds and its satisfaction always involves the infringement of someone else's prestige or dignity. And prestige is inseparable from power. This seems to be an impasse from which humanity can only escape by some miracle. But human life is made up of miracles. Who would believe that a Gothic cathedral could remain standing if we did not see it every day? Since the state of war is not, in fact, continuous, it is not impossible that peace might continue indefinitely. Once all the real data of a problem have been revealed the problem is well on the way to solution. The problem of peace, both international and social, has never yet been completely stated.

What prevents us from seeing the data of the problem is the swarm of vacuous entities or abstractions; they even prevent us from seeing that there is a problem to be solved, instead of a fatality to be endured. They stupefy the mind; they not only make men willing to die but, infinitely worse, they make them forget the value of life. To sweep away these entities from every department of political and social life is an urgently necessary measure of public hygiene. But the operation is not an easy one; the whole intellectual climate of our age favours the growth and multiplication of vacuous entities. Perhaps we should begin with a reform of our methods of scientific education and popularization, abolishing the artificial vocabulary which those methods crudely and superstitiously encourage. By reviving the intelligent use of expressions like *to the extent that, in so far as, on condition that, in relation to*, and by discrediting all those vicious arguments which amount to proclaiming the dormitive virtue of opium, we might be rendering a highly important practical service to our contemporaries. A general raising of the intellectual level would greatly assist any educational attempt to deflate the imaginary causes of strife. As things are, there is certainly no shortage of preachers of appeasement in every sphere; but their sermons, as a rule, are not intended to awaken intelligence and eliminate unreal conflicts, but rather, by inducing somnolence, to obscure real conflicts. There are no more dangerous enemies of international and social peace than those spell-binders whose talk about peace between nations means simply an indefinite prolongation of the status quo for the exclusive advantage of the French State or those whose advocacy of social peace presupposes the safeguarding of privilege, or at least the right of the privileged to veto any change they dislike. The relations between social forces are essentially variable, and the underprivileged will always seek to alter them; it is wrong to enforce an artificial stabilization. What is required is discrimination between the imaginary and the real, so as to diminish the risks of war, without interfering with the struggle between forces which, according to Heraclitus, is the condition of life itself.

From *Selected Essays 1934–43 by Simone Weil*, chosen and translated by Richard Rees, Oxford University Press, London, 1962.

CONTRADICTION

—————— ⊙ ——————

The contradictions the mind comes up against – these are the only realities: they are the criterion of the real. There is no contradiction in what is imaginary. Contradiction is the test of necessity.

Contradiction experienced to the very depths of the being tears us heart and soul: it is the cross.

When the attention has revealed the contradiction in something on which it has been fixed, a kind of loosening takes place. By persevering in this course we attain detachment.

The demonstrable correlation of opposites is an image of the transcendental correlation of contradictories.

All true good carries with it conditions which are contradictory and as a consequence is impossible. He who keeps his attention really fixed on this impossibility and acts will do what is good.

In the same way all truth contains a contradiction.

Contradiction is the point of the pyramid.

The word good has not the same meaning when it is a term of the correlation good–evil as when it describes the very being of God.

The existence of opposite virtues in the souls of the saints: the metaphor of climbing corresponds to this. If I am walking on the side of a mountain I can see first a lake, then, after a few steps, a forest. I have to choose either the lake or the forest. If I want to see both lake and forest at once, I have to climb higher.

Only the mountain does not exist. It is made of air. One cannot go up: it is necessary to be drawn.

An experimental ontological proof. I have not the principle of rising in me. I cannot climb to heaven through the air. It is only by directing my thoughts towards something better than myself that I am drawn upwards by this something. If I am really raised up, this something is real. No imaginary perfection can draw me upwards even by the fraction of an inch. For an imaginary perfection is automatically at the same level as I who imagine it – neither higher nor lower.

What is thus brought about by thought direction is in no way comparable to suggestion. If I say to myself every morning: 'I am courageous, I am not afraid', I may become courageous but with a courage which conforms to what, in my present imperfection, I imagine under that name, and accordingly my courage will not go beyond this imperfection. It can only be a modification on the same plane, not a change of plane.

Contradiction is the criterion. We cannot by suggestion obtain things which are incompatible. Only grace can do that. A sensitive person who by suggestion becomes courageous hardens himself; often he may even, by a sort of savage pleasure, amputate his own sensitivity. Grace alone can give courage while leaving the sensitivity intact, or sensitivity while leaving the courage intact.

Man's great affliction, which begins with infancy and

accompanies him till death, is that looking and eating are two different operations. Eternal beatitude is a state where to look is to eat.

That which we look at here below is not real, it is a mere setting. That which we eat is destroyed, it is no longer real.

Sin has brought this separation about in us.

The natural virtues, if we give the word virtue its authentic meaning, that is to say if we exclude the social imitations of virtue, are only possible as permanent attributes for someone who has supernatural grace within him. Their duration is supernatural.

Opposites and contradictories. What the relation of opposites can do in the approach to the natural being, the unifying grasp of contradictory ideas can do in the approach to God.

A man inspired by God is a man who has ways of behaviour, thoughts and feelings which are bound together by a bond impossible to define.

Pythagorean idea: the good is always defined by the union of opposites. When we recommend the opposite of an evil we remain on the level of that evil. After we have put it to the test, we return to the evil. That is what the Gita calls 'the aberration of opposites'. Marxist dialectic is based on a very degraded and completely warped view of this.

A wrong union of contraries. The imperialism of the working class developed by Marxism. Latin proverbs concerning the insolence of newly-freed slaves. Insolence and servility are aggravated by each other. Sincere anarchists, discerning, as through a mist, the principle of the union of opposites, thought that evil could be destroyed by giving power to the oppressed. An impossible dream.

What then differentiates the right from the wrong union of opposites[?]

Bad union of opposites (bad because fallacious) is that

which is achieved on the same plane as the opposites. Thus the granting of domination to the oppressed. In this way we do not get free from the oppression–domination cycle.

The right union of opposites is achieved on a higher plane. Thus the opposition between domination and oppression is smoothed out on the level of the law – which is balance.

In the same way suffering (and this is its special function) separates the opposites which have been united in order to unite them again on a higher plane than that of their first union. The pulsation of sorrow–joy. But, mathematically, joy always triumphs.

Suffering is violence, joy is gentleness, but joy is the stronger.

The union of contradictories involves a wrenching apart. It is impossible without extreme suffering.

The correlation of contradictories is detachment. An attachment to a particular thing can only be destroyed by an attachment which is incompatible with it. That explains: 'Love your enemies. . . . He who hateth not his father and mother . . .'

Either we have made the contraries submissive to us or we have submitted to the contraries.

Simultaneous existence of incompatible things in the soul's bearing; balance which leans both ways at once: that is saintliness, the actual realization of the microcosm, the imitation of the order of the world.

The simultaneous existence of opposite virtues in the soul – like pincers to catch hold of God.

We have to find out and formulate certain general laws relating to man's condition, concerning which many profound observations throw light on particular cases.

Thus: that which is in every way superior reproduces that which is in every way inferior, but transposed.

Relationships of evil to strength and to being; and of good to weakness or nothingness.

Yet at the same time evil is privation. We have to elucidate the way contradictories have of being true.

Method of investigation: as soon as we have thought something, try to see in what way the contrary is true.[1]

Evil is the shadow of good. All real good, possessing solidity and thickness, projects evil. Only imaginary good does not project it.

As all good is attached to evil, if we desire the good and do not wish to spread the corresponding evil round us we are obliged, since we cannot avoid this evil, to concentrate it on ourselves.

Thus the desire for utterly pure good involves the acceptance of the last degree of affliction for ourselves.

If we desire nothing but good, we are opposing the law which links real good to evil as the object in the light is linked to its shadow, and, being opposed to one of the world's universal laws, it is inevitable that we should fall into affliction.

The mystery of the cross of Christ lies in a contradiction, for it is both a free-will offering and a punishment which he endured in spite of himself. If we only saw in it an offering, we might wish for a like fate. But we are unable to wish for a punishment endured in spite of ourselves.

From *Gravity and Grace*, translated by Emma Craufurd, Routledge and Kegan Paul, London, 1952. Originally published as *La Pesanteur et la Grâce*, Plon, Paris, 1947.

[1] This aphorism gives us the key to the *apparent* contradictions scattered throughout the work of Simone Weil: love of tradition and detachment from the past, God conceived of as the supreme reality and as nothingness, etc. These contradictory ideas are true on different planes of existence and their opposition is smoothed out on the level of supernatural love. Reason discerns the two ends of the chain but the centre which unites them is only accessible to undemonstrable intuition. [Gustave Thibon]

PREREQUISITE
TO DIGNITY OF LABOUR

─────── ◎ ───────

This essay was written in Marseille in 1941. Part of it appeared in Cheval de Troie *in 1947 and it is now included in the collection made by Albertine Thévenon of Simone Weil's writings about her factory experience. The same collection,* La Condition Ouvrière *contains Simone Weil's journal and the notes she made after her day's work in the Renault, Alsthom and Basse-Indres Forges factories in Paris. In it she argues against the so-called 'rationalization' or 'taylorization' of labour, which reduces the worker to a series of gestures unconnected with reality. It dates from the period during which Simone Weil had become increasingly engaged in her struggle with the Christian church and contrasts vividly with articles written closer to the time of her employment in the factories, for example* 'La vie et la grève des ouvrières metallos'.

There is in all manual work and all work performed to order, that's to say in all real labour, an ineradicable element of constraint which would exist in even the most equitable of societies. The reason is that such work is governed by necessity and not by purpose. It is performed not for a result but because of a need, 'since you've got to make a living' as people say whose existence is spent doing just that. It means exerting effort whose sole end is to secure no more than what one already has, while failure to exert such effort results in losing it. But in human effort, the only source of energy is desire. It is not in a person's nature to desire what he already has. Desire is a tendency, the start of a movement towards something, towards a point from which one is absent. If, at the very outset, this movement doubles back on itself towards its point of departure, a person turns round and round like a squirrel in a cage or a prisoner in a condemned cell. Constant turning soon produces revulsion. All workers, especially though not exclusively those who work under inhumane conditions, are easily the victims of revulsion, exhaustion and disgust and the strongest are often the worst affected.

Existence is not an end in itself but merely the framework upon which all good, both real and imagined, may be built. When all objectives vanish and existence appears starkly stripped of everything, it no longer bears any relation to what is good. Indeed it becomes evil. And it is precisely then, when existence is substituted for all absent ends, that it becomes an end in itself, the only object of desire. When desire is directed like that towards sheer naked evil, the soul lives in the same horror as when violent death is imminent. In the past, that state could last an entire lifetime, as for example when a man disarmed by his enemy's sword found his life spared. In exchange for his life he would exhaust all his energies all day, every day, as a slave, with nothing on which to pin his hopes except the possibility of not being whipped or not being killed. The only good objective for him was existence itself. The ancients used to say that the day a man became a slave half his soul was taken from him.

A similar kind of slavery persists whenever people find themselves in the same position on the first and the last day of a month, of a year, or of twenty years' effort. The similarity lies in its being equally impossible for them to desire more than they already possess or to direct effort towards the acquisition of what is good. Effort is for survival.

The unit of time is a day and they oscillate like a ball bouncing off two walls, from work to sleep, working so as to eat, eating so as to continue to work and so on *ad nauseam*. In this sort of existence, everything is an intermediary, a means from which all finality is excluded. The manufactured object is a means. It will be sold. Who could invest in it his or her idea of the good? Material objects, tools, the worker's body and even his soul are a means of manufacturing. Necessity is omnipresent, good nowhere. This is the sole reason for people's present loss of morale. It is the unchanging, essential working condition. We must look for the reasons why in the past there has been no similar demoralization.

The emptiness of such a life is only bearable either through enormous physical strength, in which effort is scarcely perceived, or through total moral paralysis. In the absence of these, compensations are necessary. One is the hope, either for oneself or for one's children, of occupying a different position in society. Another, of the same sort, is mindless pleasure or violence. In both, illusion is substituted for objective. On Sunday, for example, people want to forget that they have to work, so they dress and spend as though they did not. Vanity has to be satisfied and illusions of power easily procured by abandon. Enjoyments of this sort act like a drug and drugs are always a temptation to those who are suffering. Revolution itself is a similar sort of compensation. It is ambition transposed to the collective level, the wild ambition that all workers shall soar above the working condition itself.

Most revolutionary feeling, though initially a revolt against injustice, often becomes very rapidly as it has done in the past, a workers' imperialism exactly analogous to national imperialism. Its aim is the total and unlimited domination of one collectivity over all humanity and all aspects of human life. The absurdity of it lies in the fact that under such a regime, the dominators, being themselves workers, would be unable to dominate. As a revolt against the injustices of society, the idea of revolution is right and proper. But as a revolt against the essential misery of the working condition it is misleading, for no revolution will get rid of the latter.

Belief in revolution holds the greater sway, however, since the misery of the working condition is more keenly felt than injustice itself. In people's minds the one is rarely distinguished from the other. The phrase 'opium of the people' which Marx used appropriately enough to describe religion when it had failed itself, applies essentially to revolution. The hope of a revolution to come satisfies a craving for adventure, of escaping from necessity, which again is a reaction against misery. In adolescence this same craving is shown in a taste for crime fiction and a tendency towards delinquency. It was naive of the bourgeoisie to believe that all would be well if they transferred to the people the principle that governs the middle classes, namely the acquisition of wealth. They did as much as they could in this direction by introducing piece-work and extending exchange between urban and rural areas. But all that did was increase dissatisfaction to the level of dangerous frustration, and the reason was simple. The acquisition of money as the object of desire and effort cannot take place under conditions within which it is impossible to become enriched. A small industrialist or businessman may enrich himself and become a big industrialist or a big businessman; a teacher, a writer or a minister is rich or poor according to circumstance but a worker who becomes rich ceases to be a worker and the same is nearly always true of a peasant. A worker cannot be smitten by the desire for money without wishing to escape, either with or without his companions, from the working condition.

The workers' universe excludes purpose. Purpose does not penetrate it except for very short periods always regarded as exceptional. The rapid development of new countries such as the US and the USSR produces change at such a rate that from one day to the next it seems there are fresh expectations, more and more things to desire and to covet. This frenzied social reconstruction was the great attraction of Russian communism, by coincidence as it happened, since it had to do with the economic state of the country and not with revolution or Marxist doctrine. When a system of metaphysics is based on brief, temporary and exceptional circumstances, as in the case of the American and the Russian, it is ill-founded. The family acquires purpose in the form of children to be brought up. But unless one aspires on their behalf to a different social position – rare as these social advances are – the prospect of children condemned to the same existence provides no relief from its painful emptiness. This emptiness weighs heavily and it is felt and suffered by many of low intelligence and little culture. Those whose position in society protects them from it cannot judge fairly the actions of those who bear it all their lives. It does not kill but is perhaps as painful as hunger, possibly more painful. It might be literally true that bread is less necessary than the relief of such pain.

There is one form of relief and one only. Only one thing makes monotony bearable and that is beauty, the light of the eternal. It is in respect of one thing only that human nature can bear for the soul's desire to be directed towards not what could be or will be, but towards what exists, and that is in respect of beauty. Everything beautiful is the object of desire but one desires that it be not otherwise, that it be unchanged, that it be exactly what it is. One looks with desire at a clear starry night and one desires exactly the sight before one's eyes. Since the people are forced to direct all their desires towards what they already possess, beauty is made for them and they for it. For other social classes, poetry is a luxury but the people need poetry as they need bread. Not the poetry closed inside words: by itself that is no use to them. They need poetry to be the very substance of daily life. Such poetry can come from one source only and that is God. The poetry can only be religion. There is no stratagem, no procedure, no reform or reversal whereby purpose can enter the world in which workers are placed by the working condition itself. But this entire world may be connected to the one true purpose. It may be linked to God. The condition of the workers is one in which the hunger for purpose that is the very being of all people cannot be satisfied except by God. And it is their exclusive privilege. They alone possess it. In all other conditions of life, without exception, specific aims govern activity. And there is not a single aim, including the salvation of one or many souls, which may not act as a screen and hide God. The screen must be pierced through detachment. For workers there is no screen. Nothing separates them from God. They have only to lift their heads. Therein lies the greatest difficulty for them. Unlike other people they do not have too much of something which must be shed with effort. They have too little of something. They have too few intermediaries. Asking people to think of God and to offer him their pain and suffering is no help at all.

People go to church specifically to pray, yet we know they could not do so unless their attention were drawn through intermediaries towards God. The architecture of the church itself, the images which fill it, the words of the liturgy and prayer, the ritual gestures of the priest are all intermediaries. By fixing attention on them it is guided towards God. How much more necessary then is the provision of such intermediaries in a place where someone goes merely to make a living! In the workplace all thought is dragged down to earth. It is clearly not possible to put up religious pictures and suggest people look at them or recite prayers while working. The only perceptible objects of attention there are the materials, the tools and the movements of work. If these very objects are not transformed into reflections of light, it is impossible for attention during work to be directed towards the source of all light. Nothing is more urgently needed than such a transformation. It is only possible if a reflective property is to be found in the matter that confronts working people. No concoction of arbitrary symbols will do. In truth there is no place for fiction, imagination or dreams. Fortunately for us a reflective property does exist in matter which is like a mirror misted over by our breath. We have only to wipe the mirror to read in it symbols inscribed in matter through eternity.

Some are contained in the Gospels. Inside a room, if one wishes to think about spiritual death being a prerequisite of true rebirth, one needs words about the seed fertilized by death alone. A sower in the act of sowing, however, may, if he wishes, through his own movements and the sight of the seed entering the earth, direct his attention towards that truth without the help of a single word. If he does not reason around it but simply looks, the undiminished attention he pays to the accomplishment of his task reaches the very highest degree of intensity.

Religious attention is justly called the plenitude of attention. Plenitude of attention is nothing other than prayer. Similarly, the image of the alienation of the soul parched by Christ is like the shrivelling of the branch cut off from the vine. In the great vineyards, pruning takes place over very many days. And likewise, contemplation of the inexhaustible truth it symbolizes can also continue day after day.

It should be easy to find shaped in the nature of things many other symbols which can transfigure not only labour generally but individual tasks themselves. Christ is the bronze serpent which shields from death those who look upon it. Yet our gaze must be uninterrupted and in order for it to be so, the things which our needs and obligations force us to look at must reflect what they prevent us from seeing directly. If a church made by human beings can be full of symbols, how much more full must the universe be. It is infinitely full of them. We must read into them.

The image in the Good Friday hymn of the Cross compared to a scales could be an inexhaustible source of inspiration to those who carry burdens, pull levers and who are by evening exhausted by the weight of things. On the scales a considerable weight placed close to the supporting point may be lifted by a relatively small weight placed at a great distance from it. The body of Christ was a very small weight but with the distance existing between heaven and earth, he counterbalanced the universe. It is often unbearably heavy, and body and soul are bowed beneath its wearying weight. But the person who is connected to heaven may support that weight, and once he has seen the connection, will not be distracted from it by weariness, tedium or disgust. He will be led back to it constantly.

In the fields, sun and sap are constant reminders of the greatest thing in the world – the fact that we live by solar energy alone. It feeds us, keeps us upright, activates our muscles and operates all our bodily actions. In its different forms it is perhaps the only thing in the universe to act as a countervailing force to gravity. It is through it that trees rise, our arms lift burdens and our motor power is driven. It comes from a source inaccessible to us and towards which we cannot move a single step. It flows down towards us always, and though bathed in it we can never seize it. Only the chlorophyll in plant life can capture it, to make with it our food. Provided that by our efforts the earth is properly prepared, solar energy through chlorophyll becomes solid and enters into us in bread, wine, oil and fruit. All peasant labour consists in the tending of this power in plants, which is a perfect image of Christ.

The laws of mechanics that derive from geometry and govern our machines contain supernatural truths. The oscillation of alternating motion is an image of the earthly condition. Everything belonging to creatures is limited except the desire within us which is the mark of our origin. The yearnings which make us seek the unlimited here on earth are therefore for us the only source of crime and error. The good contained in things is finite and so is the evil. In a general way, a given cause will produce a given effect up to a certain point beyond which, if it continues to act, the effect is reversed. It is God who imposes limit on all things and by whom the sea is bounded. In God, there is but one eternal, unchanging act which, rebounding on itself, has no object outside itself. In creatures there exist only movements directed outside themselves but which, because of their limits, are constrained to oscillate. This oscillation is a pale reflection of exclusively divine self-orientation. In our machines, the image of this link is that between circular and alternating motion. The circle is also the source of mean proportionals. There is no other perfectly exact way of finding the mean proportional between a unit and a number which is not a square than by drawing a circle. The numbers incommensurable with the unit [*les nombres pour lesquels il n'existe aucune médiation qui les relie naturellement à l'unité*] provide an image of our misery. The circle, which comes from outside in a manner which is transcendental with respect to the domain of numbers and provides the mean, is the image of the sole remedy for that misery. These truths and many others are contained in the simple image of a pulley determining the oscillating motion. Only the most elementary knowledge of geometry is needed to understand these last truths and the very rhythm of work, corresponding as it does to oscillation, helps the body to sense them. A human life-span is a very short time indeed in which to contemplate them.

Many other symbols could be found, some more intimately linked with individual workers' actions. In some cases merely by applying his attitude at work to everything else, a worker could experience the good life. Symbols might also be found for those with routine non-manual jobs. For clerks, these might come from elementary arithmetic, for cashiers, from money and so forth; the stock is inexhaustible. From then on, much could be accomplished. These great images, linked to the ideas of science and general culture, could be passed on to adolescents as part of their studies. They could be used as themes for their celebrations and theatrical ventures. New high days and holidays could be centred around them, such as the eve of that great day when a little fourteen-year-old goes to work alone for the first time. By means of these symbols, men and women could live constantly surrounded by an atmosphere of supernatural poetry, as they did in medieval times, perhaps even better than then, for why limit hope for the good?

In this way workers would be rid of the often painful

feeling of inferiority they experience and also the false confidence which slight contact with intellectualism puts in its place. Intellectuals, for their part, would be rid of their unwarranted snobbery and the equally suspect cult of fashionable ranting that sprang up a few years ago. All those who were able would unite on equal terms at the highest point of full attention, that's to say in the fullness of prayer. Those who were unable would at least know that such a point exists. They would see that the various paths leading up to that point, though separate at lower levels, as by the base of a mountain are all equally viable.

The only serious aim of schoolwork is to train the attention. Attention is the only faculty of the soul which gives access to God. Mental gymnastics rely on an inferior, discursive form of attention, which reasons. Properly directed, however, this attention may give rise in the soul to another, of the highest kind, which is intuitive attention. Pure, intuitive attention is the only source of perfectly beautiful art, truly original and brilliant scientific discovery, of philosophy which really aspires to wisdom and of true, practical love of one's neighbour. This kind of attention when turned to God is true prayer. Just as symbols can enable one to think of God while one is digging or mowing, so only a method of transforming schoolwork into preparation for this superior attention would allow an adolescent solving a problem in geometry or doing a Latin translation to think of God. Without such a transformation, intellectual work for all its apparent independence remains nevertheless servile. In order to attain intuitive attention, those with leisure to do so must exercise to their very utmost the discursive faculties which, while they remain, act as an obstacle. For those whose social function requires them to use those faculties there is probably no other method. For those whose faculties are almost completely paralysed by the fatigue of long daily labour, the possible obstacle is much reduced and the necessary wearing-down minimal. For them, the very work which paralyses, provided it be transformed into poetry, will lead to intuitive attention.

In our society, it is educational rather than economic differences that produce the illusion of social inequality. Marx, who is nearly always very powerful when describing evil, rightly denounced as degrading the separation of manual and intellectual labour. He did not know that in all domains, opposites are unified on a plane transcending both. The meeting point of intellectual and manual work is contemplation, which is no work at all. In no society does the person in charge of a machine exercise the same kind of attention as a person working out a problem. If they wish, however, and if they have a method for doing so, each, in exercising the particular kind of attention required of them by society, can allow another kind to appear and develop. This other kind of attention overrides all social obligations and constitutes a direct link with God.

If students, young peasants and workers could perceive all the various social functions as equal prerequisites to the emergence in the soul of one uniquely valuable faculty, as they perceive cogs in a perfectly straightforward machine, then equality would become a real thing. It would be the principle of both justice and order. It is only through a clear understanding of the supernatural meaning of each social function that the desirability of reform can be judged and injustice defined. Otherwise injustice will be seen inevitably and erroneously as suffering rooted in the nature of things, or undeserved suffering that results from our own crimes will be attributed to the human condition itself. Certain degrees of subordination and monotony are sufferings inherent in the very nature of work and inseparable from a corresponding supernatural meaning. Neither is degrading in itself but anything added to them is both degrading and unjust. Anything which prevents poetry from crystallizing around that suffering is criminal. It is not sufficient to rediscover the lost source of the poetry; working conditions must themselves favour its continued existence. If they are unfavourable, they kill it.

Anything which is inextricably linked with either the desire for or the fear of change should be excluded from what is essentially a uniform existence and one which should be accepted as such. First, all physical suffering except that which the nature of the work makes unavoidable, for it is impossible to suffer without hoping for relief. Hardships can scarcely be more unendurable than in this social condition. Food, lodging, rest and leisure should be such that a normal working day, taken in itself, should be free of physical suffering. Excess, too, is no less undesirable in this kind of life, for the desire for it is itself unlimited and implies a desire for a change of condition. All advertising and propaganda of all kinds, and anything designed to stimulate the desire for excess in both rural and urban workers should be regarded as criminal. There may be individual flights from the working condition either through unsuitability or the possession of different skills but for those who remain, there should be no improvement in individual well-being that is not at the same time seen as linked to the general. There should be no way for a worker to be afraid of getting too little or hope to get more than he needs. Security should be greater than in any other social condition and unaffected by the fluctuations of supply and demand.

The arbitrary in human life forces the defenceless soul both to hope and to fear. It should therefore be excluded as far as possible from work as should all unnecessary authority. A small peasant holding is thus better than a large one. It follows that big is bad where small is possible and that parts are better manufactured in a small workshop than under the orders of a factory foreman. In the book of Job, death is praised since it prevents the slave from hearing his master's voice. Harm is done each time a commanding voice is raised when a practical arrangement could have been made quietly without it.

The worst outrage, however, is violation of the workers' attention. This is perhaps an example of a sin against the spirit which is unforgivable if committed deliberately. It destroys that faculty of the soul which is the source of all spiritual action. The inferior kind of attention required by taylorized (conveyor-belt) work is incompatible with any other kind of attention since it drains the soul of all save a preoccupation with speed. This kind of work cannot be transformed and must be stopped. All technological problems should be viewed within the context of what will bring about the best working conditions. This is the most important standard to establish; the whole of society should be first constituted so that work does not demean those who perform it. It is not sufficient that they avoid suffering. Their joy must be desired also, not bought treats but the natural delights that do not cheapen the spirit of poverty. The supernatural poetry which should permeate all their lives could from time to time be concentrated in dazzling celebrations, as necessary in working life as milestones to the walker. Free working holidays like the old *tours de France* would satisfy the youthful appetite for seeing and learning. All should be done so that nothing essential is missing and the best among them may then possess in their daily lives the completeness artists seek to express in their art. If man's vocation is to achieve pure joy through suffering, workers are better placed than all others to accomplish it in the truest way.

From *La Condition Ouvrière*, Gallimard, Paris, 1951, translated by Siân Miles.

DETACHMENT

———————— ◎ ————————

Affliction in itself is not enough for the attainment of total detachment. Unconsoled affliction is necessary. There must be no consolation – no apparent consolation. Ineffable consolation then comes down.

To forgive debts. To accept the past without asking for future compensation. To stop time at the present instant. This is also the acceptance of death.

'He emptied himself of his divinity.' To empty ourselves of the world. To take the form of a slave. To reduce ourselves to the point we occupy in space and time – that is to say, to nothing.

To strip ourselves of the imaginary royalty of the world. Absolute solitude. Then we possess the truth of the world.

Two ways of renouncing material possessions:

To give them up with a view to some spiritual advantage.

To conceive of them and feel them as conducive to spiritual well-being (for example: hunger, fatigue and humiliation cloud the mind and hinder meditation) and yet to renounce them.

Only the second kind of renunciation means nakedness of spirit.

Furthermore, material goods would scarcely be

dangerous if they were seen in isolation and not bound up
with spiritual advantage.

We must give up everything which is not grace and not
even desire grace.

The extinction of desire (Buddhism) – or detachment – or
amor fati – or desire for the absolute good – these all
amount to the same: to empty desire, finality of all content,
to desire in the void, to desire without any wishes.

To detach our desire from all good things and to wait.
Experience proves that this waiting is satisfied. It is then we
touch the absolute good.

Always, beyond the particular object whatever it may be,
we have to fix our will on the void – to will the void. For the
good which we can neither picture nor define is a void for
us. But this void is fuller than all fullnesses.

If we get as far as this we shall come through all right, for
God fills the void. It has nothing to do with an intellectual
process in the present-day sense. The intelligence has
nothing to discover, it has only to clear the ground. It is
only good for servile tasks.

The good seems to us as a nothingness, since there is no
thing that is good. But this nothingness is not unreal.
Compared with it, everything in existence is unreal.

We must leave on one side the beliefs which fill up voids
and sweeten what is bitter. The belief in immortality. The
belief in the utility of sin: *etiam peccata*. The belief in the
providential ordering of events – in short the 'consolations'
which are ordinarily sought in religion.

To love God through and across the destruction of Troy
and of Carthage – and with no consolation. Love is not
consolation, it is light.

The reality of the world is the result of our attachment. It is
the reality of the self which we transfer into things. It has

nothing to do with independent reality. That is only perceptible through total detachment. Should only one thread remain, there is still attachment.

Affliction which forces us to attach ourselves to the most wretched objects exposes in all its misery the true character of attachment. In this way the necessity for detachment is made more obvious.

Attachment is a manufacturer of illusions and whoever wants reality ought to be detached.

As soon as we know that something is real we can no longer be attached to it.

Attachment is no more nor less than an insufficiency in our sense of reality. We are attached to the possession of a thing because we think that if we cease to possess it, it will cease to exist. A great many people do not feel with their whole soul that there is all the difference in the world between the destruction of a town and their own irremediable exile from that town.

Human misery would be intolerable if it were not diluted in time. We have to prevent it from being diluted *in order that it should* be intolerable.

'And when they had had their fill of tears' (*Iliad*). – This is another way of making the worst suffering bearable.

We must not weep so that we may not be comforted.[1]

All suffering which does not detach us is wasted suffering. Nothing is more frightful, a desolate coldness, a warped soul (Ovid. Slaves in Plautus).

Never to think of a thing or being we love but have not actually before our eyes without reflecting that perhaps this thing has been destroyed, or this person is dead.

[1] Yet Jesus Christ said: 'Blessed are they that mourn.' But here Simone Weil is only condemning the tears wrung from us by the loss of temporal goods – tears which man sheds over himself [Gustav Thibon].

May our sense of reality not be dissolved by this thought but made more intense.

Each time that we say 'Thy will be done' we should have in mind all possible misfortunes added together.

Two ways of killing ourselves: suicide or detachment.

To kill by our thought everything we love: the only way to die. Only what we love, however ('He who hateth not his father and mother . . .' but: 'Love your enemies . . .').

Not to desire that what we love should be immortal. We should neither desire the immortality nor the death of any human being, whoever he may be, with whom we have to do.

The miser deprives himself of his treasure because of his desire for it. If we can let our whole good rest with something hidden in the ground, why not with God?

But when God has become as full of significance as the treasure is for the miser, we have to tell ourselves insistently that he does not exist. We must experience the fact that we love him, even if he does not exist.

It is he who, through the operation of the dark night, withdraws himself in order not to be loved like the treasure is by the miser.

Electra weeping for the dead Orestes. If we love God while thinking that he does not exist, he will manifest his existence.

From *Gravity and Grace*, translated by Emma Craufurd, Routledge and Kegan Paul, London, 1952. Originally published as *La Pesanteur et la Grâce*, Plon, Paris, 1947.

FRIENDSHIP

———————— ◉ ————————

The essay from which this extract comes was given to the Dominican Father Perrin by Simone Weil on the day of her final departure from France. In it she describes four different kinds of 'implicit love of God' including love of religion or religious practices, love of one's neighbour, love of the beauty of the world and finally friendship. She attached great importance to it and wrote in her Notebooks *'Above all, never allow oneself to dream of friendship. ... Friendship is not be to sought, dreamed about, longed for but exercised (it is a virtue).' For herself, she hardly dared hope for it. In a letter to Joë Bousquet, disabled veteran of the First World War, she explains why:*

My attitude towards myself ... is to be explained ... on the level of biological mechanisms. For twelve years I have suffered from pain around the central point of the nervous system, the meeting-place of soul and body; this pain persists during sleep and has never stopped for a second. For a period of ten years it was so great,and was accompanied by such exhaustion, that the effort of attention and intellectual work was usually almost as despairing as that of a condemned man the day before his execution; and often much more so, for my efforts seemed completely sterile and without even any temporary result. I was sustained by the faith, which I acquired at the age of fourteen, that no true effort of

*attention is ever wasted, even though it may never have any
visible result, either direct or indirect. Nevertheless, a time came
when I thought my soul menaced, through exhaustion and an
aggravation of the pain, by such a hideous and total breakdown
that I spent several weeks of anguished uncertainty whether death
was not my imperative duty – although it seemed to me appalling
that my life should end in horror. As I told you, I was only able to
calm myself by deciding to live conditionally, for a trial period.*

*A little earlier, when I had already been for years in this
physical state, I worked for nearly a year in engineering factories
in the Paris region. The combination of personal experience and
sympathy for the wretched mass of people around me, in which I
formed, even in my own eyes, an undistinguishable item,
implanted so deep in my heart the affliction of social degradation
that I have felt a slave ever since, in the Roman sense of the word.*

*During all this time, the word God had no place at all in my
thoughts. It never had, until the day – about three and a half
years ago – when I could no longer keep it out. At a moment of
intense physical pain, while I was making the effort to love,
although believing I had no right to give any name to the love, I
felt, while completely unprepared for it (I had never read the
mystics), a presence more personal, more certain, and more real
than that of a human being; it was inaccessible both to sense and
to imagination, and it resembled the love that irradiates the
tenderest smile of somebody one loves. Since that moment, the
name of God and the name of Christ have been more and more
irresistibly mingled with my thoughts.*

Until then my only faith had been the Stoic amor fati *as Marcus
Aurelius understood it, and I had always faithfully practised it –
to love the universe as one's city, one's native country, the beloved
fatherland of every soul; to cherish it for its beauty, in the total
integrity of the order and necessity which are its substance, and
all the events that occur in it.*

*The result was that the irreducible quantity of hatred and
repulsion which goes with suffering and affliction recoiled entirely
upon myself. And the quantity is very great, because the suffering
in question is located at the very root of my every single thought,
without exception.*

*This is so much the case that I absolutely cannot imagine the
possibility that any human being could feel friendship for me. If I
believe in yours it is only because I have confidence in you and*

you have assured me of it, so that my reason tells me to believe it.
But this does not make it seem any the less impossible to my
imagination.

Because of this propensity of my imagination I am all the more
tenderly grateful to those who accomplish this impossibility.
Because friendship is an incomparable, immeasurable boon to me,
and a source of life – not metaphorically but literally. Since it is
not only my body but my soul itself that is poisoned all through by
suffering, it is impossible for my thought to dwell there and it is
obliged to travel elsewhere. It can only dwell for brief moments in
God; it dwells often among things, but it would be against nature
for human thought never to dwell in anything human. Thus it is
literally true that friendship gives to my thought all the life it has,
apart from what comes to it from God or from the beauty of the
world.

So you can see what you have done for me by giving me
yours . . .

There is however a personal and human love which is pure
and which enshrines an intimation and a reflection of divine
love. This is friendship, provided we keep strictly to the
true meaning of the word.

Preference for some human being is necessarily a different thing from charity. Charity does not discriminate. If it
is found more abundantly in any special quarter, it is because affliction has chanced to provide an occasion there for
the exchange of compassion and gratitude. It is equally
available for the whole human race, inasmuch as affliction
can come to all, offering them an opportunity for such an
exchange.

Preference for a human being can be of two kinds. Either
we are seeking some particular good in him or we need him.
In a general way all possible attachments come under one of
these heads. We are drawn towards a thing, either because
there is some good we are seeking from it, or because we
cannot do without it. Sometimes the two motives coincide.
Often however they do not. Each is distinct and quite
independent. We eat distasteful food, if we have nothing
else, because we cannot do otherwise. A moderately greedy

man looks out for delicacies, but he can easily do without them. If we have no air we are suffocated; we struggle to get it, not because we expect to get some advantage from it but because we need it. We go in search of sea air without being driven by any necessity, because we like it. In time it often comes about automatically that the second motive takes the place of the first. This is one of the great misfortunes of our race. A man smokes opium in order to attain to a special condition, which he thinks superior; often, as time goes on, the opium reduces him to a miserable condition which he feels to be degrading, but he is no longer able to do without it. Arnolphe bought Agnes from her adopted mother, because it seemed to him it would be an advantage to have a little girl with him, a little girl whom he would gradually make into a good wife.[1] Later on she ceased to cause him anything but a heart-rending and degrading torment. But with the passage of time his attachment to her had become a vital bond which forced this terrible line from his lips: '*Mais je sens là-dedans qu'il faudra que je crève –* '[2]

Harpagon started by considering gold as an advantage. Later it became nothing but the object of a haunting obsession, yet an object of which the loss would cause his death. As Plato says, there is a great difference between the essence of the Necessary and that of the Good.

There is no contradiction between seeking our own good in a human being and wishing for his good to be increased. For this very reason, when the motive that draws us towards anybody is simply some advantage for ourselves, the conditions of friendship are not fulfilled. Friendship is a supernatural harmony, a union of opposites.

When a human being is in any degree necessary to us, we cannot desire his good unless we cease to desire our own. Where there is necessity there is constraint and domination. We are in the power of that of which we stand in need, unless we possess it. The central good for every man is the free

---

[1] Characters in Molière's *L'Ecole des femmes*. Harpagon is a character in Molière's *L'Avare*.

[2] 'But I feel in all this that I shall be torn asunder.'

disposal of himself. Either we renounce it, which is a crime of idolatry, since it can be renounced only in favour of God, or we desire that the being we stand in need of should be deprived of it.

Any kind of mechanism may join human beings together with bonds of affection which have the iron hardness of necessity. Mother love is often of such a kind; so at times is paternal love, as in *Le Père Goriot* of Balzac; so is carnal love in its most intense form, as in *L'Ecole des femmes* and in *Phèdre*; so also, very frequently, is the love between husband and wife, chiefly as a result of habit. Filial and fraternal love are more rarely of this nature.

There are moreover degrees of necessity. Everything is necessary in some degree if its loss really causes a decrease of vital energy. (This word is here used in the strict and precise sense that it might have if the study of vital phenomena were as far advanced as that of falling bodies.) When the degree of necessity is extreme, deprivation leads to death. This is the case when all the vital energy of one being is bound up with another by some attachment. In the lesser degrees, deprivation leads to a more or less considerable lessening of energy. Thus a total deprivation of food causes death, whereas a partial deprivation only diminishes the life force. Nevertheless the necessary quantity of food is considered to be that required if a person is not to be weakened.

The most frequent cause of necessity in the bonds of affection is a combination of sympathy and habit. As in the case of avarice or drunkenness, that which was at first a search for some desired good is transformed into a need by the mere passage of time. The difference from avarice, drunkenness, and all the vices, however, is that in the bonds of affection the two motives – search for a desired good, and need – can very easily coexist. They can also be separated. When the attachment of one being to another is made up of need and nothing else it is a fearful thing. Few things in this world can reach such a degree of ugliness and horror. There is always something horrible whenever a human being seeks what is good and only finds necessity.

The stories that tell of a beloved being who suddenly appears with a death's head best symbolize this. The human soul possesses a whole arsenal of lies with which to put up a defence against this ugliness and, in imagination, to manufacture sham advantages where there is only necessity. It is for this very reason that ugliness is an evil, because it conduces to lying.

Speaking quite generally, we might say that there is affliction whenever necessity, under no matter what form, is imposed so harshly that the hardness exceeds the capacity for lying of the person who receives the impact. That is why the purest souls are the most exposed to affliction. For him who is capable of preventing the automatic reaction of defence, which tends to increase the soul's capacity for lying, affliction is not an evil, although it is always a wounding and in a sense a degradation.

When a human being is attached to another by a bond of affection which contains any degree of necessity, it is impossible that he should wish autonomy to be preserved both in himself and in the other. It is impossible by virtue of the mechanism of nature. It is, however, made possible by the miraculous intervention of the supernatural. This miracle is friendship.

'Friendship is an equality made of harmony,' said the Pythagoreans. There is harmony because there is a supernatural union between two opposites, that is to say, necessity and liberty, the two opposites God combined when he created the world and men. There is equality because each wishes to preserve the faculty of free consent both in himself and in the other.

When anyone wishes to put himself under a human being or consents to be subordinated to him, there is no trace of friendship. Racine's Pylades is not the friend of Orestes. There is no friendship where there is inequality.

A certain reciprocity is essential in friendship. If all good will is entirely lacking on one of the two sides, the other should suppress his own affection, out of respect for the free consent which he should not desire to force. If on one of the two sides there is not any respect for the autonomy of the other, this other must cut the bond uniting them out of respect for himself. In the same way, he who consents to be enslaved cannot gain friendship. But the necessity contained in the bond of affection can exist on one side only, and in this case there is only friendship on one side, if we keep to the strict and exact meaning of the word.

A friendship is tarnished as soon as necessity triumphs, if only for a moment, over the desire to preserve the faculty of free consent on both sides. In all human things, necessity is the principle of impurity. All friendship is impure if even a trace of the wish to please or the contrary desire to dominate is found in it. In a perfect friendship these two desires are completely absent. The two friends have fully consented to be two and not one, they respect the distance which the fact of being two distinct creatures places between them. Man has the right to desire direct union with God alone.

Friendship is a miracle by which a person consents to view from a certain distance, and without coming any nearer, the very being who is necessary to him as food. It requires the strength of soul that Eve did not have; and yet she had no need of the fruit. If she had been hungry at the moment when she looked at the fruit, and if in spite of that she had remained looking at it indefinitely without taking one step toward it, she would have performed a miracle analogous to that of perfect friendship.

Through this supernatural miracle of respect for human autonomy, friendship is very like the pure forms of compassion and gratitude called forth by affliction. In both cases the contraries which are the terms of the harmony are necessity and liberty, or in other words subordination and equality. These two pairs of opposites are equivalent.

From the fact that the desire to please and the desire to command are not found in pure friendship, it has in it, at the same time as affection, something not unlike a complete indifference. Although it is a bond between two people it is in a sense impersonal. It leaves impartiality intact. It in no way prevents us from imitating the perfection of our Father in heaven who freely distributes sunlight and rain in every place. On the contrary, friendship and this distribution are the mutual conditions one of the other, in most cases at any rate. For, as practically every human being is joined to others by bonds of affection that have in them some degree of necessity, he cannot go toward perfection except by transforming this affection into friendship. Friendship has something universal about it. It consists of loving a human being as we should like to be able to love each soul in particular of all those who go to make up the human race. As a geometrician looks at a particular figure in order to deduce the universal properties of the triangle, so he who knows how to love directs upon a particular human being a universal love. The consent to preserve an autonomy within ourselves and in others is essentially of a universal order. As soon as we wish for this autonomy to be respected in more than just one single being we desire it for everyone, for we cease to arrange the order of the world in a circle whose centre is here below. We transport the centre of the circle beyond the heavens.

Friendship does not have this power if the two beings who love each other, through an unlawful use of affection, think they form only one. But then there is not friendship in the true sense of the word. That is what might be called an adulterous union, even though it comes about between husband and wife. There is not friendship where distance is not kept and respected.

The simple fact of having pleasure in thinking in the same way as the beloved being, or in any case the fact of desiring such an agreement of opinion, attacks the purity of the friendship at the same time as its intellectual integrity. It is very frequent. But at the same time pure friendship is rare.

When the bonds of affection and necessity between human beings are not supernaturally transformed into friendship, not only is the affection of an impure and low order, but it is also combined with hatred and repulsion. That is shown very well in *L'Ecole des Femmes* and in

Phèdre. The mechanism is the same in affections other than carnal love. It is easy to understand this. We hate what we are dependent upon. We become disgusted with what depends on us. Sometimes affection does not only become mixed with hatred and revulsion; it is entirely changed into it. The transformation may sometimes even be almost immediate, so that hardly any affection has had time to show; this is the case when necessity is laid bare almost at once. When the necessity which brings people together has nothing to do with the emotions, when it is simply due to circumstances, hostility often makes its appearance from the start.

When Christ said to his disciples: 'Love one another,' it was not attachment he was laying down as their rule. As it was a fact that there were bonds between them due to the thoughts, the life, and the habits they shared, he commanded them to transform these bonds into friendship, so that they should not be allowed to turn into impure attachment or hatred.

Since, shortly before his death, Christ gave this as a new commandment to be added to the two great commandments of the love of our neighbour and the love of God, we can think that pure friendship, like the love of our neighbour, has in it something of a sacrament. Christ perhaps wished to suggest this with reference to Christian friendship when he said: 'Where there are two or three gathered together in my name there am I in the midst of them.' Pure friendship is an image of the original and perfect friendship that belongs to the Trinity and is the very essence of God. It is impossible for two human beings to be one while scrupulously respecting the distance that separates them, unless God is present in each of them. The point at which parallels meet is infinity.

From 'Forms of the Implicit Love of God', in *Waiting on God*, translated by Emma Craufurd, Routledge and Kegan Paul, 1951. Originally published as *L'Attente de Dieu*, La Colombe, Paris, 1950.

LOVE

---◎---

Love is a sign of our wretchedness. God can only love himself. We can only love something else.

God's love for us is not the reason for which we should love him. God's love for us is the reason for us to love ourselves. How could we love ourselves without this motive?

It is impossible for man to love himself except in this roundabout way.

If my eyes are blindfolded and if my hands are chained to a stick, this stick separates me from things but I can explore them by means of it. It is only the stick which I feel, it is only the wall which I perceive. It is the same with creatures and the faculty of love. Supernatural love touches only creatures and goes only to God. It is only creatures which it loves (what else have we to love?), but it loves them as intermediaries. For this reason it loves all creatures equally, itself included. To love a stranger as oneself implies the reverse: to love oneself as a stranger.

Love of God is pure when joy and suffering inspire an *equal* degree of gratitude.

Love on the part of someone who is happy is the wish to share the suffering of the beloved who is unhappy.

Love on the part of someone who is unhappy is to be filled with joy by the mere knowledge that his beloved is happy without sharing in this happiness or even wishing to do so.

In Plato's eyes, carnal love is a degraded image of true love. Chaste human love (conjugal fidelity) is a less degraded image of it. Only in the stupidity of the present day could the idea of sublimation arise.

The Love of Phaedrus. He neither exercises force nor submits to it. That constitutes the only purity. Contact with the sword causes the same defilement whether it be through the handle or the point. For him who loves, its metallic coldness will not destroy love, but will give the impression of being abandoned by God. Supernatural love has no contact with force, but at the same time it does not protect the soul against the coldness of force, the coldness of steel. Only an earthly attachment, if it has in it enough energy, can afford protection from the coldness of steel. Armour, like the sword, is made of metal. Murder freezes the soul of the man who loves only with a pure love, whether he be the author or the victim, so likewise does everything which, without going so far as actual death, constitutes violence. If we want to have a love which will protect the soul from wounds, we must love something other than God.

Love tends to go ever further and further, but there is a limit. When the limit is passed love turns to hate. To avoid this change love has to become different.

Among human beings, only the existence of those we love is fully recognized.

Belief in the existence of other human beings as such is *love*.

The mind is not forced to believe in the existence of anything (subjectivism, absolute idealism, solipsism, scepticism: cf. the Upanishads, the Taoists and Plato, who, all of them, adopt this philosophical attitude by way of purification). That is why the only organ of contact with existence is acceptance, love. That is why beauty and reality are identical. That is why joy and the sense of reality are identical.

This need to be the creator of what we love is a need to imitate God. But the divinity towards which it tends is false, unless we have recourse to the model seen from the other, the heavenly side. . . .

Pure love of creatures is not love in God, but love which has passed through God as through fire. Love which detaches itself completely from creatures to ascend to God and comes down again associated with the creative love of God.

Thus the two opposites which rend human love are united: to love the beloved being just as he is, and to want to recreate him.

Imaginary love of creatures. We are attached by a cord to all the objects of attachment, and a cord can always be cut. We are also attached by a cord to the imaginary God, the God for whom love is also an attachment. But to the real God we are not attached and that is why there is no cord which can be cut. He enters into us. He alone can enter into us. All other things remain outside and our knowledge of them is confined to the tensions of varying degree and direction which affect the cord when there is a change of position on their part or on ours.

Love needs reality. What is more terrible than the discovery that through a bodily appearance we have been loving an imaginary being. It is much more terrible than death, for death does not prevent the beloved from having lived.

That is the punishment for having fed love on imagination.

It is an act of cowardice to seek from (or to wish to give) the people we love any other consolation than that which works of art give us. These help us through the mere fact that they *exist*. To love and to be loved only serves mutually to render this existence more concrete, more constantly present to the mind. But it should be present as the source of our thoughts, not as their object. If there are grounds for wishing to be understood, it is not for ourselves but for the other, in order that we may exist for him.

Everything which is vile or second-rate in us revolts against purity and needs, in order to save its own life, to soil this purity.

To soil is to modify, it is to touch. The beautiful is that which we cannot wish to change. To assume power over is to soil. To possess is to soil.

To love purely is to consent to distance, it is to adore the distance between ourselves and that which we love.

The imagination is always united with a desire, that is to say a value. Only desire without an object is empty of imagination. There is the real presence of God in everything which imagination does not veil. The beautiful takes our desire captive and empties it of its object, giving it an object which is present and thus forbidding it to fly off towards the future.

Such is the price of chaste love. Every desire for enjoyment belongs to the future and the world of illusion, whereas if we desire only that a being should exist, he exists: what more is there to desire? The beloved being is then naked and real, not veiled by an imaginary future. The miser never looks at his treasure without imagining it n times larger. It is necessary to be dead in order to see things in their nakedness.

Thus in love there is chastity or the lack of chastity according to whether the desire is or is not directed towards the future.

In this sense, and on condition that it is not turned

towards a pseudo-immortality conceived on the model of the future, the love we devote to the dead is perfectly pure. For it is the desire for a life which is finished, which can no longer give anything new. We desire that the dead man should have existed, and he has existed.

Wherever the spirit ceases to be a principle it also ceases to be an end. Hence the close connection between collective 'thought' under all its forms and the loss of the sense of and respect for souls. The soul is the human being considered as having a value in itself. To love the soul of a woman is not to think of her as serving one's own pleasure, etc. Love no longer knows how to contemplate, it wants to possess (disappearance of Platonic love).[1]

It is a fault to wish to be understood before we have made ourselves clear to ourselves. It is to seek pleasures in friendship and pleasures which are not deserved. It is something which corrupts even more than love. You would sell your soul for friendship.

Learn to thrust friendship aside, or rather the dream of friendship. To desire friendship is a great fault. Friendship should be a gratuitous joy like those afforded by art or life. We must refuse it so that we may be worthy to receive it; it is of the order of grace ('Depart from me, O Lord. ...'). It is one of those things which are added unto us. *Every* dream of friendship deserves to be shattered. It is not by chance that you have never been loved. ... To wish to escape from solitude is cowardice. Friendship is not to be sought, not to be dreamed, not to be desired; it is to be exercised (it is a virtue). We must have done with all this impure and turbid border of sentiment. Schluss!

Or rather (for we must not prune too severely within ourselves), everything in friendship which does not pass

---

[1] Here 'Platonic' love has nothing to do with what today goes by the same name. It does not proceed from the imagination but from the soul. It is purely spiritual contemplation [Gustav Thibon].

into real exchanges should pass into considered thoughts. It serves no useful purpose to do without the inspiring virtue of friendship. What should be severely forbidden is to dream of its sentimental joys.

That is corruption. Moreover it is as stupid as to dream about music or painting. Friendship cannot be separated from reality any more than the beautiful. It is a miracle, like the beautiful. And the miracle consists simply in the fact that it *exists*. At the age of twenty-five, it is high time to have done with adolescence once and for all. . . .

Do not allow yourself to be imprisoned by any affection. Keep your solitude. The day, if it ever comes, when you are given true affection there will be no opposition between interior solitude and friendship, quite the reverse. It is even by this infallible sign that you will recognize it. Other affections have to be severely disciplined.

The same words (e.g. a man says to his wife: 'I love you') can be commonplace or extraordinary according to the manner in which they are spoken. And this manner depends on the depth of the region in a man's being from which they proceed without the will being able to do anything. And by a marvellous agreement they reach the same region in him who hears them. Thus the hearer can discern, if he has any power of discernment, what is the value of the words.

Benefaction is permissible precisely because it constitutes a humiliation still greater than pain, a still more intimate and undeniable proof of dependence. And gratitude is prescribed for the same reason, since therein lies the use to be made of the received benefit. The dependence, however, must be on fate and not on any particular human being. That is why the benefactor is under an obligation to keep himself entirely out of the benefaction. Moreover the gratitude must not in any degree constitute an attachment, for that is the gratitude proper to dogs.

Gratitude is first of all the business of him who helps, if the help is pure. It is only by virtue of reciprocity that it is due from him who is helped.

In order to feel true gratitude (the case of friendship being set aside), I have to think that it is not out of pity, sympathy or caprice that I am being treated well, it is not as a favour or privilege, nor as a natural result of temperament, but from a desire to do what justice demands. Accordingly he who treats me thus wishes that all who are in my situation may be treated in the same way by all who are in his own.

From *Gravity and Grace*, translated by Emma Craufurd, Routledge and Kegan Paul, London, 1952. Originally published as *La Pesanteur et la Grâce*, Plon, Paris, 1947.

CHANCE

———————— ⓒ ————————

The beings I love are creatures. They were born by chance. My meeting with them was also by chance. They will die. What they think, do and say is limited and is a mixture of good and evil.

I have to know this with all my soul and not love them the less.

I have to imitate God who infinitely loves finite things in that they are finite things.

We want everything which has a value to be eternal. Now everything which has a value is the product of a meeting, lasts throughout this meeting and ceases when those things which met are separated. That is the central idea of Buddhism (the thought of Heraclitus). It leads straight to God.

Meditation on chance which led to the meeting of my father and mother is even more salutary than meditation on death.

Is there a single thing in me of which the origin is not to be found in that meeting? Only God. And yet again, *my* thought of God had its origin in that meeting.

Stars and blossoming fruit-trees: utter permanence and extreme fragility give an equal sense of eternity.

The theories about progress and the 'genius which always pierces through', arise from the fact that it is intolerable to suppose that what is most precious in the world should be given over to chance. It is because it is intolerable that it ought to be contemplated.

Creation is this very thing.

The only good which is not subject to chance is that which is outside the world.

The vulnerability of precious things is beautiful because vulnerability is a mark of existence.

The destruction of Troy. The fall of the petals from fruit trees in blossom. To know that what is most precious is not rooted in existence – that is beautiful. Why? It projects the soul beyond time.

The woman who wishes for a child white as snow and red as blood gets it, but she dies and the child is given over to a stepmother.

From *Gravity and Grace*, translated by Emma Craufurd, Routledge and Kegan Paul, London, 1952. Originally published as *La Pesanteur et la Grâce*, Plon, Paris, 1947.

BIBLIOGRAPHY

———————— ◉ ————————

Works by Simone Weil

L'Attente de Dieu (1950) Paris: Gallimard.
Cahiers I (1951) Paris: Plon.
Cahiers II (1953) Paris: Plon.
Cahiers III (1956) Paris: Plon.
La Condition ouvrière (1951) Paris: Gallimard.
La Connaissance surnaturelle (1950) Paris: Gallimard.
Ecrits de Londres et dernières lettres (1957) Paris: Gallimard.
Ecrits historiques et politiques (1960) Paris: Gallimard.
L'Enracinement: Prélude à une declaration des devoirs envers l'être humain
    (1949) Paris: Gallimard.
Intuitions préchrétiennes (1951) Paris: La Colombe.
Leçons de philosophie (1959) Paris: Plon.
Lettre à un religieux (1951) Paris: Gallimard.
Oppresssion et liberté (1955) Paris: Gallimard.
Pensées san ordre concernant l'amour de Dieu (1962) Paris: Gallimard.
La Pesanteur et la grâce (1947) Paris: Plon.
Poèmes (1968) Paris: Gallimard.
La Source grecque (1953) Paris: Gallimard.
Sur la science (1965) Paris: Gallimard.
Venise sauvée (1955) Paris: Gallimard.

Translations of Simone Weil into English

Gravity and Grace (2002) trans. Emma Craufurd, London: Routledge.

Intimations of Christianity among the Ancient Greeks (1998) ed. Elizabeth Chase Geissbuhler, London: Routledge.

Lectures on Philosophy (1978) trans. H. Price, Cambridge: C.U.P.

Letter to a Priest (2002) London: Routledge.

The Need for Roots (2001) trans. A. F. Wills with a foreword by T. S. Eliot, London: Routledge.

The Notebooks of Simone Weil (2004) trans. Arthur Wills, London: Routledge.

On Science, necessity and the love of God (1968) Oxford: O.U.P.

Oppression and Liberty (2001) trans. Arthur Wills and John Petrie, London: Routledge.

Selected Essays 1934–43 (1962) trans. Richard Rees, Oxford: O.U.P.

Seventy Letters (1965) trans. Richard Rees, Oxford: O.U.P.

Waiting on God (1951) trans. Emma Craufurd, London: Routledge and Kegan Paul.

Waiting for God (1973) introd. Leslie Fiedler, USA: Harper Perennial.

Suggestions for Further Reading

Anderson, Pamela (1998) *A Feminist Philosophy of Religion*, Oxford: Blackwell.

Bell, Richard H. (ed.) (1993) *Simone Weil's Philosophy of Culture*, Cambridge: C.U.P.

Cabaud, Jacques (1964) *Simone Weil: A Fellowship in Love*, London: Harvill Press.

Dargan, Joan (1999) *Simone Weil: Thinking Poetically*, Albany, N.Y.: SUNY Press.

Gray, Francine du Plessix (2001) *Simone Weil*, London, Weidenfeld and Nicolson.

Griffin, Gabriele (1993) *The Influence of the Writings of Simone Weil on the Fiction of Iris Murdoch*, San Francisco: Mellen Research University Press.

Heaney, Seamus (1995) *The Redress of Poetry*, London: Faber and Faber.

Irigaray, Luce (1985) *Speculum of the Other Woman*, trans. Gillian C. Gill, Ithaca, N.Y.: Cornell University Press.

— (1993) *Sexes and Genealogies*, trans. Gillian C. Gill, New York: Columbia University Press.

Jantzen, Grace (1998) *Becoming Divine*, Manchester: Manchester University Press.

Little, J. P. (1988) *Simone Weil: Waiting on Truth*, Oxford and New York: Berg.

— (2003) *Simone Weil on Colonialism*, Rowman and Littlefield.

McLellan, David (1991) *Simone Weil: Utopian Pessimist*, London: Macmillan.

Martin, Agnes (1991) *Kunstmuseum Winterthur*, Ostfildern: Cantz Verlag.

Murdoch, Iris (1992) *Metaphysics as a Guide to Morals*, London: Chatto and Windus.

— (1997) *Existentialists and Mystics*, London: Chatto and Windus.

Nye, Andrea (1994) *Philosophia*, London and New York: Routledge.

Pétrement, Simone (1988) *Simone Weil: A Life*, trans. R. Rosenthal, New York: Schocken Books.

Rees, Rhush (2000) *Discussions of Simone Weil*, New York: SUNY.

Ruddick, Sara (1990) *Maternal Thinking: towards a politics of peace*, London: The Women's Press.

Springstead, Eric O. (1998) *Simone Weil*, Maryknoll, N.Y.: Orbis Books.

Winch, Peter (1989) *Simone Weil: The Just Balance*, Cambridge: C.U.P.

INDEX

READ MORE IN PENGUIN

In every corner of the world, on every subject under the sun, Penguin represents quality and variety – the very best in publishing today.

For complete information about books available from Penguin – including Puffins, Penguin Classics and Arkana – and how to order them, write to us at the appropriate address below. Please note that for copyright reasons the selection of books varies from country to country.

In the United Kingdom: Please write to *Dept. EP, Penguin Books Ltd, Bath Road, Harmondsworth, West Drayton, Middlesex UB7 0DA*

In the United States: Please write to *Consumer Services, Penguin Putnam Inc., 405 Murray Hill Parkway, East Rutherford, New Jersey 07073-2136.* VISA and MasterCard holders call 1-800-631-8571 to order Penguin titles

In Canada: Please write to *Penguin Books Canada Ltd, 10 Alcorn Avenue, Suite 300, Toronto, Ontario M4V 3B2*

In Australia: Please write to *Penguin Books Australia Ltd, 487 Maroondah Highway, Ringwood, Victoria 3134*

In New Zealand: Please write to *Penguin Books (NZ) Ltd, Private Bag 102902, North Shore Mail Centre, Auckland 10*

In India: Please write to *Penguin Books India Pvt Ltd, 11 Community Centre, Panchsheel Park, New Delhi 110017*

In the Netherlands: Please write to *Penguin Books Netherlands bv, Postbus 3507, NL-1001 AH Amsterdam*

In Germany: Please write to *Penguin Books Deutschland GmbH, Metzlerstrasse 26, 60594 Frankfurt am Main*

In Spain: Please write to *Penguin Books S. A., Bravo Murillo 19, 1°B, 28015 Madrid*

In Italy: Please write to *Penguin Italia s.r.l., Via Vittorio Emanuele 45/a, 20094 Corsico, Milano*

In France: Please write to *Penguin France, 12, Rue Prosper Ferradou, 31700 Blagnac*

In Japan: Please write to *Penguin Books Japan Ltd, Iidabashi KM-Bldg, 2-23-9 Koraku, Bunkyo-Ku, Tokyo 112-0004*

In South Africa: Please write to *Penguin Books South Africa (Pty) Ltd, P.O. Box 751093, Gardenview, 2047 Johannesburg*

Penguin Modern Classics

UNDER FIRE
HENRI BARBUSSE

'One of the most influential of all war novels' *History Today*

Under Fire follows the fortunes of the French Sixth Battalion during the First World War. For this group of ordinary men, thrown together from all over France and longing for home, war is simply a matter of survival, and the arrival of their rations, a glimpse of a pretty girl or a brief reprieve in hospital is all they can hope for.

Written during the War and based on his own experiences, Henri Barbusse's novel is a powerful account of one of the greatest horrors mankind has inflicted upon itself and a critique of the inequality between ranks and of the incomprehension of those who have managed to avoid active service. It vividly evokes life in the trenches – the mud, stench and monotony of waiting, while under fire in an eternal battlefield.

Translated by Robin Buss With an Introduction by Jay Winter

PENGUIN MODERN CLASSICS

THE REBEL
ALBERT CAMUS

'One of the great humanist manifestos on the 20^(th) century' *The Times*

Camus described this brilliant essay on the nature of human revolt as 'an attempt to understand the time I live in'. Published in 1951, it expresses his horror at the events of a period which 'within fifty years uproots, enslaves or kills seventy million human beings'. Hope for the future, he argues, lies in revolt, which unlike revolution is a spontaneous response to injustice and a chance to achieve change without giving up individual or collective freedom. *The Rebel* created an irreconcilable rift between Camus and his friend Jean-Paul Sartre who bitterly attacked Camus for his criticism of communism.

'*The Rebel* should be read as a daring, emotional and intellectual biography'
Olivier Todd

Translated by Anthony Bower

With an Introduction by Olivier Todd

WINNER OF THE NOBEL PRIZE FOR LITERATURE